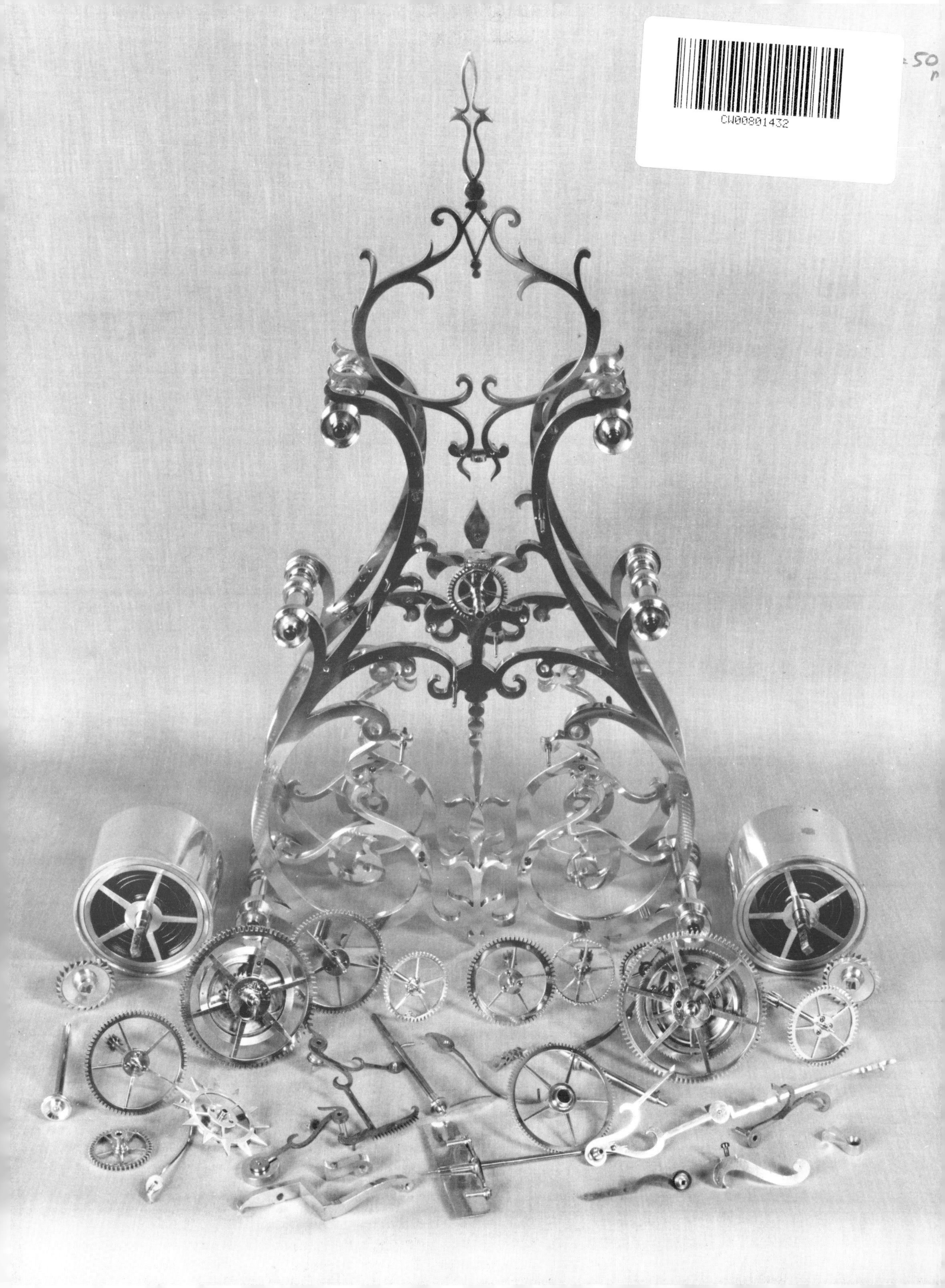

Skeleton Clocks

Plate 1. Two train skeleton clock by J. Smith & Sons, Clerkenwell (*see* p.137).

SKELETON
CLOCKS
BRITAIN 1800–1914

Derek Roberts

Antique Collectors' Club

First published 1987
© 1987 Derek Roberts
World copyright reserved

Reprinted 1996

ISBN 1 85149 256 9

The right of Derek Roberts to be identified as author of this work has been asserted by
him in accordance with the Copyright, Designs and Patents Act 1988

British Library Cataloguing-in-Publication Data
A catalogue record for this book is available from the British Library

Designed by John and Griselda Lewis

Printed in England on Consort Royal Art paper from Donside Mills, Aberdeen, by the
Antique Collectors' Club, Woodbridge, Suffolk IP12 1DS

The Antique Collectors' Club

The Antique Collectors' Club was formed in 1966 and quickly grew to a five figure membership spread throughout the world. It publishes the only independently run monthly antiques magazine, *Antique Collecting*, which caters for those collectors who are interested in widening their knowledge of antiques, both by greater awareness of quality and by discussion of the factors which influence the price that is likely to be asked. The Antique Collectors' Club pioneered the provision of information on prices for collectors and the magazine still leads in the provision of detailed articles on a variety of subjects.

It was in response to the enormous demand for information on 'what to pay' that the price guide series was introduced in 1968 with the first edition of *The Price Guide to Antique Furniture* (completely revised 1978 and 1989), a book which broke new ground by illustrating the more common types of antique furniture, the sort that collectors could buy in shops and at auctions rather than the rare museum pieces which had previously been used (and still to a large extent are used) to make up the limited amount of illustrations in books published by commercial publishers. Many other price guides have followed, all copiously illustrated, and greatly appreciated by collectors for the valuable information they contain, quite apart from prices. The Price Guide Series heralded the publication of many standard works of reference on art and antiques. *The Dictionary of British Art* (now in six volumes), *Oak Furniture* and *Early English Clocks* were followed by many deeply researched reference works such as *The Directory of Gold and Silversmiths*, providing new information. Many of these books are now accepted as the standard work of reference on their subject.

The Antique Collectors' Club has widened its list to include books on gardens and architecture. All the Club's publications are available through bookshops world-wide and a full catalogue of all these titles is available free of charge from the addresses below.

Club membership, open to all collectors, costs little. Members receive free of charge *Antique Collecting*, the Club's magazine (published ten times a year), which contains well-illustrated articles dealing with the practical aspects of collecting not normally dealt with by magazines. Prices, features of value, investment potential, fakes and forgeries are all given prominence in the magazine.

Among other facilities available to members are private buying and selling facilities, the longest list of 'For Sales' of any antiques magazine, an annual ceramics conference and the opportunity to meet other collectors at their local antique collectors' clubs. There are over eighty in Britain and more than a dozen overseas. Members may also buy the Club's publications at special pre-publication prices.

As its motto implies, the Club is an organisation designed to help collectors get the most out of their hobby: it is informal and friendly and gives enormous enjoyment to all concerned.

For Collectors — By Collectors — About Collecting

ANTIQUE COLLECTORS' CLUB
5 Church Street, Woodbridge, Suffolk IP12 1DS, UK
Tel: 01394 385501 Fax: 01394 384434
—— or ——
Market Street Industrial Park, Wappingers' Falls, NY 12590, USA
Tel: 914 297 0003 Fax: 914 297 0068

Contents

Colour Plates		page 6
Acknowledgements		8
Introduction		11
Chapter 1	The Eighteenth Century	16
	The Nineteenth century	22
	1845 1920	30
Chapter 2	Skeleton Clock Frames	49
Chapter 3	The Makers	79
Chapter 4	Wheelwork	157
Chapter 5	Escapements	179
Chapter 6	Complex Clocks	211
Appendix 1	Visit to a Clerkenwell Clock Factory	260
Index		268

Colour Plates

Plate 1	Two train skeleton clock by J. Smith & Sons	page 2
Plate 2	Skeleton clock by Merlin	14
Plate 3	Reverse of the Merlin clock	15
Plate 4	Eight day spherical clock, c.1790-1800	15
Plate 5	Skeleton clock, c.1845	25
Plate 6	Two train York Minster skeleton clock, c.1865	28
Plate 7	Chiming skeleton clock by Wm. McFerran, c.1860-70	38
Plate 8	Fretted dial	38
Plate 9	A rafter frame skeleton clock, c.1845	55
Plate 10	Ivy leaf skeleton clock	58
Plate 11	Single train skeleton clock by Morgan of Manchester	58
Plate 12	Congreve's original rolling ball clock	67
Plate 13	Timepiece by Parker	67
Plate 14	John Pace clock	93
Plate 15	Condliff pillar clock, c.1825-30	93
Plate 16	Condliff first series skeleton clock	96

Plate 17	Condliff second series skeleton clock	105
Plate 18	Condliff two train skeleton clock	116
Plate 19	John Moore & Sons clock	117
Plate 20	Skeleton clock by Haycock	117
Plate 21	Two train clock by Smith's	136
Plate 22	Two train clock by Smith's with hour strike	136
Plate 23	Three train skeleton clock by Smith's based on St. Paul's Cathedral	141
Plate 24	Evans' Scott Memorial clock	144
Plate 25	Evans' scroll frame skeleton clock	150
Plate 26	Evans' arabesque skeleton clock	150
Plate 27	French 19th century skeleton clock	159
Plate 28	An epicyclic skeleton clock	159
Plate 29	A two train clock by Edwards	177
Plate 30	Glass wheeled skeleton clock by Edwards	177
Plate 31	French 19th century skeleton clock by Royelle, Paris	180
Plate 32	Skeleton clock attributed to Evans	189
Plate 33	Skeleton clock by Dent's of London	192
Plate 34	Congreve's rolling ball clock	192
Plate 35	Skeleton clock by Smith's	210
Plate 36	Three train fusee scroll frame skeleton clock	219
Plate 37	Three train skeleton clock, with fretted and engraved chapter ring	219
Plate 38	Four train musical and quarter chiming bracket clock	226
Plate 39	The clock without case showing the mechanism and subsidiary dials	227
Plate 40	Skeletonised table regulator by Dent	234
Plate 41	A table regulator by Alexander Watkins	234
Plate 42	An astronomical skeleton clock by Shearer	243
Plate 43	An ivory timepiece dismantled prior to restoration	249
Plate 44	Two train skeleton clock with hour strike on a bell and calendar work	249
Plate 45	Congreve rolling ball clock, c.1840	252

Acknowledgements

So many people including enthusiasts, collectors, clockmakers, dealers and the staff of various magazines, auction houses and museums have assisted me so willingly and enthusiastically in the preparation of this book that I feel that in many ways it is a communal publication. Among the many people who kindly either allowed me to photograph pieces in their collection or supplied photographs the names of Norman Langmaid, Albert Odmark and Dr. S.P. Lehv stand high. Sadly, for reasons of security, it is now no longer practical for me to name the numerous other enthusiasts who gave me such free access to their treasured possessions and assisted me in every way possible, including tracking down every skeleton clock which might be of the slightest interest to me whether it was in a museum, a private collection, a hotel or even, in one case, a crematorium.

One of the most valuable contributions came from Mr. Dudley Heathcote who supplied photographs of many of the clocks which had been in the collection of his father, Major Anthony Heathcote.

Those who gave advice and assistance on specific areas are: Mr. C.W. Haycock, who advised on the skeleton clocks produced by his family; Dr. Vaudrey Mercer, who advised on the work of Dent; Mr. C.H. Bailey, Managing Director of the American Clock and Watch Museum, who kindly let me have a copy of Smiths catalogue and gave me useful advice; Mr. J. Faries of California, who gave much useful information on the work of Smith and Evans; The Time Museum, for letting me have details and photographs of various items in their collection; Mr. Charles Allix, who provided much useful information, many helpful leads and some excellent photographs of the Merlin Clock; Mr. R.J. Griffiths, F.B.H.I., Assistant Keeper Horology, Prescot Museum; Mrs. E.C. Gent, St. Helens, and Professor Alan Smith of Manchester who provided much information and advice on Condliff's clocks.

A considerable number of the clocks illustrated in this book have passed through our hands over the last twenty years and have been photographed down here at Tonbridge and the majority of the remainder have been photographed by me in the various private collections and museums visited. In this respect, I am very grateful to Sky Photographic for all the care they have taken with the numerous films they have processed and printed on my behalf. Kenneth Clark is responsible for several of the photographs taken in this country, including some of those taken at Sotheby's, for whose co-operation I am indebted.

Sotheby's, Christie's and Phillips all kindly gave me free access to their catalogue and photographic files and readily supplied all the pictures requested and various other auction houses assisted by forwarding photographs of skeleton clocks which had passed through their hands, for which I am most grateful. The only difficulty with this has been that it has not always been possible to control the quality of the photography or show details, for instance, of the escapement or other technical points which the reader might find of interest and the same remarks do, of course, apply to the photographs kindly forwarded to me by other dealers, collectors and enthusiasts.

All the escapements have been drawn by David Penney in his own skilled and inimitable style, thus enabling even someone who has only a limited knowledge of horology to understand how they work.

I shall always be grateful to my wife and son for all the tolerance and understanding they have exhibited during the last six years when I have either been writing, immersed in articles or books, or heading off to some far flung place to examine and photograph yet another skeleton clock. Even my poor dog has shown great tolerance, if not comprehension, when he has appeared on numerous Sunday mornings to be taken for his traditional long Sunday walk only to find me immersed in papers from which he could not drag me, no matter which of his numerous wheezes he employed.

I am very grateful to my long suffering secretary, Mrs. Rosemary Freeman, for her assistance with the manuscript which was speeded up in the latter stage by the introduction of a word processor by my son and herself. Mrs. Ann Wood also kindly assisted with some of the typing.

As with so many books it has taken far longer to prepare than was originally anticipated and thus I much appreciate the tolerance and understanding of John Steel of the Antique Collectors' Club during the long delay which has occurred. Finally, it would by only right and proper to thank all the staff at the Antique Collectors' Club for the care and skill they have applied to the production of this book. Inevitably this list of acknowledgements, despite my best efforts, will be far from complete and all I can do is apologise to and thank those whom I have inadvertently omitted.

Derek Roberts
1987

Figure 1. A Gothic iron chamber clock, probably made in the late 16th century, with vertical verge escapement controlled by a balance, internally toothed countwheel and a counterbalanced iron hour hand. Height 20in. (51cm).

Figure 2a, b. A small portico clock signed 'Franciscus Schwarz in Bruessel ca. 1630', which has an engraved bronze and fire gilt frame with some silver ornamentation. The back plate has cut-outs and the clock is laid out in such a way that all the mechanical components can be seen as clearly as possible, with the cross beat escapement, on which the arms have been renewed, mounted prominently at the top. Height 6¾in. (17.2cm).   *H. von Bertele Collection*

Introduction

The term skeleton clock may be taken to include any clock which has been designed with the main purpose of displaying the movement as completely as possible. In practice this usually means making the plates (or frames as they are probably more aptly termed in this context) as delicate relative to the movement as practicable, or fretting them out so that in effect one can see through them. Whereas with a bracket or longcase clock the movement is enclosed in a wooden case, thus concealing it from view, with a skeleton clock it is covered by a glass dome or sometimes a glazed brass frame and can thus be examined from all angles. Other ways which are sometimes used to assist in the display of the movement are the omission of the dial centre, the fretting out of the remaining chapter ring and on occasions the use of glass dials.

Different approaches were used in different countries, for instance in France and Austria a solid inverted Y frame was commonly employed which was very rarely skeletonised whereas in England the ornamental nature of the frame was a very important consideration when designing the clock and thus the frames were fretted out in many different ways, varying from a simple rafter design to fine arabesque scrollwork or even in such a manner as to depict famous buildings. Similar remarks apply to the dial in that on the Continent dials were usually kept solid or with just the centre omitted, whereas in England, particularly in the last half of the nineteenth century, the centre was nearly always left out and indeed in the majority of cases the remaining chapter ring was also extensively skeletonised.

An interesting technique used in France was the employment of a glass plate for the frame, which many would consider to be the ultimate in skeleton clock design as it permits one to look through it and see at a glance all the mechanical features of both the front and the back of the clock.

Many of the very early clocks such as the turret and lantern clocks (Figure 1) particularly those made in France, Italy and Germany were heavily skeletonised purely on the grounds of simplification of construction and economy in the use of materials, but it is doubtful if skeletonising was ever used as a means of displaying the movement. Some early makers undoubtedly produced clocks which they skeletonised to show off their craftsmanship as completely as possible or laid the clock out in such a way to draw attention to a fine or ingenious mechanical feature. Just such a clock is the lovely little portico clock with cross beat made by Franciscus Schwarz (*see* Figure 2).

Skeletonised Clocks

One type of clock which whilst not conceived as a skeleton clock does deserve a mention here, is a clock of relatively conventional design such as the regulator shown in Figure 6/25 which has been partly skeletonised to display as much of the movement as possible whilst still maintaining the normal clock case, which enabled the owner to see the details of a complex movement, or an unusual escapement or strike work.

FRANCE

It is probable that the skeleton clock first appeared in France in the mid-eighteenth century from the gradual evolution of the magnificent pendules de cheminée which were being produced at that time.

Whereas in England much of the finest clockmaking was carried out in the late seventeenth or early eighteenth centuries, the French achieved their best work from 1750-1830 with the arrival on the scene of such brilliant makers as Bertoud, Lepine, the Lepaute family, Janvier and Breguet to name but a few. It was the desire of makers such as these to display their superb craftsmanship to the best possible advantage which probably gave rise to the skeleton clock, reinforced by the wish of the wealthy few to show off their magnificent objets d'art as impressively as possible. It must be remembered that this was still an age of patronage and undoubtedly many of the finest clockmakers at that time, as in previous centuries, relied heavily on the support of the aristocracy.

In France the number of people able to acquire a fine clock was strictly limited, but those who could afford to buy such a piece demanded only the best and this is why the French skeleton clocks, particularly those made in the eighteenth century, although relatively few in number compared to the English skeleton clocks were of magnificent quality and frequently of considerable complexity. The French clocks incorporated calendarwork, made use of mechanical refinements such as remontoires and were often fitted with beautifully executed gridiron pendulums. The only skeleton clocks produced in appreciable quantities in France were the very attractive little clocks made in a variety of forms in the mid-nineteenth century at the time of the Great Exhibitions in both London and Paris.

One other type of French skeleton clock produced in considerable but far fewer numbers than those just mentioned were the great wheel clocks, mostly timepieces, made at the beginning of the nineteenth century.

AUSTRIA

Skeleton clocks first appeared in Austria, mainly in and around Vienna, towards the end of the eighteenth century, and although they have a superficial resemblance to those made in France because of the close links between the two countries at that time, they are in effect very different, due in large measure to the somewhat limited financial resources available in Vienna compared with France. Thus, whilst the clocks were often of great technical merit, they were, with a few notable exceptions, much simpler in conception. Remontoires and true gridiron pendulums were only used occasionally and the clocks were generally much smaller than their French counterparts and had thinner plates, but their relative simplicity and great delicacy of construction give them a charm all of their own. The early Austrian clocks are undoubtedly the most attractive, those produced after the mid-nineteenth century being much heavier in concept and more stereotyped in their design.

ENGLAND

Whereas in France the skeleton clock as an entity gradually evolved over an appreciable period of time, in England the skeleton clock seems to have appeared almost spontaneously c.1820, although a few highly specialised examples such as the one produced by Merlin (Figure 1/1) were constructed in the previous century.

The early English skeleton clocks copied the inverted Y frame (Figure 1/3) used so extensively in France, but rapidly assumed their own identity and the simple scroll frame (Figure 1/7) became the most popular design. These clocks were probably made in fairly small quantities by an appreciable number of different clockmakers and it is likely that in the case of these relatively early pieces that the name which appears on the clock is often also that of the maker.

During the period 1820-50 a few fine makers such as Condliff and the partnerships of Strutt and Wigston, and Parker and Pace produced some beautiful quality and highly ingenious clocks, but only in limited numbers. By the mid-nineteenth century the production of skeleton clocks had increased dramatically, roughly matching the rapidly increasing industrial wealth of the country, and it was at this stage that their manufacture was largely taken over by a few specialised firms such as Smith of Clerkenwell and Evans of Handsworth.

Two and three train clocks began to appear in increasing numbers, together with more complex frames (for instance those depicting well-known buildings) and dials became far more decorative. The heyday of skeleton clock production in England was probably in the thirty to forty years following the Great Exhibition of 1851. By 1890 production was slowing down and by 1910 had almost ceased as the populace swung away from what it considered to be the over ornate and excessively elaborate products of the Victorian era and adopted the classic simplicity of the Edwardian period they had entered, inspired at least in some degree by the beautifully elegant furniture designs produced by Sheraton over a century earlier.

Although the vast majority of skeleton clocks were made in England, France and Austria, some were also produced in limited numbers in other countries such as Belgium, Holland, Spain and America. No trace has been found of skeleton clocks having been manufactured in Italy, which is somewhat surprising in view of its association with the Austro-Hungarian Empire, nor is there information about any originating from Germany. It is likely that a few were commissioned to be made in Switzerland (it is thought that Breguet had some manufactured there) but so far no records exist of any bearing a Swiss clockmaker's name.

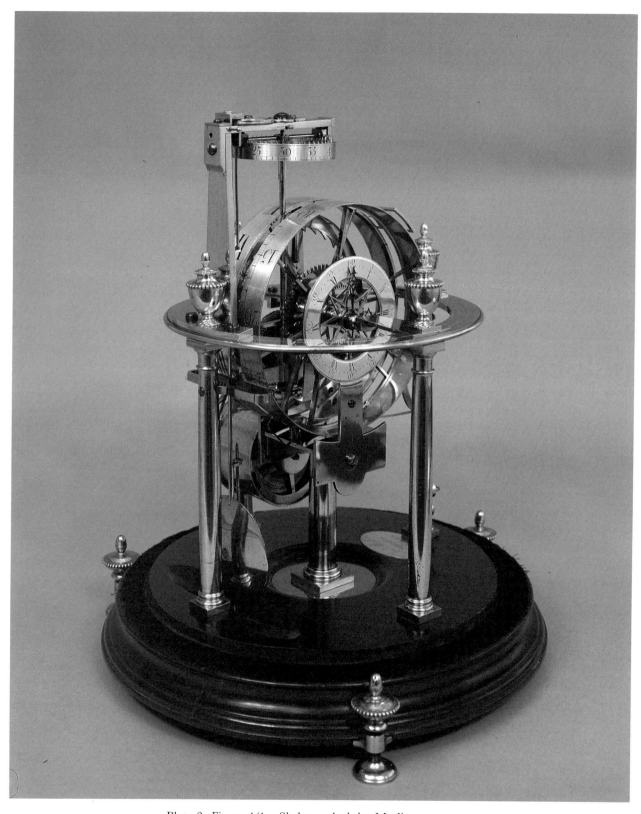

Plate 2. Figure 1/1a. Skeleton clock by Merlin.

Plate 3. Figure 1/1b. Reverse of the Merlin clock.

Plate 4. Eight day spherical clock, c.1790-1800 (*see also* Figure 1/2, pp.18 and 19).

Figure 1/1c. A skeleton clock by Merlin (*see* Plate 2 *opposite and above*) which is described in detail on pp.17 and 21. In this illustration the plumb line may be seen for setting it up. (This clock is now on permanent display at The Iveagh Bequest, Kenwood House, Hampstead Lane, London, N.W.3.) *Charles Allix, Sevenoaks*

1. The Eighteenth Century

Possibly the first skeleton clock to be conceived and constructed as such in England was that made in 1776 by John Joseph Merlin, a truly remarkable man who was born at Huy near Namur in Belgium in 1735, and when nineteen years old was invited by the French Academy of Art and Science to settle in Paris. It is interesting that Sarton, another fine Belgian clockmaker, who specialised in skeleton clocks, also worked in Paris but with Pierre Le Roy. Merlin worked in Paris for some six years prior to coming to England where he was to remain until the end of his days; he joined James Cox in 1760 soon after his arrival.

Cox was undoubtedly one of the most ingenious clockmakers of the second half of the eighteenth century. He specialised in complex musical clocks, frequently with automata, which were made principally for export to the Middle East and in particular the Far East; indeed several of his clocks may still be seen, principally in the Forbidden City in China. One of his main claims to fame was the invention of the first clock to be powered by changes in atmospheric pressure and temperature, which must at that time have been regarded as almost akin to achieving perpetual motion, and preceded the Atmos clock by some 150 years.

James Cox had a museum in Spring Gardens where for a fee people could see the ingenious clocks, automata and other devices which he had made, and it was here that Merlin worked as principal mechanic and set up his necromantic cave. The cave was similar in many ways to modern Ghost Trains in that the customers were assailed on all sides by bats, reptiles and various satanic apparitions as they passed through to the accompaniment of shrieks and horrid noises.

In 1773 Merlin left James Cox and established his own museum in Princes Street, known as Merlin's Necromantic Cave. Here he displayed many of his inventions including The Hydraulic Vase; Merlins Vocal Harp; The Circus of Cupid; The Mechanical Organ; The Machine for Blind People to play at cards; The Mechanical Table; The Antique Bust; The Portable Hygaeian Chair; The Morpheus Chair; The Mechanical Tea Table; The Review of Beauties; The Gouty Chair; The Double Escarpolet; The Barrel Harpsichord; A new Mechanical Desk; The Patent Piano Forte Harpsichord with Kettle Drums; The Patent Double Bass Piano Forte Harpsichord; The Patent Four Unison Piano Forte and The Sanctorious Balance.

The design and function of most of these inventions can now only be guessed at, but they do give some indication of his extraordinary ingenuity. Probably his main field of activity was in the design of musical instruments and these are discussed in Charles Mould's excellent article 'Merlin The Ingenious Mechanician'.[1] In this he also refers to another of Merlin's inventions, the

---

1. Mould, C., 'Merlin The Ingenious Mechanicien', *The Antique Collector*, June 1973, pp.165-9.

roller skate, which is recorded in Busby's *Concert Room and Orchestra Anecdotes:*[2] 'One of his ingenious novelties was a pair of skates contrived to run on small metallic wheels. Supplied with a pair of these and a violin he mixed in the motley group of one of the celebrated Mrs. Corneily's masquerades at Carlisle House, Soho Square; when, not having provided the means of retarding his velocity, or commanding its direction, he impelled himself against a mirror of more than five hundred pounds value, dashed it to atoms, broke his instrument to pieces, and wounded himself severely.' The shock of this incident appears to have made Merlin give up his desires to set this invention before the public, and it was left to the Americans to reintroduce the roller skate under that name in the early 1870s. Two of the inventions for which he became best known are the 'self propelled invalid carriage' or 'Gouty' chair and a personal weighing machine.[3]

Merlin seems to have made relatively few clocks, at least on his own account, but an unconventional skeleton clock signed 'Josh Merlin Inventor London' (*see* Figure 1/1 and Plates 2 and 3) was described by Charles Allix in his article 'John Joseph Merlin, A Forgotten Artist':[4] 'The main frame consists of a horizontal ring, supported on four turned columns, each topped by an urn finial. A further and larger central pillar rises from the ebonised wood base to uphold a sub-frame through which passes the centre pinion. The centre pinion has eight leaves and carries two silvered chapter rings, divided for hours and minutes respectively and read against fixed cursors. The minute ring turns in an hour with the clock. That for the hours is advanced 30 degrees at a time by a very ingenious gathering device. Lower down, and run between a side column and the central pillar, is a conventional fuzee of 16 turns with maintaining power. A chain joins the fuzee to a large barrel. The barrel caps (one at either end) each have six crossings to show the main spring. The great wheel has 96 teeth. The centre wheel has 60 teeth and drives directly a waisted and vertical 'scape pinion which is a worm or helix with a single start. The escapement, in conjunction with this ratio of 60:1, allows one tooth of the centre wheel to pass per minute. The work here suggests, perhaps significantly, the practice used to turn the fly of a music box or of an automaton. It also foreshadows the all-helical month skeletons made about 1830 by Charles McDowall (1790-1872) of Wakefield.

'The Merlin escapement is as unexpected as any other feature in the clock. It is a dead-beat verge which has a half-seconds pendulum with heavy

2. Busby, T., *Concert Room and Orchestra Anecdotes,* London 1825.

3. An exhibition of Merlin's work was held at the Iveagh Bequest, Kenwood, London (19.7.1985-26.8.1985). *John Joseph Merlin, The Ingenious Mechanic,* an exhibition catalogue produced by The Greater London Council in 1985, (ISBN 7168 15826).

4. Allix, C., 'John Joseph Merlin, A Forgotten Artist', *Antiquarian Horology,* June 1967.

Figure 1/2a

Figure 1/2a, b, c.
A particularly interesting eight day spherical skeleton clock signed and possibly made by George Jamieson (of London, Portsea and Portsmouth), c.1790-1800 (*see* Plate 4). The escapement is a two plane anchor with divided lift, i.e. the two pallets are in different planes relative to each other, thus avoiding the use of a contrate wheel. The pallet arbor runs across the top of the 'scape wheel and maintaining power is provided. The pendulum, which is similar to that on most verges in that it is not removable, has a 2½ in. (6.4cm) diameter spherical bob which is decorated with latitude and longitude lines and engraved outlines of the continents, oceans and some countries.

The indications on the clock consist, in effect, of two parts:

1 Four horizontally rotating rings which show, from top to bottom:
   a. Minutes
   b. Double twelve hours
   c. Longitude indicated by the equatorial bands calibrated 0-180, London being zero. The sun pointer may be set to read local time.
   d. A zenith ring bearing compass indications and on a flat horizontal disc are shown many parts of the world.

2 A perpetual calendar clock, having:
   a. A chapter ring which indicates Greenwich Mean Time.
   b. An orbiting ball moon commonly known as a 'Halifax Moon', one side of which is silvered and the other painted deep blue: this moon also rotates around a lunar ring showing the moon's age.
   c. The perpetual calendar consists of silvered rings rotating behind apertures at the top of the clock.

The drive to the calendar work is taken from the minute ring. The clock has rack strike on an inverted bell at the top of the central column. Because of the horizontal layout of the train, winding is effected from above. The whole is supported by a brass tripod base with adjustable feet.
Height 23in. (58.4cm).   *Albert Odmark Collection, U.S.A.*

Figure 1/2b

Figure 1/2c

Figure 1/3a, b. This fine quality skeleton clock made in the early 1820s has an inverted Y frame, a style much favoured in France in the late 18th and early 19th centuries. The narrow chapter which incorporates a seconds ring below twelve o'clock is engraved and silvered. The 'scape wheel has three crossings and all the other finely finished wheels in the train have four. A nice touch is the turning out in steel of the five finials surrounding and surmounting the cupola. An interesting feature of this clock is the use of only twelve widely spread teeth on the 'scape wheel which means that when employed in conjunction with a half seconds beating pendulum it revolves once every twelve seconds. The use of a twelve leaf pinion on the 'scape wheel arbor in conjunction with a sixty tooth wheel, i.e. a ratio of 1:5, enables seconds to be shown on the dial. The plinth on which the clock rests is of coromandel.

Height including dome 20in. (51cm).

Figure 1/3b

lenticular bob. The swing wheel has 60 teeth and shows half seconds against a silvered ring pinned to its outside close to a fixed pointer. Due to the even number of teeth in the wheel, the resting or dead faces of the verge are staggered on either side of its axis. The top potance carries a large end-stone to take the upward thrust imparted to the 'scape pinion. It also carries a continuous face-snail upon which rests the pendulum suspension for a "rise and fall". A graduated regulation dial affords fine adjustment. For coarse alterations, a standard inverted rating screw and nut are provided on the pendulum itself. At the right side of the clock within the hour chapter ring is a normal simple calendar mechanism. On the left, shrouded by the minute circle, is a small concentric meantime dial. Three levelling screws under the base enables the clock to be set up correctly in a "fore and aft" plane, and also to be put accurately in beat by observation of the plumb bob against a vertical line scribed on the foremost column. This last refinement is important because the escapement will not tolerate any sensible deviation from symmetrical conditions'.

Spherical Skeleton Clocks

A fascinating series of spherical clocks was made towards the end of the eighteenth century which varied considerably in size and complexity. All would appear to have been made by one man or firm as the workmanship is very similar and they employ a most unusual escapement which may be described as a two plane anchor with divided lift, i.e. the two pallets are in different planes relative to each other, thus avoiding the use of a contrate wheel. Who exactly designed and made these clocks is open to some doubt although it does seem most likely that they derive from one by Henry Gratte as he signed such clocks 'Invenit et Fecit Londini'.[5] The particularly fine specimen which is illustrated in Figure 1/2 has George Jamieson's name appended to it. Jamieson was a very able clockmaker and an expert on Mudge's chronometers having been in partnership with Wm. Howells and P.P. Barraud making Mudge's timekeepers up until 1799.[6]

The Nineteenth Century

Probably the first skeleton clocks were made in England c.1820, employing an inverted Y frame (Figure 1/3) similar to that already being used in France and Austria. From the beginning many features differentiated them from their Continental counterparts, for instance a fusee was usually employed. Silvered brass dials were generally favoured instead of the enamelled ones, and the centre of the dial was usually cut out to display the movement as completely as possible, whereas in France it was frequently left solid.

In the majority of cases the numerals were engraved and black waxed prior to silvering, but in some instances, as with English carriage clocks and some small mantel clocks at this period, the numerals were painted on after silvering. In those instances where the dial was fire gilded the numerals could only be painted on, for if waxing had been carried out prior to gilding it would have been burnt out when the chapter ring was heated up over the charcoal. It is virtually impossible to wax in and rub down engraved numerals after gilding without causing damage. Whereas on the Continent bezels were commonly fitted to the dials of skeleton clocks, in England this feature was usually omitted except on some early clocks such as that by Whitehurst & Son of Derby (Figure 1/5) which shows a strong French influence, and those of a few specialist makers such as Condliff.

A clock which well illustrates the Continental origins of the English skeleton clock is that shown in Figure 1/4. It has many of the features seen on French skeleton clocks of the early nineteenth century such as an inverted Y frame

---

5. 'Sphere Clock by Henry Gratte', *Horological Journal*, Feb. 1951, pp.94-5.

6. Jagger, C., 'Paul Philip Barraud', *Antiquarian Horological Society*, London 1968, p.98, Plate XIX a, b.

Figure 1/4. An English skeleton clock, c.1820, showing strong Continental influences such as the enamelled chapter ring, the inverted Y frame with a diamond shaped cut out at the top and a great wheel virtually the same size as the dial, but the train with chain fusee and recoil escapement is typically English; the base is veneered in mahogany. Height 11in. (28cm). *Phillips*

Figure 1/5. A particularly interesting skeleton clock which at first sight would appear to be French in origin with its attractively finished inverted Y frame, which is D shaped in cross section. The highly decorative feet and the use of ornamental collets, together with a white marble plinth embellished with ormolu and the fancy bezel are reminiscent of French work and it may well be that many of these components were brought in from France. However, the chain fusee movement is undoubtedly English despite the offset 'scape wheel at the top of the frame which is usually a Continental feature. The barrel, which is skeletonised, is signed around its periphery by the eminent makers Whitehurst & Son, Derby, and dated 1829.
Height 11in. (28cm). *Phillips*

with a diamond shaped cut out at the top, a large great wheel and an enamelled chapter ring, but the workmanship is typically English.

The early English skeleton clocks were generally only timepieces but were constructed to a high standard and often showed considerable individuality either in the construction of the frame or the escapement, which is well illustrated by the clocks shown in Figures 1/3 and 1/5. The clock in Figure 1/3, for instance, has a half second pendulum with a beautifully executed 'scape wheel of only twelve teeth which thus revolves every twelve seconds, but seconds are shown on the dial by taking the seconds hand off the intermediate fourth wheel which has a 5:1 ratio with the 'scape pinion. Other points to note are the thickness of the frame, the relatively deep oil sinks to reduce friction at the pivots and the fact that all the spires are turned out of steel to provide a contrast to the brass.

Figure 1/6a, b. A skeleton timepiece of eight days duration signed by Savage of Salop (presumably John) who is recorded as working between 1828-35. This clock, which would date from the beginning of Savage's work period, has an inverted Y frame and a particularly well laid out train comprising a great wheel with chain fusee, a centre wheel a little larger than the dial of the clock (and thus apparently running around its periphery) and a 120 tooth 'scape wheel with recoil escapement. An unusual feature is the relatively wide radiusing of the crossings at the periphery of the wheels. The frame rests on a brass plate which is cut out to allow the barrel to be partially recessed into the base. Height 13½ in. (34.3cm).

The Time Museum, Rockford, U.S.A.

Figure 1/6b

Plate 5. Skeleton clock, c.1845 (*see* Figure 1/15, p.36).

Figure 1/7a, b. Two skeleton timepieces both probably made in the 1830s with identical frames (which were probably supplied by Edwards of Stourbridge who could even have made the entire clocks) but with different feet, dials, hands and bases. The clock in Figure 1/7a is by William Brooksbank of Bradford and that in Figure 1/7b by Scott of Leeds; both have six spoke wheelwork.

It is interesting to note that of the four early inverted Y frame skeleton clocks illustrated (Figures 1/4, 1/5 and 1/6) no less than three have large great wheels, a practice much favoured in France in the late eighteenth and early nineteenth centuries. A refinement on this theme, again of Continental origin, is the admirable way in which the intermediate wheel on the skeleton clock by Savage in Figure 1/6 has been made just a little larger than the chapter ring so that it appears to run around its periphery.

Prior to 1830 the chapter rings normally had a smooth outline and were not fretted out, but after this period they gradually became more ornate. Up until this time it would appear likely that the clockmaker made his own frames but subsequently bought them in as it is relatively common to see skeleton clocks with similar frames, but finished in different ways (*see* Figure 1/7), for instance bearing different types of chapter rings, brass feet and train layouts.

The majority of skeleton clocks signed prior to 1845 probably bear the name of the maker, but after this time it is increasingly likely that it will be the retailer's name and not that of the manufacturer on the clock, but this varies greatly from maker to maker. Edwards of Stourbridge, for instance, never signed any of his clocks, whereas Condliff in all probability signed some fifty per cent, the proportion being much higher on his earlier pieces, thus the name

Litherland appeared increasingly on Condliff's clocks as the century progressed, possibly because Litherland manufactured escapements for Condliff but it could also mean that he took over more and more of the marketing of Condliff's clocks as the years went by. Other designers and makers who usually signed their clocks were Parker and Pace, Strutt and Wigston, Moore, McDowall, and occasionally Dent, but in all these cases the design and appearance of their clocks is so highly individual that they can generally be recognised at a glance, which is certainly not true of the majority of other makers.

(When discussing the evolution of the skeleton clock during the nineteenth century one finds that makers such as Condliff are so far outside the general pattern that they are best excluded and treated individually (*see* pp.98-113).)

By the early 1830s, after a period of about ten years, the angular inverted Y frame skeleton clock had gone out of favour to be succeeded by the simple scroll frame, which took the form of relatively small single train clocks frequently with solid chapter rings (Figure 1/7a), although by the middle of the decade it was already becoming popular to fret these out (*see* Figure 1/7b).

Rafter frame skeleton clocks (Figure 1/16) appeared upon the scene shortly after the scroll frame and were also fairly small clocks. The skeleton clocks shown in Figure 1/8 are interesting in that although the frames are very similar, the details, for instance the dial, hands, feet, wheelwork, etc. are different. These clocks could in some ways be regarded as transitional as the frames are a combination of scroll and rafter designs; both incorporate passing strike, a feature popular in skeleton clocks throughout the century.

Skeleton clocks seem to have been much favoured as gifts in Victorian times and therefore quite frequently bear presentation plaques which give an indication of when the clocks were made or at least retailed. One such clock shown in Figure 1/8a was presented to the Reverend Samuel by the Teachers of the Mayfield Church Sunday School as a token of their esteem and regard on June 28th, 1838; another (Figure 1/14b) bears a label under its base which reads 'This clock was bequeathed to Mr. Robert Whitmore by Admiral the Honourable Sir Courtenay Boyle May 1844', possibly implying that it was made a little earlier. Some of the more important skeleton clocks were obviously specially commissioned and made with the recipient in mind such as the skeleton by Condliff shown in Figure 3/17 which is decorated with a stag, an elephant, a lion, cupids, sphinxes, two racehorses and a boat, all of which presumably relate to the activities or possessions of the original owner.

Although the majority of skeleton clocks employed a recoil escapement with pendulum the use of a balance wheel is also often seen, indeed Condliff employed it for the majority of his early clocks. It appears to have been fairly common to offer the balance wheel as an alternative to the pendulum on clocks which were similar in most other respects. Figure 1/14 shows a clock which appears quite regularly with both pendulum and balance wheel escapements. In the majority of cases, as with mantel clocks, those to which balance wheels

Plate 6. Two train York Minster skeleton clock, c.1865 (*see* Figure 1/20, p.41).

Figure 1/8a, b. Two clocks with similar frames but with different dials, hands, feet and plinths; both have passing strike on the hour, a feature popular on skeleton clocks throughout their period of construction. One has five, and the other six spoke wheelwork. That shown in Figure 1/8a is signed G. & T. Hammond of Manchester and interestingly bears a presentation plaque which reads 'Presented to the Revd Samuel by the Teachers of the Mayfield Church Sunday School as a token of their esteem and regard June 28th 1838.'

Overall height 15½ in. (39.4cm).

Figure 1/8a. Schoonhoven Museum, Holland
Figure 1/8b. Phillips

were fitted were relatively small and the main reason for fitting the balance was presumably to make the clocks readily portable. There can be few more hazardous procedures than carrying a skeleton clock complete with a glass dome and a pendulum swinging wildly around inside with every step one takes. This manoeuvre must have accounted for an appreciable percentage of all the domes which have been smashed over the last century and a half.

Whereas Condliff and certain other specialised manufacturers had produced relatively complex clocks quite early on in the life of the skeleton, the majority of makers had contented themselves with making simple timepieces. By the 1840s more striking clocks were starting to appear on the market such as that seen in Figure 1/13 which is unusual in having a seconds ring above twelve o'clock and which also incorporates strike/silent regulation. Quarter chiming skeleton clocks had also appeared but at this stage were usually relatively compact and had far simpler frames than the later clocks.

Figure 1/9a, b. A fine quality single train skeleton clock with passing strike, resting on a well finished moulded brass plinth. Note the large great wheel, the attractively turned screwed pillars with thick dished collets and the substantial frames. The clock, which is signed by Jordan of Manchester (who is recorded as working from 1834-51), would have been made c.1840.

The use of plinths on which to rest the frame (Figures 1/10 and 1/13) appears to have originated c.1840, but was not confined to any one area of the country, examples having been seen, for instance, in clocks believed to have been made in London, Liverpool and Manchester, which lends credence to the belief that many of the clockmakers throughout the country were by this period (and indeed much earlier) buying in components from specialised suppliers in London and elsewhere.

1845-1920

As the 1840s progressed the production of skeleton clocks rapidly increased until by the time of the Great Exhibition in 1851 they were being manufactured in very considerable numbers. From the earliest days the main areas of production had been based in the Midlands, London and Liverpool

Figure 1/10a, b. A relatively early two train skeleton clock of highly individual design which, like that shown in Figure 1/9, has a moulded brass base. In addition there are two rectangular plinths which in turn support the bottom of the scroll frame. The train layout is unusual in that the fusees are on almost the same level as the spring barrels. Note the detailed finish on the hammer. *E. Wright*

and this trend was to continue until by the 1850s probably ninety per cent of all skeleton clocks were being made in these areas. At the same time their manufacture was being taken over by a much smaller number of relatively large firms, the principal ones being Smith's of Clerkenwell in London, and Evans of Handsworth in Birmingham.

At this stage the whole approach to the manufacture and marketing of skeleton clocks, as with many other products, was to change. The manufacturers produced a standard range of clocks such as those illustrated in Smith's catalogue (part of which is shown in Figures 3/43a, 3/44b, 3/45b, 3/46a and 3/47a, c, d) and sold these to jewellers and other retailers throughout the country, who usually affixed their names to the clocks prior to selling them, which explains why although Smith's for instance produced a vast quantity of clocks during the second half of the nineteenth century one seldom finds such a clock signed by them. By having a standard range of products and producing

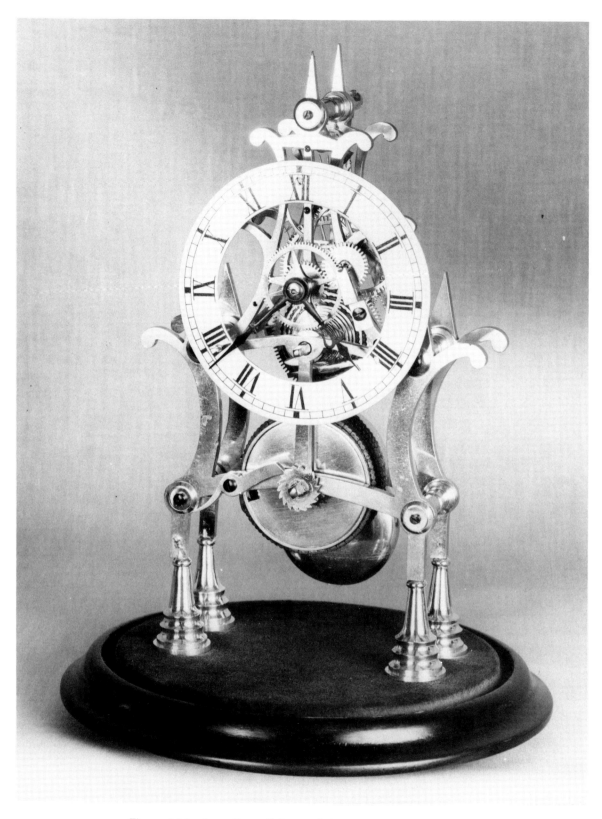

Figure 1/11. A small scroll frame skeleton clock with four and five spoke wheelwork, c.1840.
Overall height 11in. (28cm).

Figure 1/12. A compact twin fusee skeleton clock incorporating striking and repeating on a bell, probably made by Edwards of Stourbridge in the early 1840s. The upper part of the finial is missing.
Overall height 16in. (40.6cm).

each design in relatively large numbers the cost of manufacture could be appreciably reduced, the more so as many of the components such as wheels, pinions, chapter rings, pendulums and bases would be interchangeable between several different designs. It was also relatively easy for the manufacturers to supply a basic clock design finished to different specifications, as with car manufacture today. Thus the basic scroll frame skeleton clock (Figure 1/18 right) which must have been produced in tens if not hundreds of thousands, was available either with a wood or marble base, with or without passing strike, with gut or chain fusee and with different styles of chapter ring.

It was very difficult, if not impossible, for the small clockmaker to survive against such competition, particularly when one bears in mind the massive and ever increasing imports of wall and mantel clocks from France, Germany and America. Only those clockmakers who were large enough to meet the competition or who produced very high quality products for the limited top end of the market managed to stay in business.

By the 1850s all the basic skeleton clock designs had evolved including the inverted Y, scroll, rafter, Gothic and architectural frames, and these were mainly developed and elaborated upon as the century progressed. The clocks tended to become much larger and the frames far more ornamental; the scroll frames became more decorative and frequently incorporated a floral motif such as ivy leaves (Figure 1/19) or fuschias. The representation of buildings became more elaborate, York Minster being the most frequently depicted (Figure 1/20); the height of the Evans' version of this clock including base and dome was 24in.-26in. (61cm-66cm).

The quality of the clocks varied enormously from the simplest of timepieces produced to the minimum standard compatible with reliable service, up to the magnificent musical clocks (Figure 1/21) and other complex clocks, often produced to special order and to the highest possible standards (Figure 6/1 and Plate 35) frequently for special presentation purposes. Indeed the skeleton clock, judging by the number of plaques that exist, appears to have assumed the role of presentation clock par excellence during the second half of the nineteenth century. Whilst many clocks tended to become extremely 'fussy' and excessively ornamental, others were beautifully conceived and made. Such a clock is the arabesque skeleton (Figure 2/11) which sometimes has two and occasionally three frames; the great delicacy of this design and the care with which the frames are fretted out and finished makes them a joy to behold.

Dials and Hands

Up until the 1840s the dial usually consisted of a solid silvered chapter ring of regular outline together with simple spade, moon or fleur-de-lis hands, but as the century progressed the designs of chapter rings became far more elaborate. At first the chapter ring was just lightly fretted out (Figure 1/23) leaving each

Figure 1/13a, b. This compact but substantial twin chain fuse skeleton clock with rather unsightly gong strike has good six spoke wheelwork and the interesting feature of a second ring above twelve o'clock which incorporates strike/silent regulation; it is signed by Benjn Russell of Norwich and would date c.1840.

Anthony Woodburn, Le...

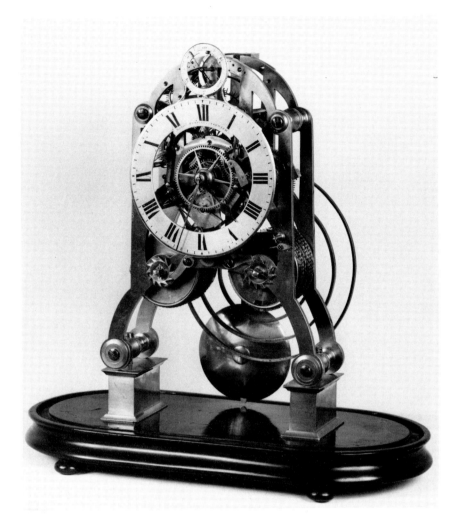

Figure 1/13b

Figure 1/14a, b. This attractive little clock is interesting in that it is dated 1844 which gives a guide as to the time when this particular style was made, and which was later to evolve into the far larger and more elaborate architectural clocks, most of which depicted cathedrals. The same design was used for both pendulum and balance wheel clocks; the advantage of the latter, apart from portability, was that a seconds hand could be easily provided.

Sir George White

Figure 1/14b

Figure 1/15. A somewhat more decorative skeleton clock than those previously illustrated, c.1845 (*see also* Plate 5). Note the scalloping of the inside and outside of the chapter ring and the elaboration of the scroll frame, which might be considered to be the forerunner of the ivy leaf skeleton. As in Figure 1/14 this design is to be seen with both pendulum and balance wheel regulation.
Height 10in. (25.5cm).

Figure 1/16. A simple skeleton timepiece, with the rafter frame resting on twin brass plinths, c.1840. Signed on a plaque on the base 'Durrant, London'. Clocks with similar frames to this were made in many different forms, sometimes with unusual escapements and in other instances with the addition of calendarwork.

Plate 7. Chiming skeleton clock by Wm. McFerran, c.1860-70 (*see* Figure 1/21, p.41).
Private Collection

Plate 8. Fretted dial (*see* Figure 1/27, p.43).

Figure 1/17. Relatively few chiming skeleton clocks were made prior to 1845. This very compact example, probably made c.1840 has a simple frame which is in some ways transitional between the rafter and the far more elaborate cathedral frames which were produced in great numbers in the second half of the nineteenth century.
Overall height 20in. (51cm).   *Phillips*

Figure 1/18. A selection of skeleton clocks spanning the years 1840-90. Left to right: 1. A lyre shaped skeleton clock, probably made by Dent's, c.1850. 2. A small skeleton clock of Gothic design, c.1840-5. 3. An unusual skeleton clock with twenty-four hour dial by Smith's of Clerkenwell, loosely based on Westminster Abbey. 4. A small scroll frame clock with balance wheel made towards the end of the century. 5. The standard scroll frame timepiece with passing strike which must have been produced in much greater numbers than any other design of skeleton clock in the second half of the nineteenth century.

Figure 1/19. A fully skeletonised ivy leaf skeleton clock of which the decorative frame carefully follows the outline of the delicately fretted out chapter ring.

numeral either resting on a small island of silvered brass or standing alone, and at the same time the dials began to vary in outline (Figure 1/23) scalloping being popular in the initial stages, rapidly progressing to the far more elaborate dials seen on the skeleton clocks produced from 1850 to 1900.

A popular feature was the individual display of each numeral on a shield, lozenge or heart shaped background (Figure 1/24). In other instances the whole design of the chapter ring became far more fanciful (Figure 1/25) often depicting flowers and leaves and being engraved (Figure 1/26) as well as fretted out. Whilst some of these designs can only be described as clumsy, others, as with the arabesque frame, are delicate in the extreme (Figure 1/27) and very carefully executed. On occasions the chapter ring is built up in two layers, the upper part basically consisting of the fretted out silvered numerals which is then laid on to a gilded or polished brass background (Figure 1/28). In other instances the chapter ring is cast as one, with the numerals already incorporated and raised above the background, which is usually matted. A contrast finish is then produced, usually either a matt gilt background with polished gilt numerals, or a combination of silver and gilt (Figure 1/29).

Figure 1/20. A good quality two train York Minster skeleton clock striking and repeating the hours on a gong with passing half hour strike on a bell, c.1865, (*see also* Plate 6). Although this clock has a plaque bearing the name Lister and Son, Newcastle on Tyne, this would have been the name of the retailer, the maker being Evans & Son, Handsworth. The rosewood base is a replacement. Overall height including dome 26in. (66cm).

Figure 1/21a

Figure 1/21a, b. A fine quality musical and quarter chiming skeleton clock, c.1860-70 (*see also* Plate 7) with dead beat escapement signed on the chapter ring 'Wm McFerran, Manchester', probably the retailer. The massive scroll frame, which is fully skeletonised, is supported by very heavy pillars. The chapter ring, some 12in. in diameter, has raised numerals and is fretted, engraved and painted and the extraordinarily elaborate hands including their centres have been similarly treated; there is also applied painted fretwork to either side of the pendulum bob. The musical movement (which is in the base) is wound from one side and has regulation for Change, Play and Stop. There is a selection of three tunes which it plays on the hour after the strike or at will; the duration of the musical movement is approximately four days and the clock goes eight days on one winding.
Height 22in. (56cm). *Private Collection*

Figure 1/22. A Gothic style skeleton clock with hour strike on a gong and half hour strike on a bell, c.1850. The lever escapement with balance is mounted vertically at the top of the frame. The chapter ring is very fully fretted out, the background being completely removed from each numeral and even the narrow periphery of the chapter ring has been pierced.

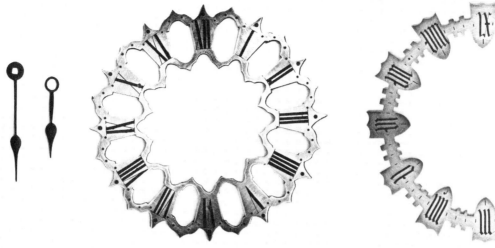

Figure 1/23. Simply fretted out, engraved and silvered brass chapter ring.

Figure 1/24. A dial design favoured by Evans of Handsworth in which each numeral rests on a shield shaped plaque.

Figure 1/25. An elaborately fretted out chapter ring, basically floral in design on a skeleton clock by Smith's of Clerkenwell.

Figure 1/26 (*above right*). A highly ornamental dial with floral decoration which is not only pierced out in the form of hearts but is also engraved, c.1865-75.

Figure 1/27. A fine quality dial which has been fretted out and engraved with great delicacy (*see also* Plate 8). A similar design is also sometimes to be seen with the centre omitted.

Figure 1/28. A Gothic style skeleton clock, c.1850-5, on which the chapter ring is built up in two layers, the top or outer one of silvered brass bearing the numerals laid on a gilded background.

Figure 1/29. A gilded dial in which the raised numerals are cast as an integral part of the chapter ring. A contrast is then produced, as in this instance, by using a matt gilt background and polished numerals or by silvering only the numerals. This particular clock was produced by Evans of Handsworth.

Figure 1/30. A selection of hands used on skeleton clocks made c.1860-90.

Figure 1/31. A beautifully delicate triple plated arabesque skeleton clock with the relatively rare feature of raised white enamelled plaques for the blue Roman numerals. *Private Collection*

The use of raised enamelled plaques for the numerals was a practice usually confined to the Continent, but is occasionally seen on English skeleton clocks (Figure 1/31) principally those made by Evans of Handsworth. It would seem likely that they were imported in view of their similarity to those used on French clocks at that time.

The dial layout, as on certain other clocks, varies considerably. Whereas the vast majority have centre sweep minute and hour hands, a 'regulator' dial layout with subsidiary minute and hour dials (Figure 6/21a) is also occasionally seen as are calendarwork, moon phases and various other additional indications. The hands on the later skeleton clocks, particularly those with elaborate dials, tend to be heavy in design and stamped out (Figure 1/30) and whilst they look clumsy they do at least have the merit that it is possible to see them easily, which is by no means usually the case with skeleton clocks.

Dating of Clocks 1850-1900

Whereas it is reasonably easy to give an estimate of the date of manufacture of the earlier skeleton clocks, on the later pieces it is far more difficult as designs tended to become standardised and continued for a relatively long period of time, largely because the clocks were being made on a volume production basis. Once a manufacturer had geared himself up to produce a particular design of skeleton clock and had invested heavily in the relevant patterns and moulds he would be reluctant to discontinue that line, at least until the demand for it had fallen away. Thus one sees two skeleton clocks such as, for instance, the York Minster manufactured by Evans, identical in every way but bearing presentation plaques dated some thirty to thirty-five years apart.

The heyday of the English skeleton clock, particularly so far as numbers made is concerned, was probably encompassed by the years 1845-85. By the end of this period production was already beginning to tail off and by the end of the century the number of clocks being produced must have been quite small. [A letter from an employee of Smith & Company of Clerkenwell, who was apprenticed to them in 1912, states that by that time the production of all striking and chiming skeleton clocks had been discontinued they had just four employees left working on skeleton timepieces, making them from wooden moulds.]

In Figure 1/32 is shown a simple skeleton timepiece with passing strike which would probably have been made early in the twentieth century. It will be noted that this is contained in a glazed wooden case, a feature relatively common at that time, probably to try and make it a more desirable furnishing piece and revive its flagging sales.

Although the production of skeleton clocks virtually ceased with the advent of the First World War their manufacture has never been entirely discontinued. Occasionally clocks are seen bearing the influence of art nouveau

Figure 1/32. This clock, contained in a glazed oak case would have been made at the beginning of this century. The employment of a decorative wooden case was probably an attempt on the part of the manufacturers to revive the flagging fortunes of the skeleton clock.   *Phillips*

or art deco and at the same time reproductions of earlier designs were produced intermittently both between the two wars and even right up to the present time. Indeed there are probably more skeleton clocks being produced today either as reproductions or as new designs than at any time during the last sixty years.

2. Skeleton Clock Frames

The early English skeleton clocks, like their Continental brethren, usually employed just a simple inverted Y frame, but the whole concept of the English skeleton rapidly changed as it was realised how important it was to employ a decorative frame which appealed to the general public. The types which evolved can be divided into the following categories: (a) Rafter, including the inverted Y frame (b) Gothic (c) Scroll (d) Floral (e) Architectural.

Rafter Frame

The earliest and simplest of the rafter frames was the inverted Y, mostly employed during the first ten to fifteen years of skeleton clock production. Some resembled those which had been produced in France during the previous twenty to thirty years (Figure 2/2) whereas others were made more decorative by the addition of a cupola and spire to the top (Figure 2/1) which gives them a decidedly Regency air, but only a very limited number of skeleton clocks were produced in England employing the Y frame.

Many of the rafter frame skeleton clocks were made in London and frequently bear relatively well known names such as Carter, Viner and Dwerrihouse. Possibly because of the simplicity of the frame, unusual escapements and other mechanical refinements were often fitted to these clocks. In Figure 2/4 (*see also* Plate 9) a clock is illustrated which shows both the day of the week and the phases of the moon above the main dial: it is signed by Patterson of Walworth who was probably the retailer. In Figure 2/3 is seen another clock with virtually identical frame, but signed by Viner. This clock is unusual in that it has a pin wheel escapement, which is relatively rare on English clocks, with seconds on a subsidiary dial above twelve o'clock, and is provided with beat regulation, maintaining power and a wood rod pendulum, thus giving it all the ingredients of a table regulator. It is interesting to speculate as to whether these clocks were made by the same maker or if their frames were obtained from the same source.

Another skeleton clock, with the simplest of all rafter frames, is that by Blaylock of Carlisle (Figure 2/5) who was almost certainly the maker; it has many mechanical refinements such as Graham dead beat escapement with the pallets (most unusually) spanning the top pillar, maintaining power and a wood rod pendulum, which has been cut away at the top to leave space for the adjustable fly mounted on the backplate.

Gothic Frame

The simple Gothic frame, sometimes quite closely resembling the rafter frame, probably first appeared in the late 1830s. The earliest, generally relatively small, simple timepieces (Figure 1/14), were produced with both pendulum and balance wheel controlled escapements. This design, which was the forerunner of the cathedral skeleton clocks, was to stay in production for the rest of the century and appeared in many different forms including striking and

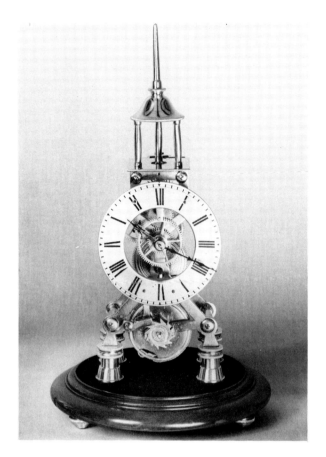

Figure 2/1. A simple inverted Y frame skeleton clock surmounted by a cupola which would date from the 1820s. Overall height 13in. (33cm).

Figure 2/2. A small inverted Y frame skeleton timepiece resting on a moulded brass plinth, signed on the gilded dial (which has painted numerals) 'Dwerrihouse, Ogston & Bell' — c.1830-35. Although it has a short, fast beating pendulum, suitable gearing enables it to show seconds above the main dial. Height 9in. (23cm). *Sotheby's*

chiming clocks. Figure 2/6, which shows a fine quality piece with six heavy decorative pillars, seconds above twelve o'clock and a large balance wheel mounted vertically on the backplate, has a gilded dial with painted numerals and would date c.1840.

A more elaborate frame design produced either as a timepiece or as a striking clock is shown in Figure 2/7; this particular example which has half hour passing strike on a bell, hour strike on a gong and a wood rod pendulum with pewter bob was probably made by Evans, c.1860, is an interesting half way house between the basic Gothic design and the full cathedral skeleton clock.

Scroll Frame

The simple scroll frame was particularly popular in the late 1830s and '40s (Figure 2/9) but remained in use throughout the entire production of the skeleton clock. Indeed more skeleton clocks have been produced employing scroll frames than any other type. Smith's of Clerkenwell favoured their use and many of the designs to be seen in their catalogue incorporate a scroll frame. Undoubtedly the most beautiful examples were those made by Condliff,

Figure 2/3a, b, c. A rafter frame skeleton clock by
Viner & Co., London, c.1845, with a gilded brass dial
very similar to that on the Dwerrihouse clock seen in
Figure 2/2, the only difference being that the centres of
the main and seconds dials are decorated with fan
tracery. Unusually for an English clock it has a pin
wheel escapement, a form of dead beat, and this
together with the maintaining power, wood rod
pendulum with beat regulation and seconds hand makes
it akin to a table regulator. The brass plinths rest on a
gold leafed wood base which in turn is supported by a
brass inlaid ebonised base.
Height 16in. (40.5cm).   *Albert Odmark Collection, U.S.A.*

Figure 2/3b

Figure 2/4, *see* Plate 9, p.55.   Figure 2/3c

Figure 2/5a

Figure 2/5b

Figure 2/5a, b, c. A highly individual striking rafter frame skeleton clock, c.1845, by Blaylock of Carlisle, who was almost certainly the maker and is known to have produced some fine quality clocks including a particularly good striking longcase regulator. This clock has many interesting features including dead beat escapement, the pallets spanning the top pillar, maintaining power and a wood rod pendulum supported by a very heavy bracket fixed to both the front and back plates, a practice favoured by many fine regulator makers. There is a cut out to one side of the top of the wood rod to clear the relatively large externally mounted fly. A nice refinement is the spirit level let into the base. *Private Collection*

Figure 2/5c

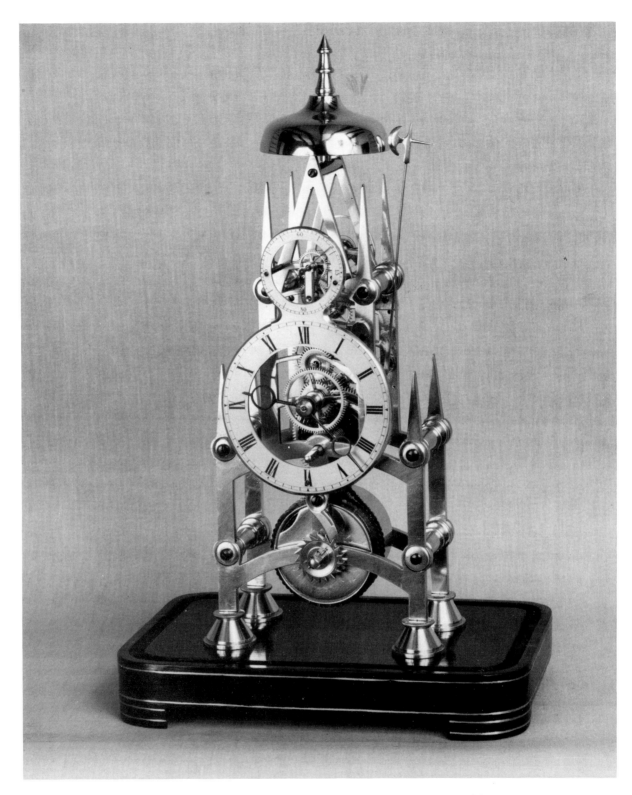

Figure 2/6. A fine quality single train skeleton clock in the Gothic style, with six substantial and attractively turned pillars, which has a gilded brass dial with painted numerals, a practice much favoured around this time (1830-50) not only on skeleton clocks but also carriage and small mantel clocks. A large balance wheel mounted vertically on the backplate enables seconds to be shown above the main dial. The clock rests on a rectangular brass inlaid ebonised base with matching dome.
Height 17in. (43cm).

Figure 2/7. A fairly large Gothic style two train skeleton clock with half hour passing strike on a bell and hour strike on a gong. The frame has been carefully designed so that the pendulum may be seen in motion from the front of the clock. This clock, which was probably made by Evans of Handsworth, c.1860, was also produced as a simple timepiece either with or without passing strike.

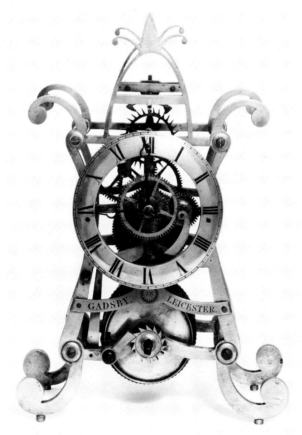

Figure 2/8. A simple and highly individual chain fusee timepiece, c.1840, signed 'Gadsby Leicester No. 6', who was probably the maker. *Sotheby's*

Plate 9. Figure 2/4. A skeleton clock with a very similar rafter frame to that seen in Figure 2/3 which poses the question, were the two clocks made by the same maker, or did their frames come from the same supplier? The silvered brass dial on this particular clock, which is signed 'G. Paterson, Walworth', and would date c.1845, is unusual in having subsidiaries for days of the week and phases of the moon; it also has a compass mounted on the base between the two brass plinths.
Height 17in. (43cm).

Figure 2/9a, b. Two scroll frame skeleton clocks made in the 1840s. At this stage the dials were still of relatively simple design with scalloping on the inner and outer edges. Both have six spoke wheelwork, chain fusees and attractively skeletonised barrels. The striking clock is signed on the chapter ring by Hatfield & Hall of Manchester, who were almost certainly the retailers. *Sotheby's*

Figure 2/10. Condliff undoubtedly produced the most attractive scroll frame skeleton clocks but unfortunately only in very limited numbers when one compares his output with that of Evans and Smith. This great wheel clock was the simplest of all his designs, even the fusee being eliminated; nothing on it is overdone, the frame is of excellent proportions, the chapter ring is narrow, the hands delicate and of fine quality and the platform base which rests on ball feet is well executed. The fitting of a gong or even a bell on to or near the frame would obviously seriously marr the appearance of the clock, thus the passing hour strike has been concealed in the base, as was the rule with most of Condliff's clocks. *Christie's*

Figure 2/11a, b. The arabesque skeleton is considered by many to be the most graceful ever produced and certainly the extreme delicacy of the frame and the gently curving lines are very appealing. They were made either as single or two train clocks and sometimes, as on this example, a third frame was added to support the dial, which adds greatly to their attraction. The wood rod pendulum with pewter bob can just be seen beneath the spring barrel. Although none of these clocks have been signed by the maker it is fairly safe, judging by the details of the construction of this example, to attribute it to Evans of Handsworth. It was supplied with various different dials (*see also* Figure 1/31) some of which have been seen on other clocks by Evans such as his York Minster (Figure 3/58a). The hands on this particular clock are probably not original. In the rear view of the clock the pendulum has been omitted so as to show the details of the frame more clearly.

Figure 2/12. A delicate ivy leaf skeleton clock of particularly open design made by Smith's of Clerkenwell in the third quarter of the 19th century.

Figure 2/11b

57

Plate 10. Figure 2/13a. This ivy leaf skeleton clock employs exactly the same frame as that shown in Figure 2/12 but its appearance has been completely changed by fitting a particularly attractive fretted out and engraved dial, the omission of passing strike and the use of different feet.

Plate 11. Figure 2/14. A large and highly individual single train skeleton clock signed by T. Morgan of Manchester who was almost certainly the maker. Despite the frame (which employs trailing fuschias as its motif) being nearly ⅜in. (1cm) thick it still shows great delicacy of design and execution. In this instance a relatively large great wheel has been employed. This clock would have been much more expensive to produce than the standardised designs manufactured by Evans and Smith. Height 22in. (56cm).

Back view of Plate 10 (Figure 2/13b).　　　　　　Back view of Plate 11 (Figure 2/14b).

which can be clearly seen in the stripped down clock illustrated in Figure 3/18c, and the little timepiece with going barrel and passing strike built into the base in Figure 2/10. Mr. Condliff was certainly not going to spoil the appearance of this exquisite little clock by cluttering it up with a coiled gong.

The arabesque (Figure 2/11) was probably the ultimate development of the scroll frame: the extreme delicacy of this design and the very high standard to which these clocks were fretted out and finished makes them a joy to behold. They were made as single and two train clocks and whereas some had only two frames the best examples also had a third frame which supported the dial and added greatly to the depth and overall appeal of the clocks.

Floral Designs

Most of the frames based on floral designs may be considered to be an elaboration of the simple scroll frame; some such as Figure 2/14 had considerable delicacy of design whereas others tended to be fussy and over ornamented. A popular design, probably from Smith & Son, was that shown in Figure 2/12 in which the train is run vertically up through the clock thus leaving the inside of the fully fretted out dial as clear as possible. It will be noted that the floral motif is continued on the chapter ring with thistles and clover leaves between the numerals.

Figure 2/15. A good quality ivy leaf timepiece, with chain fusee and wood rod pendulum with pewter bob, probably made by Evans, c.1850-60.   *G.K. Hadfield*

Figure 2/16. It is difficult to conceive of more elaborately fretted out frames than those seen on this clock, which is signed by James Gowland and dated 1851, which makes one wonder if it was made for the Great Exhibition. Although the outline is basically architectural the decoration is all floral with vases of flowers depicted at the bottom of the frame, and thistles, sprays of flowers and foliage occupying every available space between the vertical bars. The dial has been fretted out as fully as possible and this against the background of such a complex frame makes it almost impossible to tell the time. The two train movement which strikes the hours on a gong has a half seconds pendulum, half dead beat escapement and rests on a three tier rectangular brass base.   *Private Collection*

A clock with a relatively early floral frame based on fuschias is that by Morgan of Manchester (Figure 2/14), a highly individual maker who produced several interesting clocks including a complex longcase regulator (*see also* Plate 11). The quality of finish on this clock is very high and although it appears to be delicate the frames are no less than ⅜ in. (1cm) thick: this must have been a time consuming clock to make.

The clock shown in Figure 2/16 must be one of the most extensively fretted out skeleton clocks ever produced; although the outline of the frame is basically architectural, the decoration is floral. Vases of flowers rest on the lower edge, sprays run up between the vertical bars and gracefully executed foliage appears throughout the frame. This clock illustrates to a nicety the adage that one does not buy a skeleton clock to tell the time. Seeing the fully fretted out numerals

Figure 2/17. This famous landmark in Edinburgh which was built in memory of the eminent Scottish poet Sir Walter Scott following his death in 1832, was commenced in 1840 and completed some six years later at a total cost of over £16,000. The memorial stands some 200ft. high, is 55ft. square at the base and the highest gallery may be reached by climbing 287 steps. John Steell's statue, which is twice life size, was sculpted out of Carrara marble. It rests on a marble block weighing some thirty tons which was specially imported for the purpose. *Edinburgh District Council*

Figure 2/18. The first of Evans' Scott Memorial clocks, which was made for the 1851 Great Exhibition, was presented to the retiring Postmaster of Handsworth. Following his death Evans bought the clock back and it has remained in the family until comparatively recently when Miss Phyllis Evans presented it to the Birmingham City Museum and Art Gallery where it is now on display. The two train clock strikes the hours on a gong and has a balance wheel mounted vertically at the top of the front plate. Far more detail is present than on the majority of architectural skeleton clock frames, which usually consist of sheets of flat fretted out brass; for instance the individual stones are represented on either side of the arch. Indeed the whole design has a truly three dimensional effect.
City Museums and Art Gallery, Birmingham

is difficult enough but here the hands completely blurr into the background. The problem of reading the time with skeleton clocks explains why quite frequently the hands are painted white or occasionally red.

Architectural Frames

Skeleton clocks with frame designs based on famous buildings first appeared in the mid-nineteenth century. The inspiration for most of these was probably the relatively simple Gothic frames being produced from c.1835-40 onwards.

Evans was one of the first to make a clock with an architectural frame; his Scott Memorial (Figure 2/18) and his two other best known were those based on Westminster Abbey (Figure 2/21) and York Minster (Figure 2/26). Over the years he probably produced more clocks of this type than any other maker and these relatively large clocks were always made to the highest standards.

The architectural frame most often seen which was made by Smith's is that based on Lichfield Cathedral (Figure 2/28), but they also produced a fairly simple Westminster Abbey clock (Figure 2/24) which was considerably smaller than Evans' version, and illustrated one based on Tom Tower, Christ Church, Oxford in their catalogue (Figure 2/35b). Undoubtedly the finest architectural clocks Smith's made were those featuring St. Paul's Cathedral (Figure 2/34) and Brighton Pavilion (Figure 2/31); these large clocks, which were only made in limited numbers, were probably for exhibition purposes or to special order.

Besides the skeleton clocks based on well-known buildings, others appear from time to time which were probably made on a one off basis, possibly for presentation. Examples of those which have been seen include one inspired by a lighthouse, and another reputed to be a copy of part of the conservatory at Syon House (Figure 2/36).

The Scott Memorial

Sir Walter Scott was undoubtedly one of the most revered of Scottish poets and thus following his death on 21st September, 1832, it was decided to erect a monument in his memory. An appeal was made for subscriptions and architects were invited to submit suitable designs, three prizes each of £50 being given to the best ones produced, but it was not until 1838 that George Meikle Kemp's design was finally decided upon, building commencing some two years later. Unfortunately Kemp was drowned in 1844, two years before the memorial was completed. For its inauguration huge crowds came from all over Scotland despite the appalling weather.

It is scarcely surprising in view of the immense popularity of Scott at that time and the interest in his memorial that Evans chose it as the model for his first architectural skeleton clock which he showed at the Great Exhibition in 1851. This large and complex clock contained much detail, even showing the individual blocks of stone in the lower main columns and accurately depicting the flying buttresses. Such was the success of this design that Evans started producing similar clocks in large numbers, a sales campaign in Scotland being particularly successful, but none of the clocks sold were as elaborate as that made for the Exhibition. Initially the frames used were very similar to the prototype and contained just as much detail (Figure 2/19); the same escapement was employed mounted vertically at the top of the front plate but the elaborate marble base was omitted. A small number of clocks were produced with this fine quality cast frame and later the design was simplified by employing flat fretted out frames. Most of the Scott Memorial clocks

Figure 2/19. An early Scott Memorial skeleton clock with a frame very similar to that used by Evans on the clock he displayed at the Great Exhibition, but without the elaborate marble base.

Nigel Raffety, London

Figure 2/20. The standard Scott Memorial skeleton clock produced by Evans either as a single or two train clock and with balance wheel or pendulum controlled escapement. He also made a version with a detented 'coup perdu' (lost beat) escapement which enabled seconds to be shown on a subsidiary dial above six o'clock. The Scott Memorial clocks were produced in sizes ranging from 14in.-24in. (35.6cm-61cm), this one being 19¾in. (50cm) overall.

produced were simple timepieces although striking clocks were also made and on occasions a two train clock with pump action quarter chime on two bells is to be seen. Some, as on the original clock, employed a balance wheel escapement whilst others used a pendulum. Probably the most interesting examples, which are comparatively rare, are those which employ a detented coup perdu escapement.

The clocks were produced in different sizes and this may have some bearing on the position in which the statue of Scott was placed. In the earlier clocks

Figure 2/21. A skeleton clock by Evans of Handsworth based on Westminster Abbey. The two train clock has passing half hour strike on a bell, which in this instance is of traditional shape, and hour strike and repeat on a gong. There is a third frame which carries the dial, one of Evans' standard designs with the numerals cast integrally with the chapter ring. An attractive feature is the small additional frame at the front representing the porch of the building.
Overall height 26in. (66cm).

he was usually housed within the monument and generally rested on a white marble plinth but in some instances, particularly with the smaller frames, the figure was positioned farther forward. Whereas the positioning of Scott seems to have remained fairly constant, considerable artistic licence was taken so far as his dog was concerned, which appears not only to the right or left of Scott but also in the foreground (Figure 2/20).

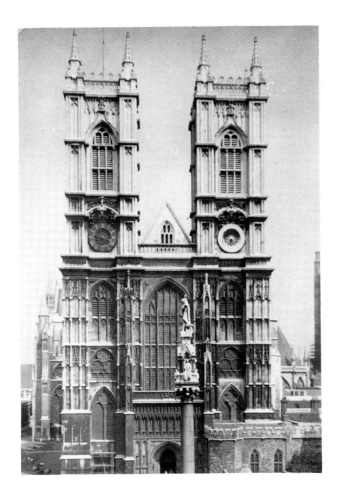

Figure 2/22. Westminster Abbey. Note the division of each tower into tiers and the four finials on top of each, two at the front and two at the back.

Dean and Chapter of Westminster Abbey

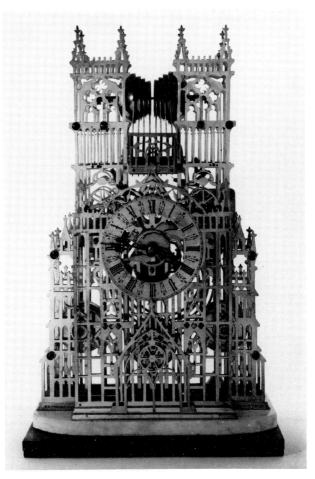

Figure 2/23. Another of Evans' Westminster Abbey skeleton clocks, which chimes the quarters on eight bells. In some instances the bells were mounted transversely in two groups of four, as on the clock illustrated, which is undoubtedly the most attractive grouping, and in other cases the bells were placed in one nest running from front to back. The chapter ring is different from that on the clock in Figure 2/21 and the way in which the towers have been fretted out has also been varied, possibly because of the eight bell chime, but the overall design and size of all Evans' Westminster clocks whether they be two or three train is always the same. Originally this clock would have had a two tier marble base as in Figure 2/21. It is very difficult to date these clocks accurately as they were made over a long period of time but most would probably have been constructed between 1855-85.

Sotheby's

York Minster and Westminster Abbey

The origins of York Minster go back a long way, the Archbishopric being established by St. Paulinus around AD600. The first church was placed on the site of the Roman military headquarters; the present building, the largest gothic church in England, dates from the thirteenth century (although the western towers were not finished until 1472) replacing that built by Edward the Confessor some 200 years earlier. Evidence of the previous buildings, including the Roman one which stood on the site, may be seen in the crypt.

Figure 2/24. A much simpler version of Westminster Abbey by Smith's of Clerkenwell; this example is a timepiece with four spoke wheelwork, passing strike on the hour and a delicately fretted out chapter ring.   *Christie's*

Since the seventeenth century Westminster Abbey has been the traditional place for the coronation of English monarchs and also the site where many of them have been buried. It is interesting to note that in the eighteenth century the clockmakers Tompion and Graham after their deaths were given the honour of burial in the Abbey, which gives some indication of the high standing of the best English clockmakers at that time.

Considerable confusion exists regarding the skeleton clocks made by Evans based on Westminster Abbey and York Minster, which is in part due to the fact that neither is as accurate a representation of the building as the one based on the Scott Memorial, but if the frames are compared with the actual

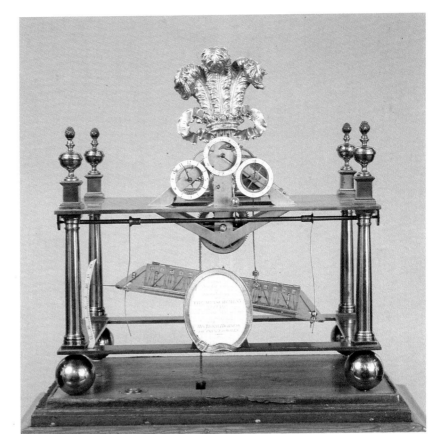

Plate 12. Congreve's original
rolling ball clock (*see* Figure 3/1a,
p.78).

Plate 13. Timepiece by Parker
(*see* Figure 3/11, p.92).

Figure 2/25. The magnificent west front of York Minster. The nave was built in the first part of the 14th century but the two towers were not added until 1472.

The Dean and Chapter, York Minster

Figure 2/26a

Figure 2/26a, b, c. Two skeleton clocks by Evans of Handsworth, both based on York Minster and with virtually identical frames. The clock shown in a, b has passing half hour strike on a bell and hour strike on a gong, which can be clearly seen in the rear view. The well made wood rod pendulum with cylindrical pewter bob was a design frequently used by Evans. This particular clock which bears the plaque of the distributor Lister & Son, Newcastle, has a decorative two tier rosewood base which is a replacement. The second clock (2/26c) chimes the quarters on eight bells mounted above the spires; it can be seen that they are in a higher position than that used on the Westminster clock, although when they are in one nest from back to front their position is somewhat lower (*see* Figure 3/58).

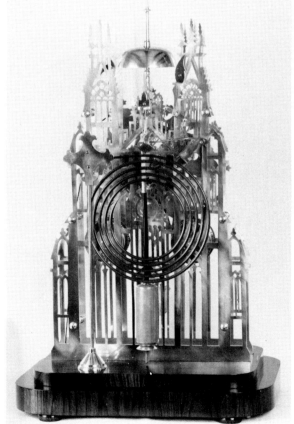

Figure 2/26b

Figure 2/26c.

buildings (Figure 2/22 and 2/25) the difference immediately become apparent, for instance each tower of Westminster is surmounted by four spires, two at the front and two at the back with castellations between. Similarly, the towers are clearly divided into sections by horizontal mouldings and all these features are represented on Evans' Westminster clocks. To the left of the picture of the Abbey may be seen one of the two side towers which are set back from the frontal elevation and these again are usually represented on the Westminster clock, depth being created by employing a third frame carrying the dial. A porch is also frequently provided in the form of a small additional fourth frame, but this can create some confusion as it appears to have been modelled more closely on that of York Minster than Westminster Abbey.

Undoubtedly Evans' representations of Westminster Abbey are more convincing than those of York Minster. It will be seen from the illustrations that the frontal elevation of York Minster differs appreciably from that of Westminster: for instance there are stepped extensions at the sides which are reflected in the frame of the clock where they are sometimes left flat or in other cases angled forwards. Similarly the two towers are stepped in as they rise up and each tower is surmounted by three spires at the front as opposed to the two on Westminster. Smith's also produced a skeleton clock based on Westminster, but it was smaller and much less elaborate than that made by Evans (*see* Figure 2/24).

Figure 2/27. The building of Lichfield Cathedral was started c.1300 and the magnificent west façade seen here was completed some 100 years later.   *Rackhams, Lichfield*

Lichfield Cathedral

The See was established by St. Chad in AD669 as the principal centre of Christianity in the kingdom of Mercia, the most important English kingdom at that time. Lichfield is unique in that it is the only English cathedral to have three stone spires, the central one was damaged in the Civil War and was later rebuilt. The present cathedral was commenced at the beginning of the thirteenth century, the choir, transepts, chapter house and nave were built during the first fifty years and the magnificent west façade, which is the aspect copied by the skeleton clock manufacturers, was completed c.1300.

This cathedral appears to have been a popular subject for skeleton clock frames and a line drawing of one is included in Smith's catalogue of 1865. In

Figure 2/28. A fine pair of Lichfield Cathedral skeleton clocks in which only the chapter rings differ, complete with the original rosewood brackets, by Smith and Sons, Clerkenwell (formerly in the collection of Major Heathcote). This particular design is shown in their catalogue (*see* Figure 3/44b).
Height of clocks 17½ in. (44.5cm).

Figure 2/28 may be seen two of the clocks actually made by Smith's, both on their attractive original rosewood Gothic style brackets. The only difference between the two clocks is in the style of the chapter ring. It will be noted that whereas the cross and other decorations on the spires are much larger than on the actual building in most other respects the representation is reasonably accurate.

In Figure 2/29 is a smaller version of the Lichfield clock, with the decoration missing from the top of the spires, in which the frame design has been simplified and much of the detail omitted.

Figure 2/29. A somewhat simpler version of the Lichfield Cathedral clock, without any mounts to the top of the spires. Height 14in. (35cm). *Phillips*

Figure 2/30. The Royal Pavilion, Brighton. Only the great onion shaped central dome is depicted on the skeleton clock frames. The Royal Pavilion was originally reconstructed from an existing house by Henry Holland in the late 18th century and subsequently rebuilt by John Nash in 1811 who transformed it for the Prince Regent into something of a fantasy palace by adding domes, pinnacles and minarets. The interior was equally exotically furnished, mostly in the 'Chinese taste'. The Royal family ceased to use the building in 1845 and it was then purchased by the town. Subsequently it was damaged by fire but since then it has been magnificently restored, much of the original furniture and pictures being returned to it by the Queen. The Pavilion is open to the public and the superb kitchens where many a fine banquet was prepared can be viewed; one can even read the menu for the last meal served there, which comprised some thirty-two courses.

The Royal Pavilion and Museum Department, Brighton

Figure 2/31. The central dome of the Royal Pavilion, Brighton, depicted on a skeleton clock by Smith's of Clerkenwell. This particular example (formerly in the collection of Major Heathcote) was converted to dead beat verge escapement by Peter Bonnert of Maidstone in 1968. Originally it would have been surmounted by a fretted out plinth carrying a figure and there would have been lions mounted on either side of the chapter ring as in Figure 2/32. The design and execution of this clock are of great delicacy: the frame is carefully fretted out with floral decoration between the bars; the snail is skeletonised and the various cocks, brackets and other mechanical features of the clock are attractively shaped and finished; the conventional pendulum with brass cased lenticular bob strikes the hours on a gong. The chapter ring, which is illustrated in Smith's catalogue, is of fine quality and complements the frame excellently, bears the plaque of the distributor Frodsham & Keen of Liverpool. The base on which it rests, as with so many skeleton clocks, is a replacement.
Height of clock 18in. (46.7cm).

Brighton Pavilion

George IV, whilst still Prince of Wales, first visited Brighthelmstone (as it was then called) in 1783, when it was only a village and was just starting to become a fashionable resort following the adoption of the new pastime of sea bathing. The Prince leased a house in the Steine, close to that where his wife (formerly Mrs. Fitzherbert) lived.

Figure 2/32. This two train Brighton Pavilion skeleton clock, in good original condition, still has the lions to either side of the chapter ring (a feature popular with Smith's) and is surmounted by a boy blowing a trumpet. The velvet covered plinth, which rests on a two tier white marble base, is also original. The design of the chapter ring is the same as in Figure 2/31 and appears to have been used on all the Brighton Pavilion skeleton clocks produced by Smith's. This clock bears the screwed on plaque of M. Rhodes of Bradford, the retailer.

Brighton was obviously much to Prince George's liking as he commissioned Henry Holland to enlarge his house and provide it with a central rotunda. In 1811 George III lost his sanity and Prince George was appointed Regent. As a result of this his plans for the enlargement of his house became much more grandiose, large sums of money being spent on the kitchens, entrance hall, long gallery and State Apartments. John Nash, the Prince Regent's Surveyor, was called in to advise on the building and added pinnacles, minarets and in particular the onion shaped dome which is the part of the Royal Pavilion which is represented on skeleton clock frames.

Only a small number of clocks based on Brighton Pavilion appear to have been made, and all, except for minor details, are identical, even to the chapter rings. Of five examined three still had lions on either side and on the other two there were signs that they had originally existed. One was surmounted by an eagle, two by a youth blowing a horn and on the other two the figure had been removed, in one instance to make way for a dead beat verge escapement. All the clocks were two train with attractively skeletonised snails for the strike and five spoke wheelwork. One bore a plaque by Frodsham & Keen of Liverpool and another was signed by M. Rhodes of Bradford but these were almost certainly just retailers. Various mechanical details and in particular the design of the delicately fretted out chapter ring, which is identical with one illustrated in Smith's catalogue, make it almost certain that the maker was Smith's of Clerkenwell, although the standard of finish is considerably higher than on the majority of their clocks. A further factor in support of this hypothesis is that the lions present on three of the clocks appear to be almost identical to those known to have been used by Smith's on various other skeleton clocks.

St. Paul's Cathedral

The original St. Paul's was destroyed in the Great Fire of 1666 and by 1670 Sir Christopher Wren had already prepared his first plans for a replacement. By 1673 the final designs were approved and in 1675 the foundation stone was laid, but the cathedral took thirty-six years to complete.

Figure 2/33. St. Paul's Cathedral. The present cathedral, which was designed by Sir Christopher Wren in 1673 and completed some thirty-eight years later, is undoubtedly one of the largest and finest cathedrals in Europe. The exterior of the cathedral has recently been cleaned for the first time since it was built and now looks magnificent, as the fine carved decoration by Francis Bird, Caius Gabriel Gibbs, Edward Pierce and Grinling Gibbons can now be clearly seen. The most impressive aspect of St. Paul's is probably the west front and it is this which is depicted on Smith's skeleton clocks.

Figure 2/34. Smith's superb skeleton clock based on St. Paul's Cathedral which was exhibited at the Great Exhibition of 1851. This particular clock (which was formerly in the collection of Major Heathcote) was exhibited in the 'Follies and Fantasies' Exhibition at the Brighton Art Gallery in 1971. The clock employs Graham dead beat escapement, has Harrison's maintaining power, strikes the hours on a gong and plays either Westminster or Whittington chimes at each quarter, a selection lever being provided above six o'clock. The bells are ingeniously housed within the Great Dome and because of this do not detract from the overall appearance of the clock and its attempt to copy the silhouette of St. Paul's. All the components are finished to a very high standard and attractively decorated; note for instance the tails of the clicks (one of which is replaced) and the way in which the various levers and cocks have been shaped. The chapter ring, typical of Smith's work, is delicately fretted out and engraved; a nice touch is the mounting of a crown above each numeral.
Height 28½ in. (72.5cm).

The West front with the steps leading up to it, the turrets surmounted by spires on either side and the great dome set back in the centre, was the perspective chosen by Smith's when they designed the skeleton clock which they displayed at the Great Exhibition of 1851. This large and impressive clock of superb quality rested on a stepped base of a similar design to that used on their Lichfield Cathedral clocks. How many of the St. Paul's clocks were made is not known but the number must have been small as only two have been seen.

Figure 2/35a, b. Tom Tower, Christ Church, Oxford, and Smith's skeleton clock based on it which is illustrated in their 1865 catalogue.   *2/25a Thomas Photos, Oxford*

Tom Tower, Christ Church, Oxford

The buildings of the Universities of Oxford and Cambridge are amongst the oldest and most beautiful in the land and thus it is scarcely surprising that at least one and probably more were used as the basis for the design of skeleton clocks, particularly as they would then be likely to find a ready sale to the occupants, both past and present, of the relevant college. Smith's design which was shown in his catalogue (Figure 2/35b) was based on Tom Tower, Christ Church, Oxford, but it is likely that various other designs which have not been attributed with any certainty, were also based on the Colleges of Oxford and Cambridge.

It is believed that several other buildings besides those already mentioned were used as the basis for skeleton clock frames but as it proved impossible to identify them with any certainty they have been omitted.

Figure 2/36. A fine skeleton timepiece of delicate and attractive design reputed to have been based on part of the conservatory of Syon House.   *David Symonds*

Figure 3/1a

Figure 3/1c

Figure 3/1d

Figure 3/1b

Figure 3/1a, b, c, d. Congreve's original rolling ball clock which he presented to the Prince Regent in 1808 and which was subsequently given to the Royal Regiment of Artillery, Woolwich, of which Congreve was an officer. The clock now lives amongst the cannons in the Museum of Artillery at The Rotunda, Green Hill, Woolwich which is run by The Royal Artillery Institution; it bears a plaque which reads 'This first experiment of a new Principle for the measurement of time, invented by William Congreve Esq. and humbly presented to His Royal Highness The Prince of Wales. 1808. Gravel & Tolkein Fecit.' This clock is markedly different and in many ways finer than the rolling ball clocks which were subsequently produced, as it is weight driven, the movement is more delicate and there is a degree plate to one side (3/1c) which shows the angle of the table and may thus be used as an indicator for fast/slow regulation. The beautifully executed table which employs a ball only ¼ in. (6mm) diameter, tilts every thirty seconds and above each gate through which the ball passes seconds are indicated in two second divisions. The clock has delicate separate enamelled chapters for seconds, minutes and hours.
The overall height with stand is 5ft. (152.4cm).   *The Royal Artillery Institution, Woolwich*

3. The Makers

SIR WILLIAM CONGREVE

William Congreve, the son of a baronet to whose title he succeeded in 1814, was a man of many parts; born in 1772, in 1791 he joined his father who was in charge of the Royal laboratory at Greenwich at that time. His principal claim to fame was his invention of what came to be known as the 'Congreve Rocket' which was used both on land and at sea during the latter part of the Napoleonic wars, and was successfully employed at the siege of Copenhagen in 1807. Indeed Congreve himself commanded a rocket company at the battle of Leipzig in 1812. He became a Fellow of the Royal Society, a Member of Parliament, a friend of King George IV and in 1814 succeeded his father as Comptroller of the Royal laboratory and second Baronet.

Although it is doubtful if Congreve ever made a clock he was a gifted and ingenious horologist, producing in his time two highly individual clock designs, the rolling ball clock which now bears his name and that which he described as having 'an extreme detached escapement'.

Congreve's Rolling Ball Clock

In 1808 Congreve patented his rolling ball clock[1] in which a small metal ball rolls down a groove in the form of a zigzag cut in a flat metal plate which is first tilted in one direction and then the other (Figure 3/1). The ball is designed to complete its passage from one end of the table to the other every thirty seconds and when it arrives at the end of its travel moves a pivoted metal bar which releases the train; the hands are thus advanced and the table tilted in the opposite direction, when the ball starts on its return and indeed endless journey. The table controlled by the ball thus acts as the escapement.

Although Congreve only patented his clock in 1808, the same year he gave it to the Prince of Wales, it is possible that this clock (Figure 3/1) was made several years earlier, as a clock by Bryson of Edinburgh is in existence, which, it is understood[2] bears a plaque stating that it was constructed in 1803 and is a copy of Congreve's invention. In view of this it can only be assumed that either Bryson saw Congreve's original clock prior to 1803, or more likely, that the plaque has been misinterpreted and a 3 confused with an 8, an easy mistake to make. (Unfortunately it has not proved possible to examine the clock to elucidate this query).

Whilst Congreve almost certainly thought that his invention was original, in fact this is not the case, as is true with so many 'inventions'. Clocks were devised and made at the end of the sixteenth century and in the early seventeenth century based on Galileo's law that bodies on equally inclined planes roll

---

1. Turner & Devereux, 'William Congreve and his Clock', Occasional Paper No.2. 1972. This is a reprint of the patent granted to Congreve in 1808, with an introductory note and a portrait.

2. Drake, T.A.S., 'Congreve Clocks', *Antiquarian Horology*, Vol. I No. 11, 1956.

Figure 3/2. An early 19th century Congreve rolling ball clock made to his design by John Moxon who was responsible for the construction of the two Congreve skeleton clocks in the Royal Collection (Figures 3/5 and 3/6). The chain fusee movement has three narrow chapter rings showing hours, minutes and seconds with the hands mounted directly on to the arbors of three wheels. Every thirty seconds when the ball reaches the end of its travel it strikes an arm which turns a connecting link and lifts a detent from one of two teeth on the rim of the 'scape wheel which then turns through 180° (see Figure 5/15c). The table, which is pivoted on two circular supports, is tilted by a cranked rod linked to a disc fixed to the back of the seconds arbor; built into this disc is a fine rack and pinion mechanism which may be used to adjust the angle of tilt and thus the timekeeping. Above the grooves are fourteen gates each of which has a window displaying the number of seconds on a revolving bar. When the table is tilted in one direction 2-28 in even numbers are displayed and in the reverse direction 32-58. The clock, some 16in. (43cm) high, is complete with a glazed showcase and even has a wooden travelling box and the original winding key. *Sotheby's*

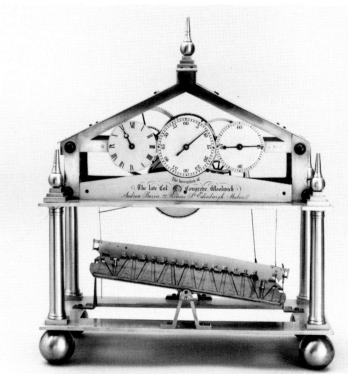

Figure 3/3. A Congreve rolling ball clock (formerly in the possession of Ambrose Congreve, Esq.) which bears the inscription 'The Invention of the late Col. Congreve, Woolwich. Andrew Barrie, 24 Princes St., Edinburgh, Maker.' implying that it was made shortly after Congreve's death in 1828. It seems likely that this clock was inspired by Bryson who made a similar example in Edinburgh in 1803. Unlike the earlier clocks the table of this version tilts every fifteen as opposed to thirty seconds, probably for greater reliability, which also has the advantage that the ball traverses the table once every second and thus seconds can be displayed on the silvered bar contained in the gate above the table which rotates four times per minute. *Sotheby's*

Figure 3/4. Several Congreve clocks have been produced which closely resemble Moxon's (Figure 3/2). Whilst the one shown here, which has a thirty second table and built in spirit level is anonymous, others have been seen bearing the names of various makers such as French, Royal Exchange, and there is an example at Quex House, Kent with the inscription 'I.P. Powell, Esq., Quex House, 1820'. It seems likely that these clocks were all made either by one man, most probably Moxon, or from the same drawing supplied by Congreve.   *Sotheby's*

through the same distances in the same time.[3] In 1595 Christoph Margraf suggested to Emperor Rudolf II that clocks should be constructed which were regulated by this means, at the same time explaining to the Emperor the impossibility of achieving perpetual motion with these clocks. Margraf was granted a patent and constructed several clocks based on this principle (an example of his work is in the Kunsthistorisches Museum in Vienna) and the idea was adopted by several leading clockmakers in Augsburg, Paris and Rome.

The principal difference between these clocks and Congreve's was that they employed a series of rolling balls, one entering a channel at exactly the same time as another left it. These clocks should not be confused with the famous rolling ball clocks such as those made by Nikolaus Radeloff of Schleswig, in which the ball provides the motive power for driving the clock by running down through a spiral cage and as it does so presses against a vertical bar and forces the mechanism to rotate.

The first of Congreve's clocks (Figure 3/1) which was weight driven, was made for him by Gravel and Tolkein and is now in the Rotunda at Greenwich, but all subsequent examples (Figures 3/2 and 3/3) are spring driven. The spring driven versions normally have a table with fifteen channels which tilts

3. Bertele, H. von., 'The Rolling Ball Time Standard', *La Suisse Horlogère,* No.3 September 1956 and No.4 December 1956.

every thirty seconds, the ball thus taking two seconds to traverse each channel. A refinement is the display of seconds in an aperture above each channel. When the table is tilted in one direction 2-28 in even numbers are displayed in the windows and when the table is reversed 32-58 appear. Congreve's rolling ball clocks are amongst the most fascinating pieces of horology ever to have been produced and almost invariably attract attention wherever they are placed. (It is amazing how many people still remember the example made by Dent's which stood in their shop window in Pall Mall until the late 1960s.) Because of their almost universal appeal they have been reproduced more extensively than practically any other type of clock and with widely varying results. The main problem with the design, even when the clock has been perfectly set up, is that the frictional resistance to the ball as it runs down the inclined plane varies greatly with the cleanliness of both the ball and the grooves; even the handling of the ball with bare hands is sufficient to affect the timekeeping or even stop the clock. It is for this reason that the clock should always be kept under a protective cover, the ball cleaned every week and the table every month.

These clocks have been the downfall of more amateur and some professional horologists than any other and it should always be remembered that the larger the table and the greater the angle of tilt the faster the ball moves and the more reliable the clock will be. Whereas with a large clock a thirty second table may be satisfactory, with a small clock one tilting every fifteen seconds is much to be preferred.

The Extreme Detached Escapement

From the mid-eighteenth century onwards increasing importance was given to detaching the pendulum from the influence of the escapement as obviously any variation or fluctuation in the power transmitted to the pendulum will affect its arc of swing and thus its isochronicity. This was a problem which was to occupy the minds of many famous clockmakers such as Cumming, Hardy, Reid and Le Roy and was also a matter which obviously concerned Congreve as in 1808 he took out a patent on what he termed his 'extreme detached escapement' in which the pendulum, under its own momentum, drives a count wheel which releases the train each minute to impulse the pendulum. In practice it would seem likely that little was achieved by this ingenious device. His patent No. 3164 dated 24th August, 1808 reads: 'That he accomplished the same effect by a simple pendulum. A light spring wheel of thirty teeth is unconnected with anything but the seconds hand and a pair of pallets. Another pallet, on the same stock, is connected with a large wheel of sixty teeth. On the face of this wheel are sixty pins, and a lever acting on these locks the wheel. On the face of the little wheel is one pin. A seconds pendulum being set in motion, the pallets drive the little wheel, and, at the sixtieth second, the pin discharges the lever from the pins of the large wheel. This, being thus

Figure 3/5. The two train chain fusee skeleton clock, shown here with the dial removed, was originally ordered for Carlton House and subsequently transferred to Buckingham Palace where it remains. It is fitted with maintaining power and one train is planted behind the other. The clock is inscribed 'Extreme Detached Escapement' across the top of the frame and below 'Invented by Wm Congreve, Esq., J. Moxon Fecit'. Unfortunately the original escapement has been removed and replaced by a spring detent chronometer escapement manufactured by Charles Frodsham & Co. As originally conceived it would have had a dial similar to that of the Time Museum Clock (Figure 3/7), thus displaying to the full Mr. Congreve's ingenious but ill-fated design.

Photograph by Gracious Permission of Her Majesty the Queen

unlocked, starts forward from the action of the first mover, and one of its teeth striking the pallet of the large wheel, gives motion to the pendulum. When the pin on the little wheel has passed the lever, the lever relocks the large wheel for another fifty nine seconds.'

There are records of at least five clocks which were fitted with Congreve's extreme detached escapement; two which were made by Moxon were first acquired for Carlton House but were eventually moved to Buckingham Palace. One of these (Figure 3/5) which is inscribed 'Extreme Detached Escapement',

Figure 3/6

Figure 3/7a

Figure 3/6. This seconds beating weight driven longcase regulator (which like that in Figure 3/5 was also purchased for Carlton House) has suffered a similar fate to the spring driven clock, having had its original escapement removed and its dial changed by Charles Frodsham in 1879. The pride which Congreve took in the clock is evinced by the fully glazed case surrounding the movement, the effect of which is now marred by the solid chapter ring.

Photograph by Gracious Permission of Her Majesty the Queen

Figure 3/7a. This skeleton clock, similar in many respects to the Buckingham Palace clock in Figure 3/5 is signed along the bottom of the front frame 'Invented by Wm Congreve Esq.'; although it bears no maker's name it would seem likely to have been made by Moxon. The fusee is mounted at the top of the frame. Hours are shown at the top, minutes in the centre and seconds on the apparently overlapping third chapter ring.

The Time Museum, Rockford, U.S.A.

is spring driven and the other is a weight driven longcase with seconds beating pendulum (Figure 3/6), but sadly they have both had their original escapements removed. A similar clock to that in Figure 3/6 but which still has its original escapement (Figure 3/7a, b) is now in the Time Museum, Rockford, U.S.A. and two far more decorative clocks with a different form of Congreve's escapement may be seen in Figures 3/8 and 3/9.

Figure 3/7b. The escapement of 3/7a.

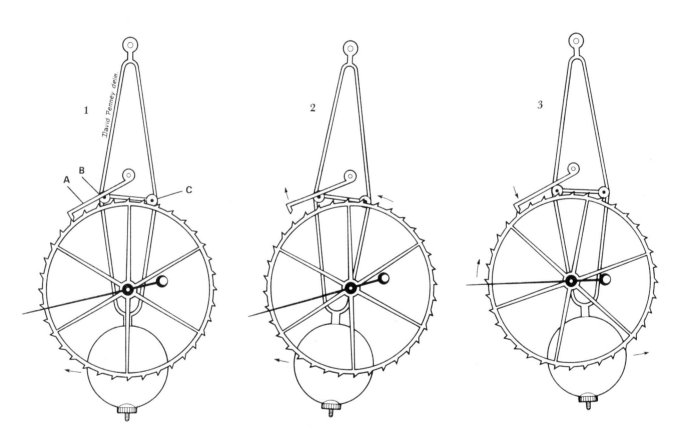

Figure 3/7c. The escapement is detached.

1. The pendulum is at bottom dead centre and moving to the left the detent (A) is firmly locked on a tooth of the 'scape wheel.

2. As the pendulum moves to the left the pin (B) on the left hand side of the pendulum lifts the detent (A) and unlocks the 'scape wheel which then rotates until a tooth engages the pin (C) on the right of the pendulum and gives it an impulse.

3. As the pendulum swings to the right the detent is allowed to drop on to and lock the 'scape wheel.

Figure 3/8a

Figure 3/8b

Figure 3/8c

Figure 3/8a, b, c, d. This clock, which is believed to have been Congreve's personal clock, was owned by his family until 1950 and is still fitted with his 'Extreme Detached Escapement'. The pendulum drives a count wheel which releases the train once a minute to impulse the pendulum. The count wheel, the arbor of which also carries the seconds hand, is mounted at the top of the train and is connected to the 'scape wheel by a line which may be seen passing down through a tube on the right hand side in Figure 3/8c. All the wheelwork is very delicate and finely executed. *Mr. D. Olson, California*

Figure 3/8d

Figure 3/9. A skeleton clock very similar to that seen in Figure 3/8 but bearing the inscription 'William Congreve London. Invenimus et Patenti 11th September 1808.'

Norman Langmaid Collection, U.S.A.

Figure 3/8d. Congreve minute impulse free pendulum regulator.

Tooth (A) of wheel (L) is held by detent (B). When one minute has passed, wire (H) is pulled by pin on upper wheel (not shown here). This raises detent (B) off tooth, allowing wheel to move forward. Arm (C), on the same shaft as (B), is also raised, placing detent (D) in path of pin (C), which is immediately locked in temporary position. Arm (E), which is jointed on arm (K), is now in path of hipp trailer (F), but as pendulum moves left, trailer passes over arm (E) without disturbing it. As pendulum moves right, trailer (F) depresses jointed arm (E), unlocking pin (C) from detent (D). Wheel (L) now moves forward and tooth (M) contacts pendulum impulse piece (J), giving impulse to pendulum. Detent (B) now locks next tooth, and jointed arm (E) returns detent (D) to resting position. Pendulum inertia carries upper wheel around for one minute until pin again raises arm (B), unlocking next tooth.

For Figure 3/8e *see* next page.

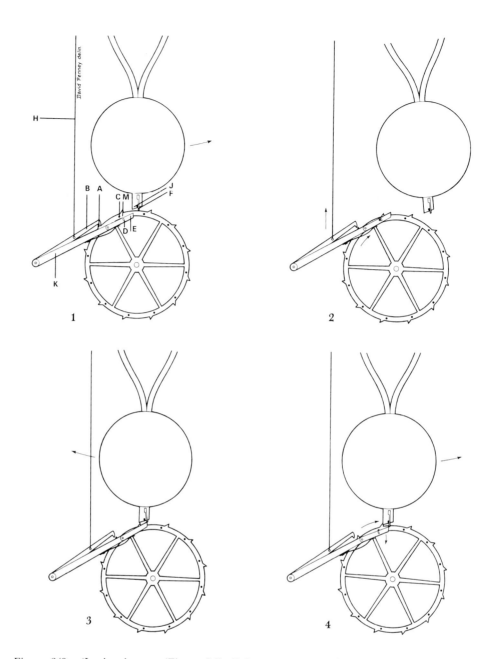

Figure 3/8e. (In the close up (Figure 8d) all the components of the escapement except the count wheel may be seen.)

1. This shows the pendulum at bottom dead centre and moving to the right. At this stage the detent (B) is locking the 'scape wheel tooth (A).

2. Every minute the count wheel mounted at the top of the clock lifts the line (H) which then raises the detent (B) off the tooth and unlocks the 'scape wheel (L), allowing it to rotate. Arm (K) on the same shaft as (B) is also raised placing detent (D) in the path of pin (C) which is immediately locked in temporary position. Arm (E) which is jointed on arm (K) is now in the path of the toggle (F) (similar to a Hipp Toggle) attached to the bottom of the pendulum.

3. As the pendulum swings to the left the trailer (F) pivots and passes over the arm (E) without disturbing it.

4. When the pendulum swings back to the right, trailer (F) depresses the jointed arm (E) unlocking pin (C) from detent (D) and allows the wheel to move forward when one of its teeth (M) hits the pendulum at (J) and impulses it. Detent (B) now locks the next tooth and the jointed arm (E) returns detent (D) to its original position. The pendulum now drives the upper count wheel round for another minute until the process is repeated. (N.B. In these drawings fewer teeth are shown on the 'scape wheel than are on the actual clock.)

Figure 3/10. A small timepiece typical of the work of Parker and Pace; this example being signed by the latter. Although at first sight these clocks appear somewhat plain and uninteresting, with their simple circular solid backplates, closer examination reveals their quality and the time which must have been spent on their construction. The beautifully finished oval base plate with tapering sides and the shield shaped front plate must have been very time consuming to produce. On this example the plinth on which the dome rests is brass cased but their plinths are more commonly made of mahogany. An interesting feature is the pendulum clamp which passes up through the base and screws on to the thread on the bottom of the pendulum.

Height 10in. (25.4cm).

PARKER AND PACE OF BURY ST. EDMUNDS

The names of these two men are so inextricably linked that it is impossible to consider them separately. It is by no means uncommon to find two clocks, one signed by Parker and the other by Pace, which are identical in every other way. The probable explanation, for which there is unfortunately no documentary proof, is that Parker was the clockmaker and Pace the retailer and probably also the designer.

JOHN PACE

John Pace was born in London in 1783. At around that time two other clockmakers with the same name were recorded as working in London and may well have been related to him; Thomas (1788-1840) and John who was working from 1790. (Other Paces are recorded as clockmakers in London as early as 1630.) The local trade directories record that John Pace worked in Bury St. Edmunds as a jeweller and watchmaker for some fifty-three years until 1857 when his wife died and he moved to Chelmsford. He remained there until he died on 14th June, 1867.[1] He was a deeply religious man who was a member of the Society of Friends, or Quakers as they are more commonly called. Several mentions are made of his untiring, industrious and above all his ingenious nature:

An extract from the *Norwich and Bury Post* may be of some interest:

> 'Death of Mr. John Pace: Our obituary records the death, at a ripe old age of Mr. John Pace, who for many years was a highly respectable resident in this town, where he carried on the business of a silversmith and watchmaker. During his earlier days Mr. Pace gave many proofs of his mechanical ingenuity; examples of which, in the shape of clocks constructed to go for years without winding-up, were exhibited at the International Exhibition of 1851. His keen appreciation of any advance in scientific knowledge led him to adopt with readiness any new invention of importance; and we believe that the inhabitants of Bury were on one occasion startled by the brilliant appearance of his shop, he being the first to substitute gas-light for the dimness of former days. His kindness of heart and desire to help forward any good object, especially of an educational character, caused him to be widely esteemed outside the boundaries of the religious community to which he belonged, at a time when members of the Society of Friends suffered in various ways from the lack of that catholicity of spirit which is more widely diffused in our own day.'

As stated above he exhibited at the Great Exhibition in 1851 and an extract from the catalogue reads as follows:

---

1. *To a Father's Memory.* By his Children 1867. Printed for private circulation only. Kindly lent by the family.

'PACE, J., Bury St. Edmunds — Inventor, Designer and Manufacturer.

Skeleton clock, which goes three years. This period is obtained by the use of six springs, the united force of which is 250lbs. They are enclosed in six barrels or boxes: three are connected with chains to a fusee on the right hand, and three to one on the left.

Pyramidical skeleton timepiece, which goes three months. The dial is placed at the bottom of the clock to show the motion of all the wheels; the Graham's dead beat escapement, and the hands moved by a simple mechanism. [This description is similar to that of the clock illustrated in Figure 3/14.]

Barometer of highly-positioned brass, containing three glass tubes supported by scrollwork. The centre-tube is the barometer and those on each side move on index work by means of wheel-work, they turn the hands on two dials, one for night and the other for day, indicating the state of the barometer.'[2]

An extract from *Suffolk Clocks and Clockmakers*[4] reads as follows:[3]

'PACE, JOHN. BURY ST. EDMUNDS. 1823-1855.

Watch and clockmaker and Jeweller in Abbeygate Street' from 1823 to 1855, in various directories. The later ones give the address as No.19. John Pace was a Quaker and of an inventive nature, as can be seen from the fact that he patented a night time-piece (No.6,506) in 1833 (Britten), and also from the many elaborate skeleton clocks bearing his name. (See *Skeleton Clocks*, by F.B. Royer-Collard.) He had acquired a high reputation even before the end of the last century, as can be seen from a catalogue description of one of his clocks in the Hengrave Hall sale (1897) — 'A fine old English striking clock, in shaped upright Spanish mahogany case, with brass mounts, made by John Pace, Bury.' There are two watches at 8 Angel Hill, Bury St. Edmunds. 8 day longcase clock, painted dial in tall, imposing lacquered case (about 8ft. tall).

BENJAMIN PARKER

Much less is known about Benjamin Parker than John Pace, but he is recorded as working as a gunsmith at 30 Churchgate Street in 1839, Chalk Lane in 1844 and 9 Chalk Lane in 1855. The fact that Parker is recorded as a gunsmith by no means precludes his work as a clockmaker and indeed it would seem likely that he made all the clocks signed by both John Pace and himself but that Pace had a strong influence on their design and marketed all those which bear his name.

---

2. *Official Descriptive and Illustrated Catalogue of the 1851 Crystal Palace Exhibition*, Vol. I, Section II, Class 10, p.419.

3. Haggor, A.L. and Miller, L.F., *Suffolk Clocks and Clockmakers*, 1974, Thames Printing Works, Ramsgate.

Figure 3/11a, b. This timepiece, which is signed on the front of the oval base by Parker, is unusual in having a very delicate and beautifully finished scroll frame (*see also* Plate 13). The wheelwork is six spoke and the spring barrel is skeletonised. Height 12in. (30cm).

Their Clocks

The clocks of Pace and Parker are different from all other skeleton clocks except those of Strutt & Wigston to which they bear several marked similarities.

The chapter rings are completely fretted out so that they consist in effect of thin inner and outer rings with Arabic numerals between them. Minute divisions are represented on the outer ring by a series of dots. The movements rest on substantial oval or occasionally rectangular brass bases with tapering sides and the name on these, whether it be that of Parker or Pace, is always beautifully engraved and in the same hand. The thick plates, which are generally solid, frequently have chamfered edges.

The Strutt clocks, which normally have virtually identical chapter rings, rest on substantial oval brass bases with tapering sides and have relatively heavy frames which are basically scroll in form and are not dissimilar from those seen on some of the Parker and Pace clocks. Strutt, who probably worked in conjunction with Wigston, was either strongly influenced by Pace and Parker (or vice versa) or possibly they had a working relationship.

Plate 14. John Pace clock (*see* Figure 3/15, p.97).

Plate 15. Condliff pillar clock, c.1825-30
(*see* Figure 3/16, p.98).

Figure 3/12. A rare year duration timepiece skeleton clock signed 'B. Parker, Bury St. Edmunds' on the front and upper chamfered edge of the beautifully finished rectangular brass base, which has tapering sides. (This clock was formerly in the collection of Major Heathcote and featured in the Asprey/Nielson Exhibition in 1975.)[1] The very heavy scroll frame, which is more functional than beautiful, is ⁹/₁₆ in. (8mm) thick. Four massive 3in. (7.6cm) mainsprings are employed to drive the clock (two on either side) and there are two fusees which drive the first intermediate pinion which has thirty-two leaves; this high number was probably adopted in part to decrease friction but mainly to reduce the load on any one leaf. The wheel carried on the same arbor as this pinion drives a further intermediate pinion and the wheel on this arbor drives the centre pinion. There are two wheels between the fusee and centre wheel. Each pair of barrels works in tandem: thus when winding the chains are drawn off the upper barrels and on to the fusees and at the same time the lower chains are drawn from the lower to the upper barrels. The fusee winding arbors are reversed and thus the clock is wound from the rear.

In contrast to the massive nature of the rest of the clock, the centre, intermediate, 'scape wheel and motion work, which may all be seen inside the chapter ring, are relatively light, have very delicate crossings and are carried by long and attractively shaped cocks. The 'scape wheel, as on virtually all long duration clocks, has been kept as small as possible to reduce the power required to a minimum. The pendulum employs three steel rods and a brass bob with decorative turning. The subsidiary dials indicate the days of the month and the weeks of the year.

---

1. Catalogue of the Asprey/Neilson Exhibition of Fine Antique and Decorative Clocks, 10th-20th June, 1975.

Figure 3/13. A year duration clock (again from the Heathcote collection) this time signed by John Pace whose name appears on the front of the oval base. Although the plates are lancet shaped with scrollwork at the base the clock is basically similar to that in Figure 3/12 employing four spring barrels and two fusees. An attractive feature is the rings showing the days of the month and the weeks of the year which appear to be intertwined. The use of this technique permits much larger rings to be employed.

Figure 3/14. A most unusual pyramidal shaped skeleton clock signed on the tapering oval base by John Pace and numbered 247, which is similar to the clock referred to in the Great Exhibition catalogue (*see* p.91). The advantage of mounting the dial at the bottom is that all the wheelwork is clearly visible above it and in this case has been mounted vertically with the delicate dead beat escapement at the top. The pendulum, which has an axe shaped bob, may be regulated by means of the screw seen at the top of the plates. These, in typical Pace fashion, are all carefully chamfered at their edges. Height 14in. (35.5cm).

The number of clocks produced by Parker and Pace was relatively small but undoubtedly the design most commonly seen is that shown in Figure 3/10. The chapter ring and base are typical of their work; the plates are solid but the chamfered edges and the front one is in the form of a shield. The wheelwork is five spoke and everything is well finished; a similar but much more delicate clock may be seen in Figure 3/11 (*see also* Plate 13).

In addition to their timepieces they produced a fascinating series of clocks, most of which were of long duration and frequently had calendarwork; the durations of which vary from eight days to three months, a year and even three years. It is not known how many year going clocks were made by Parker but one other similar clock in addition to Figures 3/12 and 3/13 is still in existence, and a three year clock signed by Pace was shown at the Great Exhibition of 1851.

Plate 16. One of Condliff's first series skeleton clocks (*see* Figure 3/17, p.100).

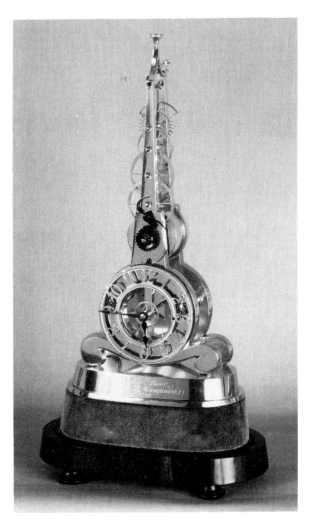

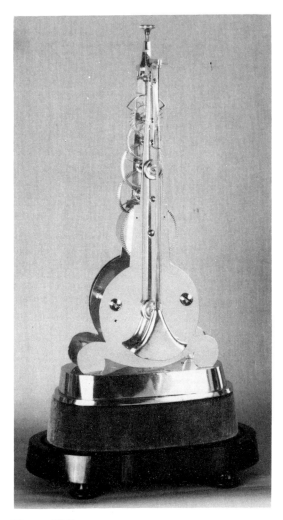

Figure 3/15a, b, c. A similar clock to that seen in Figure 3/14 with a gilded chapter ring, chamfered plates, dead beat escapement and screw regulation for fast/slow at the top of the frame (*see also* Plate 14). A most unusual feature is the mounting of a pulley at the rear of the centre wheel arbor behind the backplate from which a cord runs down to drive the minute arbor. The clock has a going barrel which gives a duration of eighteen days and is signed 'John Pace, Bury St. Edmunds, No.253' on the front of the brass base.
Height 15in. (38cm).

Figure 3/15b.

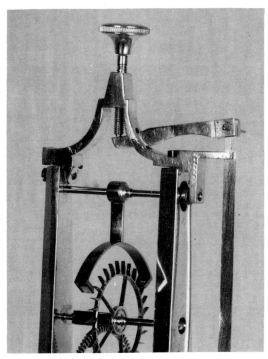

Figure 3/15c.

Figure 3/16a, b. An early example of a Condliff pillar clock, probably made between 1825 and 1830, which has the rectangular baseplate typical of Condliff's work with the barrel set into it and four rising pillars to support the skeletonised movement (*see also* Plate 15). It will be noted that a simple engraved and silvered chapter ring is employed at this stage and that the barrels have not been skeletonised. The going train, situated to the left of the clock, is provided with maintaining power. The chains may be seen running obliquely from the base plate to the fusees and the rear view shows the line passing from the movement into the hollow base which contains the gong and hammer (*see also* Figures 3/18g, h).

Figure 3/16c. Condliff's beautifully executed and very decorative escapement photographed from the rear. The top of the helical balance spring is held in the serpent's mouth and a large brass seconds beating balance is employed which permits the use of a centre sweep seconds hand. The lever escapement has jewelled dead beat pallets. To the right of the escapement is the line which passes down into the base to actuate the strike work.

THE CONDLIFF FAMILY

Liverpool began to expand rapidly in the early eighteenth century as its importance as a port increased; the principal imports were sugar from the West Indies, hides, tallow, Irish linen, cloth and tobacco, and amongst the exports were salt, coal, pottery and textiles. Indeed trade generally and in particular between England and America was showing a dramatic rise in both quantity and range at this period.[1]

Watchmaking was well established in the city by this time, as suppliers to the London trade for at least the previous fifty years. (It is interesting that one Liverpool made watch may be dated prior to 1610.)

By the early 1700s all the tools and components for the manufacture of complete watches were being made in Liverpool and the surrounding areas. One London clockmaker writing at the beginning of the eighteenth century attributed the invention of all the principal clockmaking tools to watchmakers working in Liverpool.

The advent of the Industrial Revolution was to speed the expansion in Liverpool of trade in general and watchmaking in particular until by around 1800 a higher proportion of the population must have been employed in watchmaking than in practically any other city in the realm. Chronometer production had started in Liverpool by 1800, the first recorded maker being Hornby, but rough movements were probably supplied to the London trade somewhat earlier than this.

It is against this infrastructure, with the wealth of talent and experience gained over the previous century and a half that James Condliff set up at 32 Gerard Street, Liverpool in 1816. The clock manufacturing business which he founded was to become one of the most successful in the city (and indeed the country), capable of undertaking the manufacture of virtually any type of clock from a simple wall clock to a fine chiming turret clock, but it is probably for his superb regulators and skeleton clocks that Condliff is best known. Between 1816 and 1827 he worked in Gerard Street and Fraser Street, more precise details are given on p.113.

After 1827 he worked with Joseph (possibly his brother) continuing at Fraser Street, probably his workshops, and also at Clare Street. In 1846 a branch was opened at Everton under Joseph's name and in the same year John's name appears for the first time in conjunction with premises at Mount Vernon. At this stage the relationship between these members of the family has not been properly established. Branches were also started shortly after this in Tranmere and Gloucester Street. The fourth Condliff to appear in connection with the business was Thomas who is recorded as working in Fraser Street in 1867 and was still working there in 1914 but had retired by 1925. The firm continued into the 1940s when the stock was sold off by auction.

---

1. Hyde, F.E., *Liverpool and the Mersey, the development of the Port 1700-1900,*

Figure 3/17a, b, c. Another example of a Condliff first series skeleton clock (*see also* Plate 16) probably made some ten to fifteen years later than that shown in Figure 3/16. The whole clock is far more ornate having a carved and inlaid mahogany base and numerous decorative mounts, mostly in a classical vein, with simple cupids around the arch, an elephant and stag resting just below the chapter ring, sphinxes (a popular feature in Regency and early Victorian times) on either side of the large balance with a lion in front of the left hand barrel. To the right of the balance are two racehorses which probably relate to the commencement of the Grand National in Liverpool in 1839. The feet on which the base rests have a Regency look. Although no presentation plaque is present it would seem likely that this clock was made for a specific person and may well have been designed to reflect his various interests. The two train movement has pump action quarter chime on two gongs mounted in the base and the skeletonised snail in the centre of the dial which controls this is very much a decorative feature of the clock. The fine wheelwork has six crossings and maintaining power is provided and can be seen quite clearly in the rear view of the clock. The enamelled chapter ring has an engine turned outer and a smooth inner bezel. An additional wheel has been provided in the striking train, situated to the left of the clock, which is presumably to take care of the additional duration of run required for the quarter striking but it also has the added advantage of producing symmetry in the run of the two chains.

Norman Langmaid Collection, U.S.A.

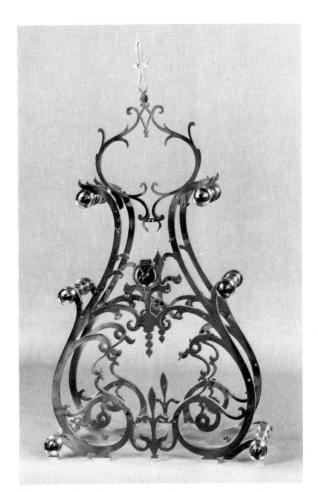

Figure 3/18a. This second series clock, which must be one of the most attractive ever produced by Condliff, has been chosen to illustrate in some detail not only the fine quality of his design and the execution of his work, but also the attention to detail and the characteristic features of his skeleton clocks (*see also* Plate 17). Although his three train clocks (Figure 3/20) may be more complex and have the appeal of a quarter chime, the somewhat wider frame required and the row of bells mounted to one side of the frame undoubtedly detracts from their appearance. This clock, which has the retailer's plaque on the front (Joseph Mayer of Liverpool) is also stamped on the back by Condliff. All the wheels have either five or six crossings and each wheel is screwed on to its collet; the barrels are skeletonised and the balance is mounted within the top of the frame. The silvered chapter ring, which has an outer brass bezel, has a recess on its inner aspect which may indicate that it had a glass inner dial graduated 13-24 as on the clock shown in Figure 3/19. The wooden bases of Condliff's clocks showed considerable variety of design to suit each clock but were all of fine quality; this example is crossbanded with rosewood and has solid rosewood moulds around its upper edge.

Figure 3/18b. The extreme delicacy and excellent symmetry of Condliff's frames is well illustrated here; both trains and all the underdial work have been removed. The top of the frame provides an ideal setting to highlight his escapement.

Figure 3/18c. A complete breakdown of the clock which shows just how much work is involved in its construction.

Figure 3/18d. The strikework. Note the quality of all the wheels with their fine crossings and narrow rims and the way in which they are screwed on to their collets, which demonstrates how much attention has been given to the design of each component to make it look attractive.

Figure 3/18e. Condliff's lever escapement with helical spring to the large balance is reminiscent of chronometer work: to watch it oscillating back and forth within the confines of the beautifully executed scroll frame is a fascinating experience.

The last entry that can be located for James is 1884 but whether he was working until this time is open to some doubt as a skeleton clock in the City of Liverpool Museum which is signed 'James Condliff, Liverpool' and dated 1862 has a plaque on the rear which reads 'This clock was made entirely by Thomas Condliff for the late James Condliff'. It is conceivable that this plaque was put on at a later date or that there was another James Condliff, but these explanations seem somewhat unlikely.

The business continued at Fraser Street and also various other addresses until it finally closed in 1923. Interestingly it is recorded that the turret clock at Winstanley Hall was repaired by the Condliffs in 1905, 1914 and 1922.

James Condliff was a man of exceptional talent: not only was he of an inventive turn of mind and had a great depth of technical knowledge and ability but he also had a keen artistic flair and it was probably this, as with so many of the most successful clockmakers before him (of which Joseph Knibb is a prime example), which made him so successful. The design of his skeleton clock frames (Figure 3/18b) and even the individual components have seldom been equalled and never bettered by any other maker although some have been conceived on a far more grandiose scale and may initially be more impressive. Similar remarks can also be applied to the components (Figure 3/18c, d). To keep the design of his skeleton clocks as 'clean' and attractive as possible the striking mechanism, usually with a gong, was concealed inside a hollow base (Figure 3/18g), but when quarter chiming on eight bells was provided the bells were usually mounted at the top and to one side of the frame.

A consistent feature of virtually all Condliff's clocks was the flat rectangular brass base supported by brass ball feet and decorated with fretwork; the front of this base carried the signature of the maker or distributor.

Condliff designed and produced three distinct series of clocks, the first being the pillar clock, an example of which is shown in Figure 3/16. The second

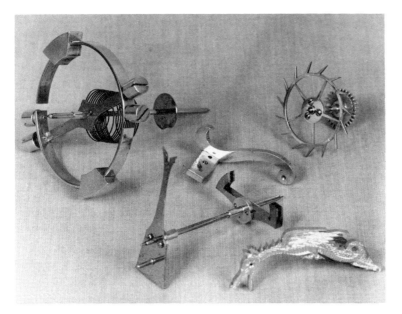

Figure 3/18f. The components of the escapement with jewelled dead beat pallets, jewelled impulse pin, a large seconds beating bi-metallic balance which runs in jewelled pivot holes and a helical balance spring. The serpent, a characteristic of so much of Condliff's work, may be seen in the foreground.

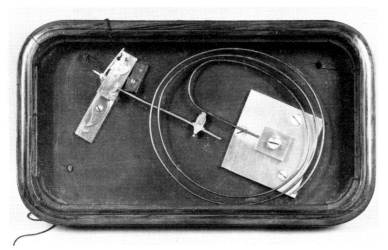

Figure 3/18g, h. The rosewood base with its top removed to reveal the gong mounted on a substantial brass block. The vertical pull of the cord by the strikework is transferred to a horizontal motion of the hammer by a cranked lever acting on pins fixed to the cylindrical base of the hammer arm.

series made use of a beautifully designed scroll frame and the third series, usually produced as a simple timepiece, sometimes with passing strike in the base, employed a going barrel with great wheel. It is difficult to put any precise dates on the production of the various series of clocks and undoubtedly there was a considerable overlap, particularly between the second and third but it would seem likely that the first series was produced between 1825-50, the second series from 1850 to c.1870 and the third series from 1855-60.

An interesting and attractive feature of Condliff's work, particularly in his second series clocks, is the way in which he constantly varied the design of the frame and the wooden base, albeit often only to a minor degree, to give each clock its individual character, regardless of the very considerable expense involved in, for instance, making up new frame patterns. This point is well illustrated by comparing Figures 3/18a and 3/19. Only some of the finest makers such as Breguet consistently went to such lengths.

Plate 17. Condliff second series skeleton clock (*see* Figure 3/18, p.101).

Figure 3/19. This clock which is signed by James Condliff is basically similar to that shown in Figure 3/18 but is quarter chiming on two gongs mounted in the base which has been made somewhat deeper to accommodate them. A further variation is the employment of a glass dial with two contrasting rings numbered I to XII and 13 to 24.
Height, including dome, 22in. (60cm).
Sotheby's. Details provided by Strike One

Figure 3/20. A fine three train quarter chiming skeleton clock signed 'James Condliff, Liverpool' on a decorative plaque on either side of the baseplate. The presentation inscription in the centre reads: 'This timepiece was presented to Joseph Crook, Esq., M.P. by the workpeople in bleachworks as a token of their very high esteem and gratitude for his noble, patriotic and disinterested exertions in pursuing through Parliament THE BLEACHERS 10 HR BILL. 1860'. The plaque is interesting in that it throws some light on the struggle going on at that time to control some of the less desirable aspects of the Industrial Revolution, and is also useful in that it gives a firm date for the production of this chiming clock.

It will be seen that the frame has been made somewhat wider to accommodate the three trains and that the bells have been mounted to one side of the top of the frame which undoubtedly detracts from its appearance, but at this time chimes were in great demand, stimulated in large measure by the completion of Big Ben.

The eight pillar movement employs very delicate wheelwork with six crossings and skeletonised barrels. Two chimes are provided and the change lever for these is immediately in front of the bells with strike/silent regulation in a similar position on the other side of the clock. As usual the hour strike is on a gong in the base. The silvered chapter ring has inner and outer bezels and employs unusual Roman numerals which seem to have been used on several of his clocks around this period. The well executed walnut base complements the clock beautifully; a nice touch is the slots cut in the top to let out the sound. (A very similar clock is in the Merseyside County Museum and is marked on the base 'International Exhibition 1862'.)
Sotheby's

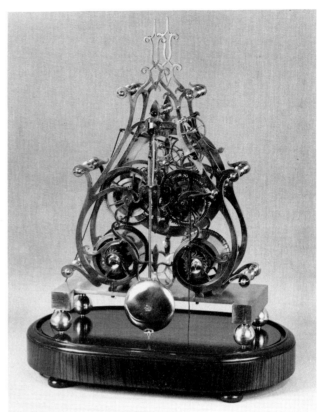

Figure 3/21a, b. This clock, made by Condliff but marketed by Litherland, Davies & Co. whose name appears on the plaque and is the first pendulum clock to be described here, was probably made in the 1860s and the adoption of the pendulum may well have been occasioned by the need to keep down prices to compete with manufacturers such as Smith's and Evans. Although the frame is basically similar to that on the other second series clocks, the base appears somewhat wider, which is accentuated by the closing in of the top part of the frame because there is no longer any need to accommodate the balance wheel. In all other respects the clock is similar to those with a balance. The workmanship is up to Condliff's usual high standard. The wheelwork has five crossings, the barrels are skeletonised and a finely skeletonised snail with star wheel is used for the repeat. The narrow chapter ring is silvered brass.
Overall height 16½ in. (42cm).

First Series

In the first series of clocks the movement, which has arched plates, is supported by four pillars (Figure 3/16a) rising from a flat rectangular base. A very similar clock to that illustrated was presented to William Scoreby in 1833 and this clock probably predates it by a few years. An interesting feature is the recessing of the barrels into the brass base, thus necessitating a long run of chain to reach the fusees, which was undoubtedly done to keep the entire centre of the clock clear in order to focus attention on the spectacular balance complete with its helical spring oscillating back and forth (Figure 3/16c).

The incorporation of a balance was probably decided on for several reasons: a) The strong influence the watch making industry would have had in Liverpool at that time. b) The importance of the chronometer to a maritime city such as Liverpool and the ever increasing numbers of these instruments being produced. c) The fascination of watching a large seconds beating balance, such as those produced by Condliff, in action, which of course had the added advantage that a centre seconds hand could be provided.

In the design of the whole escapement Condliff's artistry can clearly be seen. A fascinating feature is the serpent whose mouth acts as a pinning point for the balance spring (Figure 3/16c). (A breakdown of a somewhat similar escapement on a second series clock may be seen in Figure 3/18f, in which the dead beat pallets are jewelled, there is a jewelled impulse pin and the bi-metallic balance has jewelled pivots.) The barrels are solid which is unusual and may be an early feature, as in nearly all his later clocks the barrel covers are crossed out. The base is relatively plain and this again may suggest an early date. The chapter ring, which has bevelled edges, is engraved and silvered and a skeletonised snail can be seen within this.

A somewhat later and more elaborate clock may be seen in Figure 3/17, in which a more complex base is provided and both Georgian and Regency influences would seem to be provided by the classical figures of cupids mounted above the clock and the sphinxes resting on either side of the balance. To the left is shown a barge and on the right are two racehorses, which probably relate to the Grand National which commenced in Liverpool in 1839; it could well be that the person to whom this clock was presented was a famous racehorse owner. The stag and the elephant resting below and on either side of the dial may also have been placed on the clock for personal reasons. Brass bezels are fixed on the inner and outer aspects of the chapter ring, which may well have been in part for decorative purposes but also enabled either a glass centre or an inner chapter ring to be provided thus giving the clock a twenty-four hour dial (Figure 3/19). Because of the friability of the glass these centres are often missing but their original presence can be assumed if there is a recess on the inside of the inner bezel to receive them.

Condliff made two train clocks with pump action quarter chime and in these instances both the two quarter chiming and the hour gongs were placed in the base. Figure 3/17 shows just such a clock. The snail with its additional steps may be seen in the centre of the chapter ring.

Second Series

In the second series of skeleton clocks Condliff produced a delicate scroll frame (Figure 3/18) and the top of this was adapted to accommodate the balance, again with helical balance spring, thus displaying it very attractively at the top of the clock. The scroll frame design also enabled him to produce clocks which chimed the quarters on eight bells, these being mounted to one side of the top of the frame. Although these clocks were technically interesting and had the appeal of a quarter chime they were not quite as pleasing to look at as his classical two train scroll frame clocks because of the loss of symmetry. The brass baseplate and the hollow wooden base were retained. The shape of the frame seems to have been modified a little over the series, the lower part being

Figure 3/22. A quarter chiming skeleton clock by James Condliff similar in most respects to that shown in Figure 3/20, but the clock is controlled by a pendulum (not shown here) instead of a balance, and this permits the narrowing of the top of the frame which in turn simplifies the accommodation of the eight bell chime. The design of the clock is somewhat simpler than that in Figure 3/20 in that there is no choice of chimes; the bezel has been eliminated from the chapter ring and the base is more restrained. Overall height 20in. (51cm). *Christie's*

Figure 3/23a. A particularly interesting two train skeleton clock almost certainly made by Condliff but marketed by Henry Foster of Liverpool whose name appears on the plaque (*see also* Plate 18). It is, in effect, an amalgamation of the first and second series designs. Eight instead of the usual four pillars of the first series clocks are employed. The barrels, which have solid covers, have been raised to occupy most of the space between the baseplate and the movement which is normally filled by the balance.
The movement is supported by a much simplified scroll frame surmounted by a two headed serpent which surrounds and supports the balance with its helical spring. The chapter ring has decorative inner and outer bezels and a centre sweep seconds hand is provided. *R. Wauson Collection, U.S.A.*

somewhat wider on some clocks, probably those produced at a later date. A conventional anchor escapement with pendulum was also used occasionally instead of the balance, and the quality of these movements was also very fine.

Third Series

A third series of clocks was designed and produced, probably from the mid-1850s onwards, in which a scroll frame was again employed but of somewhat smaller and simpler design. Made as timepieces, sometimes with passing strike, these clocks employed a greatwheel which was somewhat larger

Figure 3/23b. The clock rests on a substantial gilded brass base and is protected by a rectangular base and dome.

Figure 3/23c. The rear view shows the quarter snail mounted on the backplate and the lines passing through slots cut in the brass base to reach the levers actuating the gong hammers.

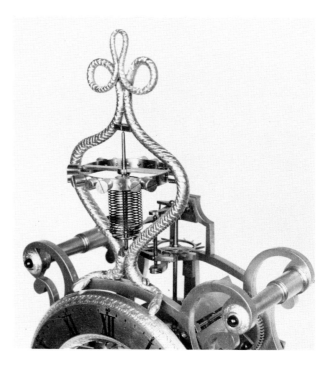

Figure 3/23d. The typical Condliff escapement with his magnificent balance and helical spring surrounded by a coiled two headed serpent.

Figure 3/24. A typical third series skeleton clock by Condliff, marketed by Litherland, Davies & Co. of Liverpool. Characteristic features are the employment of a going barrel with a great wheel at least as large as the chapter ring, a simple but delicate and well designed scroll frame and a relatively narrow silvered chapter ring. The platform base with ball feet as used on his first and second series clocks is retained. These clocks were offered with or without passing strike in the base. All of these clocks appear to have employed a pendulum with either dead beat or recoil escapement.
Height 13in. (31cm).   *Christie's*

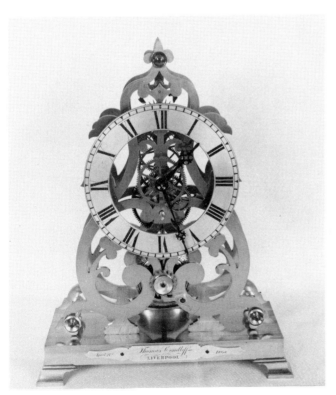

Figure 3/25a, b. A relatively late single train skeleton clock signed by Thomas Condliff and dated April 21st, 1868. The scroll frame, although reminiscent of the earlier clocks, is far heavier. Note how the platform base which is supported by bracket feet, has been cut away to accommodate the pendulum.

in diameter than the chapter ring, and a going barrel, an unusual feature for an English clock. It is likely that the production of these clocks was stimulated by ever increasing competition from such large scale manufacturers as Smith's in London and Evans in Birmingham, but although the clocks were simpler and thus cheaper to produce than Condliff's other clocks the design and quality of construction were still excellent.

A most interesting clock is shown in Figure 3/23, which is a combination of many of the features contained in both the first and second series clocks. A rectangular base is employed with eight instead of the usual four pillars rising up from this to support the movement, which instead of being arched has what is basically a scroll frame. Surmounting this is a two headed serpent the coils of which are arranged in such a way that the balance and its helical spring are contained within. The solid spring barrels occupy most of the space between the movement and the base plate which rests on a substantial moulded brass plinth.

A skeleton clock by Thomas Condliff, dated April 21st, 1868 is shown in Figure 3/25, which although it still retains the brass rectangular base typical of all the other Condliff clocks has a frame and chapter ring similar to many of the skeleton clocks being produced by other makers at that period.

Condliff Retailers

The Condliff family signed more of their skeleton clocks than the vast majority of makers, but they still relied on retailers and other clockmakers to sell much of their stock and of these Litherland, Davies & Co. were by far the most important.

LITHERLAND, DAVIES & CO.

Peter Litherland (1756-1804) was a fine watchmaker, amongst whose achievements was the invention of the rack lever. After his death the firm continued firstly under the name of Litherland, Whiteside & Co. and from 1816 (the same year as James Condliff started working in Liverpool) the firm became known as Litherland, Davies & Co. Although their name frequently appears on skeleton clocks over quite a long period of time there is absolutely no indication that they made anything other than watches and chronometers and all the skeleton clocks signed by them are identical with those produced by Condliff whose name will usually be found in addition to theirs, but stamped at the rear of the base plate. It would seem likely that Litherland's used the extensive contacts generated through their high volume of watch sales to retail Condliff's clocks, and also that they assisted in the manufacture of the escapements, as they are recorded as escapement manufacturers to the trade and indeed Ann Litherland is listed as such, working at 62 Brownlow Hill in 1825.[2]

---

2. Mercer, R.V., 'Peter Litherland & Co.', *Antiquarian Horology,* June 1962.

Figure 3/26a, b. A most unusual single train skeletonised table regulator signed by John Condliff of Liverpool, the design and construction of which is unlike anything else produced by the Condliff family. The substantial frame is delicately pierced out and this and the wheelwork with its arched crossings is very much in the idiom of earlier French practice. The silvered brass dial has the layout of an English regulator with a centre sweep minute hand and subsidiaries for the seconds and hours, winding being effected through the centre of the latter. There is dead beat escapement, maintaining power, beat regulation and a wood rod pendulum with cylindrical bob. *Patric Capon*

Other Outlets

Whereas with some of the high volume skeleton clock makers the names appearing on their clocks (usually on a plaque) came from all over the country and were obviously retailers, in Condliff's case, the retailers were usually from Liverpool and were often recorded as clockmakers, such as Evans.

Condliff — Information from Liverpool directories

	James	Joseph	John	Thomas
1816	32 Gerard St.	—	—	—
1818	65 Circus St.	—	—	—
1821	67 Circus St.	—	—	—
1823	5 Fraser St.	—	—	—
1827	"	Shaws Brow	—	—
1829	"	Clare Street	—	—
1831	"	" "	—	—
1841	"	" "	—	—
1846	"	Everton	Mount Vernon	—
1849	"	"	" "	—
1851	"	Tranmere	Gloucester St.	—
1867	—	—	—	Fraser St.

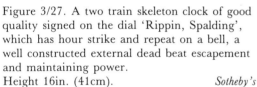

Figure 3/27. A two train skeleton clock of good quality signed on the dial 'Rippin, Spalding', which has hour strike and repeat on a bell, a well constructed external dead beat escapement and maintaining power.
Height 16in. (41cm).   *Sotheby's*

Figure 3/28. A skeleton timepiece signed 'Barrauds, London. 725', and as befits a chronometer maker everything is finished to a high standard. The great wheel is larger than usual, all the wheelwork is five spoke with delicate crossings, the barrel covers are skeletonised and the 'scape wheel is particularly well executed.

Sotheby's

RIPPIN, SPALDING

Several clocks, all virtually identical to that in Figure 3/27 have been seen over the last ten to fifteen years and all except one have borne the name Rippin, Spalding, which leads one to believe that they were made by him. Two Rippins are recorded as working in Spalding in the nineteenth century: James (possibly the father) who is known to have worked there from 1828-35 and another James (possibly the son) from 1868-76, but it is conceivable that there was just one maker who worked from 1828-76. The clocks, which have a most unusual egg shaped frame, are always two train and have external dead beat escapement and maintaining power.

BARRAUD'S, LONDON

Barraud's were well known for the fine quality of their clocks and in particular their ships' chronometers, but like Dent's they only appear to have produced one series of skeleton clocks and even these were probably made in very small numbers. The example shown here is also illustrated in the book on Paul Philip Barraud.[1]

---

1. Jagger, Cedric, The supplement to 'Paul Philip Barraud', *The Antiquarian Horological Society,* 1968.

Figure 3/29a, b. A particularly small eight bell skeleton clock which employs a ninth bell for the hour, signed at the base of the rear frame 'John Moore & Sons, Clerkenwell' and numbered 11560. The height of the movement is only 10½ in. (26.5cm). It has several interesting features for although only two train it has pump action quarter chime for the first three quarters; it winds from the rear, possibly to avoid any chance of disturbing or damaging the centre sweep seconds hand (missing), there is a lever escapement mounted vertically at the top of the backplate and maintaining power is provided. The frames are similar to, but less elaborate than the Norwich Union clock in Figure 3/31 and relatively simple feet are provided, which rest on a mahogany board supported by a decorative ormolu base. *Norman Langmaid Collection, U.S.A.*

Figure 3/29b

MOORE & SONS, CLERKENWELL

Both Handley and Moore were apprentices of Jn. Thwaites at 39 Clerkenwell Close at the end of the eighteenth century and in 1802 formed the well known partnership of Handley & Moore. G. Handley died in 1824 leaving Moore to continue the business under the name of Jno. Moore & Sons. It is believed that

Plate 18. Condliff two train skeleton clock (*see* Figure 3/23, p.109).

John Moore died in 1842, when the business was continued by his son George until his death in 1894 at the age of eighty. At the time of the Great Exhibition they were recorded as working at 38 Clerkenwell Close.

It is not known how many skeleton clocks were made by John Moore but at least five are recorded, three of which are illustrated here. In the *Descriptive and Illustrated Catalogue* of the 1851 Great Exhibition, Moore & Sons, who are described as manufacturers, are listed as having a month duration chiming

Plate 19. Figure 3/30a. John Moore & Sons clock
(*see* p.118).

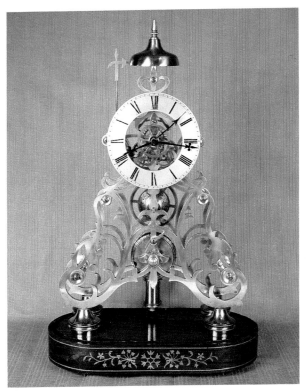

Plate 20. Skeleton clock by Haycock, c.1870
(*see* Figure 3/35, p.122).

skeleton clock on display and also another skeleton clock. Although the
Norwich Union clock (Figure 3/31) is much larger and more elaborate than the
other two it is interesting to notice that both clocks have the same highly
unusual frames somewhat akin to the designs seen in circular church windows.
Possibly the best way of describing the shape of the frames is by comparing
them to a fully opened out peony with twelve petals, with the centre of each
petal removed.

Figure 3/30b. A very similar clock to Figure 3/29 but with a more elaborate base, signed and numbered on the frame 'John Moore & Sons, Clerkenwell, London 11477' and also numbered on the barrels (*see also* Plate 19). Height without dome 14in. (36cm).

Figure 3/31a, b. This superb quality clock, which can only be described as massive, weighs some 225lbs (105kg.), and was made by John Moore & Sons of Clerkenwell for the Great Exhibition of 1851. The triple chain fusee movement chimes the quarters on eight bells mounted centrally behind twelve o'clock, the nest running from front to back. Despite the size of the clock there is much delicacy of design, the hands for instance being much lighter than on the average skeleton clock and the chapter ring has been fretted out as completely as possible, the numerals being laid on circular green enamelled discs which are connected together with fine scrollwork. The frame feet are decorated with green champlevé enamel and an unusual feature is the gilded overlay applied to the pendulum bob. The substantial carved mahogany base is attractively decorated with vine leaves and a plaque in the centre bears the inscription 'Auro Praevalet Veritas'. Clocks with similar bases often contain a musical movement (Figure 1/21) but this is not the case in this instance. (This clock was purchased by Mr. Joseph Langhorn, M.R.C.S. who lived at Spencer House, Cobham, and it was he who bequeathed it to the Norwich Union in 1878 where it has remained in their headquarters in Norwich ever since.)

John Moore & Sons are believed to have made two other such clocks, one of which was bought by the Tsar of Russia and is now in the Hermitage Museum in Leningrad, and the other went to the United States and cannot now be traced. The similarity in overall concept of the clocks shown in Figures 1/21, 6/7 and 6/9 makes one wonder whether these were also made by Moore.

Norwich Union. Mr. Greg Chandler

Figure 3/31a

Figure 3/31b

WILLIAM SMITH OF MUSSELBURGH

William Smith set up as a clockmaker in Musselburgh in Scotland in 1847 and continued working there until 1903. In the late 1840s he hit upon the ingenious idea of using rubber instead of a metal spring to drive a clock and thus designed one which would be suitable for this purpose (Figure 3/32). His solution was to house the rubber spring in a hollow vertical column and in the majority of his clocks this was fretted out so that all could see his marvellous invention which he submitted to the Society of Arts in Edinburgh on 30th April 1849, which they described as:

> 'Description and drawing of a time-piece moved by a spring of Vulcanized Caoutchouc, read at a meeting of the Society of Arts held at Edinburgh, 30th April 1849, by William Smith, Musselburgh, for which the Society's Silver Medal, value five sovereigns, was awarded. The author stated that he conceives the superiority of this spring to consist in its perfect invariability from the absence of friction, and the simplicity of its application, being in the form of a ring, one end of which is passed through a piece of steel with an eye, to which is attached a hook connecting it with the pulley, both ends being fixed at the bottom of the column by a steel pin passed over them.'

Unfortunately it was not realised at that time (and certainly not by William Smith) that rubber, which is essentially a polymer of isoprene obtained by coagulating the milky juice of various plants, is susceptible to oxidation by air and particularly so when under strain, as it would be in this case. In those days antioxidants had not been discovered so the rubber spring would probably oxidise relatively rapidly, leading to cracks in the rubber and additional failure. Modern day formulations for both natural and synthetic rubbers contain ingredients to prevent oxidation and thus it is likely that a similar design, if constructed today, might well be successful.[1,2]

It is because of the foregoing reason that all the clocks made to this design have had the rubber replaced by a steel coiled spring. It may well be that Smith realised the defect inherent in his design during his lifetime and used a steel coil spring on some of his later clocks.

The quality of these clocks is always quite high and the design of all the movements is similar. His earlier clocks are signed 'Wm. Smith. Musselburgh, Maker & Inventor' and these usually have the spring visible inside the column (Figures 3/32 and 3/33), whereas on those which are probably a little later and may have been fitted with a steel spring in the first instance, which is concealed (Figure 3/34), they are just signed 'W. Smith Musselburgh'.

1. Information supplied by Dr. P. Wright, Technical Manager, Dunlop Ltd., Manchester.
2. Stern H.J., *Rubber Natural & Synthetic,* McLauren & Sons.

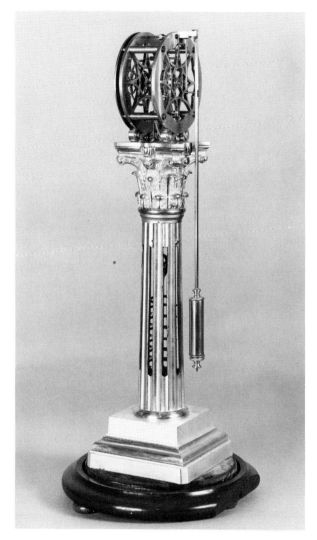

Figure 3/32a, b, c. A fine quality eight day pillar clock signed 'Wm. Smith Musselburgh. Maker & Inventor'. The plates of the movement are attractively fretted out, the delicate wheelwork is five spoke and the coiled spring, together with its pulley and chain, may be seen within the column. Height 18in. (38cm).

Figure 3/32c

Figure 3/33. Another skeleton clock signed 'Wm. Smith. Musselburgh. Maker & Inventor' in which the main column is made up of six smaller columns through which the spring passes. The movement is virtually identical to that seen in Figure 3/32c. Height 16in. (41cm).

Figure 3/34. This clock is signed 'W. Smith Musselburgh', the spring in the column is concealed and the plates are fretted out in a different manner. All the other details of the clock would appear to be the same as in Figures 3/32 and 3/33. Height 15in. (38.5cm).

The problem with these clocks, which are of eight day duration, is the very small travel of the spring as it is obviously essential that its elastic limit is not exceeded otherwise the spring will be permanently damaged, and that it has a reasonable 'set up' to provide the minimum power required to keep it going.

Because of these parameters the strength of the spring and the number of its coils have to be chosen quite carefully as there can only be a few turns on the fusee. Obviously the longer the coil spring the greater its possible elongation and the easier it is to get a more even force on the fusee via the chain but unfortunately only a relatively short spring can be used otherwise there is insufficient travel for the clock to run its full eight days.

Figure 3/35a, b. A fine quality skeleton clock made by Haycock of Derbyshire, c.1870, with a substantial silvered scroll frame some ¼ in. (6mm) thick and seven well turned pillars (*see also* Plate 20). Graham dead beat escapement is used in conjunction with a centre sweep seconds hand and a steel rod pendulum with cylindrical brass bob. A particularly interesting feature is that the clock runs for a month on one winding. The rear view shows the extra wheel incorporated in the train to achieve this.
Height 20in. (50.5cm).   *Norman Langmaid Collection, U.S.A.*

THE HAYCOCK FAMILY OF CLOCKMAKERS

Joseph Harlow started his clockmaking business in Ashbourne, Derbyshire, c.1740. His son, Samuel, who was the best known clockmaker of the Harlow family, wrote *The Clockmakers Guide,* original copies of which are now very rare. Another son John was in business as a maker of clock pinions and ironwork for clocks at a workshop in Compton, Ashbourne, along with his son Thomas.

In 1816 the Haycock brothers John and Thomas came from Staffordshire and after being in the employ of the Harlows at their clock, iron and pinion making business for some ten years, took it over and ran it in their own name. In 1860 the Haycocks built a new works off Station Street for the manufacture of all types of clocks; by this time Thomas Haycock had two sons who were involved in the business, Thomas junior, and William. After a few years William left and commenced in business on his own account near Church Street, Ashbourne, also as a clockmaker.

Figure 3/36. A truly massive skeleton timepiece of fine quality by Haycock of Derbyshire, here seen completely dwarfing a French Great Exhibition timepiece.

Figure 3/37. This was the last skeleton clock produced by Haycocks and was given to Henry Haycock (the grandfather of Charles Haycock, the present owner of the firm) on the occasion of his wedding in 1903. The pattern which was used to make the dial is still in existence.   *Charles Haycock*

Both brothers produced skeleton clocks at their respective works to their own individual designs. These clocks were of conventional English skeleton clock form with fusee movements and either recoil or dead beat escapements; most were of eight day duration but one by Thomas Haycock has been seen which runs for a month on one winding (*see* Figure 3/35). The majority of the clocks were timepieces with or without passing strike, but striking and quarter chiming clocks were also produced which were all of high quality.

Thomas Haycock junior died in 1906 after which this business (known as Thomas Haycock & Son) closed down. Meanwhile the other brother William Haycock had built the present Southcliffe Works, also at Ashbourne, in 1897, but although a few skeleton clocks were made there, their production was soon discontinued. The patterns used by this branch of the firm for their skeleton clocks are still in existence and are regarded as being the only original examples to have survived.

The firm is still run by the direct descendants of the original Haycock brothers and continues its clockmaking tradition by producing high quality longcase and bracket clocks and regulators. Unfortunately no records were kept of the number and type of skeleton clocks made by the family although they were produced in appreciable numbers. It is thought that the firm started to make skeleton clocks c.1865 and production had virtually ceased by 1900. The very last clock to be made was that given to Henry Haycock, the grandfather of the present owner Charles Haycock on the occasion of his marriage in 1903 (*see* Figure 3/37).

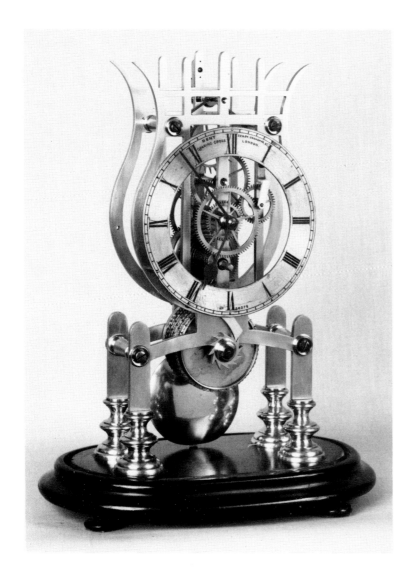

Figure 3/38a, b. An attractive lyre shaped skeleton timepiece made by Dent's, c.1851, signed on the dial 'Dent, 33 & 34 Cockspur St. Charing Cross, London. Number 24078'.[1] Height 11in. (30cm).   *J.M. Wild*

DENT'S OF LONDON

Possibly because of their pre-eminence as clockmakers, particularly during the second half of the nineteenth century when they were basking in the glory of having constructed the most famous clock in the world, Dent's signed their products more frequently than most other makers. It is likely that the addition of their name increased both the saleability of the clock and its value. As relatively few skeleton clocks have been seen which are signed by Dent's it is reasonable to suppose that the numbers they made were small, but they do appear to have constructed, c.1850, an attractive little series of lyre shaped clocks which are so distinctive in their design that they almost certainly have all come from the same maker. The smallest of these (Figure 3/39) is only 5½in. (14cm) high and the largest, a striking clock, is 13in. (33cm) (Figure 3/40).

1. Mercer, V., *Edward John Dent and His Successors,* The Antiquarian Horological Society, 1977.

Figure 3/39a, b. A miniature skeleton timepiece, c.1850, which although signed on a plate between the clock and the wood base 'Simmons & Company, Quadrant, Regent St.' may safely be attributed to Dent's. The chain fusee movement has four well turned baluster pillars, anchor escapement and a brass rod pendulum with fixing clamp. To give some idea of scale, the clock is shown in Figure 3/39b in front of a full size quarter chiming skeleton clock. Height of movement 5½in. (14cm); chapter ring 2½in. (6.3cm) diameter.   *Albert Odmark Collection, U.S.A.*

Figure 3/39b

Figure 3/40. A small twin fusee lyre shaped skeleton clock striking and repeating on a gong; unlike the other two clocks by Dent illustrated in Figures 3/38 and 3/39, it rests on scroll supports, has dead beat escapement and is signed on the chapter ring 'Dent, London. No.20789', which would seem to suggest a date of c.1846. (Interestingly, with the clock is a letter from E. Dent & Co. confirming their manufacture of the clock.)
Height 13in. (33cm).   *Christie's, New York*

Further Makers

STRUTT AND WIGSTON, MCDOWALL AND JAMES EDWARDS

Besides those already mentioned at least three other makers were celebrated for their individual designs. 1) Strutt who with Wigston produced a fascinating series of clocks with epicyclic gearing, 2) McDowall who made clocks with helical gears and 3) James Edwards of Stourbridge who used wheels with beautiful cut glass centres. These makers are discussed in the chapter on wheelwork (*see* Chapter 4).

Various other makers produced skeleton clocks on a one off or even a limited production basis but by and large they had no characteristic features which would make them readily identifiable or indeed of any special interest.

EVANS OF HANDSWORTH (BIRMINGHAM) AND SMITHS OF CLERKENWELL (LONDON)

The two makers who between them probably produced more skeleton clocks than all the others put together were Smith's of Clerkenwell and Evans of Handsworth. The vast majority of skeleton clocks produced by these makers were made in the second half of the nineteenth century, by which time the practice of makers signing their clocks had almost ceased, indeed it is doubtful

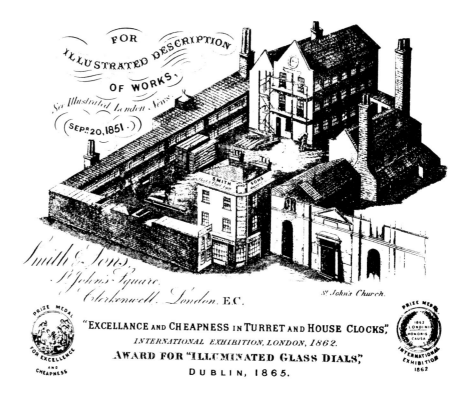

Figure 3/41. The cover of Smith & Sons' catalogue.

SMITH & SONS,
ST. JOHN'S SQUARE (next St. John's Church), CLERKENWELL,
LONDON, E.C.

8-Day Skeleton Clocks and Timepieces, with Shades and Marble Stands complete.	Common. £ s. d.		C. Warranted. £ s. d.		2nd Quality. £ s. d.		Best. £ s. d.
No. 160.—Scroll pattern	... ...		... ...		... ...		2 10 0
„ 184.—New ditto, strike One	... ...		... ...		... ...		3 5 0
New Gothic, strike One	... ...		... ...		... ...		3 10 0
Ditto ditto, Timepiece	... ...		... ...		... ...		3 0 0
„ 222.—Lion and Eagles gilt	... ...		... ...		... ...		6 0 0
„ 188.—Lichfield Cathedral, strikes on gong	... ...		... ...		... ...		9 0 0

All the above with Chains and Marble Stands.

No. 230.—York Minster, strikes half-hours on bell and hours on gong ...... £10 to £12.
Christ Church, Oxford, ditto ditto ditto .... £12.
Mediæval Gothic Registered design, half-hours on bell & hours on gong £12.
Chime Skeleton Clocks, quarter-hours on 8 bells & hours on gong, £25 upwards.
Regulators of various designs, in Carved or Plain Cases, from ...... £10 10s.

Mercurial, Dr. Lardner's, Gridiron, and other Compensating Pendulums.

8-day Weight Clocks, in cases complete, from .... £3 15s.

Nos. 89, 90, 91.—Outside Illuminated Dials for Watchmakers, Railway Stations and Public Buildings, commencing at £25.

NEW AND ELEGANT DESIGNS IN STOCK.

Quarter Clocks in Elaborate Carved Cases, chiming on 4, 8, or 12 Bells, and Striking on Gong.

DETECTOR CLOCKS, £5.

Fillery's Detector Clocks, ½-hour bell, double dials, £7.

GLASS SHADES FOR COVERING & PROTECTING ALL ARTICLES LIABLE TO INJURY BY EXPOSURE.

Shades for Jewellery, with Trays complete, of every description.

MATERIALS.

Brass Work, Clock Springs, Dials and Clock Wheels in Sets, Fusees, Springs, Barrels, Clock Chains, Steel and Iron Work, Gut Lines, Clock Hands, Winders, Keys, and Pendulums. Superfine prepared Watch Oil. Watch Glasses of every description. Mahogany Watch Glass Boxes.

F. PICKBURN, Printer, Bowling Green Lane, Clerkenwell, E.C.

Figure 3/42. An extract from Smith & Sons' price list.

Figure 3/43a. Smith's 'Lion and Eagles gilt' from their catalogue (*see* p.129).

if Evans put his name to as much as five per cent of his output and the percentage from Smith's would have been far less, largely due to the consumer boom at that time and the corresponding strength of the retailers, who frequently insisted on having their own names affixed to the clocks. Their position was strengthened by the flood of clocks being imported from France, Germany and America.

It is difficult to attribute a particular clock to any one maker, but there are several important factors which help attribution:

a) Smith's produced a catalogue illustrating some of their skeleton clocks and from this various designs can be positively identified.

b) Examination of these clocks reveals certain characteristic features in their manufacture such as the design of the frame and dial (including the way in which they have been made and their thickness); the manner in which the wheelwork has been crossed out and the size of specific wheels; the shape of the hammers and indeed many other details which help to build up a dossier of the features of Smith's clocks which in turn enables identification even if they cannot be positively attributed by referring to the catalogue or any other means.

c) More of Evan's clocks are signed than Smith's and from the existing records it can be seen that he was responsible for various designs such as the Scott

Memorial clock (*see* Figures 2/18 and 2/20), and the fine clocks with detented coup perdu escapements which appeared on both the Scott Memorial, an attractive scroll frame clock and one with a Gothic frame.

Because both manufacturers were involved in volume production they standardised their components which were virtually interchangeable from clock to clock and were not altered over quite a long period of time. Thus by identifying the components it is frequently possible to identify the clock.

Interestingly, the ranges of clocks produced by Smith's and Evans, whilst superficially similar, were in fact with few exceptions, quite different from each other and in many ways complementary, which may well have been more by design than accident. At least three clocks signed by Smith were undoubtedly made by Evans, which leads one to believe that on occasions they sold each other's products, as was the case with clock manufacture in England almost since its inception. If Evans, for instance, was geared up to make a large clock based on York Minster it would make little sense for Smith to do likewise as the cost of patterns, etc., would make it uneconomic unless he were producing a long run.

At this stage some of the basic differences between the products of the two manufacturers can be summarised whilst bearing in mind that in many instances it is the summation of many design features rather than any single one which is most likely to identify the clock.

Evans' clocks are, on the whole, larger and more substantial than Smith's with thicker plates and chapter rings and must have been more expensive to make. The vast majority of Evans' clocks have six spoke wheelwork as opposed to the four or five used on most of Smith's, although some of Smith's fine clocks such as those based on Brighton Pavilion used six spokes, and indeed it is not uncommon to see the same frame design with both five and six spoke wheelwork. Evans used a relatively large hour wheel almost 2in. (5cm) in diameter whereas Smith's were 1½ in. (3.8cm).

The Frames. Evans concentrated much of his efforts on producing clocks based on various buildings such as Westminster Abbey (Figure 2/21) and York Minster (Figure 1/20) which were usually quite large clocks, the York Minster for instance averaging 26½ in. (67cm) with base and dome, whether a two train or a three train clock. Smith's skeleton clocks with architectural frames were smaller, and on the whole less accurate portrayals of the buildings, but the exception to the rule is a superb series he produced in very small numbers and probably mainly for exhibition purposes such as the St. Paul's Cathedral (Figure 2/24) and Brighton Pavilion clocks (Figure 2/31).

Besides the architectural clocks, Evans produced a substantial scroll frame skeleton to which he fitted either a balance wheel escapement, a detented coup perdu (Figure 3/63), or an anchor escapement with pendulum, and in at least one instance a chronometer escapement (Figure 3/66).

Figure 3/43b, c. Smith's 'Lion and Eagles gilt', illustrated in their catalogue and priced at £6.0s.0d. It is relatively common for either the eagles, lions or both to be omitted or lost. (Note the mock gridiron pendulum and the three tier brass base quite frequently used on their clocks.) This particular clock is signed by S. Rutter, the retailer. Height 17in. (43.2cm) without dome.

Figure 3/43c

Probably the most attractive clocks he made were those with arabesque frames, (Figure 3/67) often with an additional third frame to carry the dial; their beauty of line and extreme delicacy is in marked contrast to his substantial architectural clocks, indeed it is almost as if he was saying 'There, I can do it if I want to'.

Smith's probably produced a greater quantity of skeleton clocks than Evans and tended to concentrate on smaller and more delicate timepieces, usually with scroll or floral frames. On occasion they were decorated with a pair of lions (Figure 3/43) and/or eagles and occasionally even incorporated a compass.

Chapter Rings. The basic difference in the approach of Smith and Evans to the design of their chapter rings is in many ways similar to that for their frames. Evans' chapter rings were of thick cast brass and usually had a relatively simple design; occasionally they consisted of a conventional silvered ring; in other instances they were made with raised gilt or silvered Roman numerals standing out against a matted background (Figure 1/29) and possibly the commonest design was a series of interlinked plaques, often shield shaped, with each one bearing a single numeral (Figures 1/24). Evans occasionally made use of enamelled plaques (Figure 1/31) which he probably imported from France.

Smith's chapter rings are far thinner and more extensively fretted out (Figure 1/25) as are the frames and are in some ways more attractive than Evans', although on occasions the fretwork becomes a little excessive and they are far more liable to damage.

Pendulums. Evans used the conventional English bracket clock pendulum for the majority of his clocks but also sometimes employed the wood rod with cylindrical pewter bob (Figure 3/68) particularly on his two and three train York Minster and Westminster Abbey clocks and occasionally made fully compensated pendulums (Figure 3/65).

Smith's made use of the standard English pendulum with lenticular brass bob and in addition used a mock three rod gridiron pendulum on some of his more decorative clocks.

Hammers and Hammer Springs. The hammer head employed by Evans is usually hatchet shaped, fairly substantial (Figure 3/67) and has a conventional English hammer return spring whereas the hammer employed by Smith is in the shape of a halberd, nearly always of the shape seen on the clock in Figure 3/45, and sometimes a simple coil spring is used.

The foregoing list should, when used in conjunction with the illustrations of the clocks which are known to have been made by Evans or Smith, enable one to differentiate quite readily between the products of the two makers. Once one becomes really familiar with these clocks it will become apparent that not just

Figure 3/44a, b. Smith's striking version of Lichfield Cathedral, which has a similar brass plinth to the clock shown in Figure 3/43. The frame corresponds very closely to drawing no.188 in their catalogue where it is priced at £9.0s.0d., with chains, marble stand and dome.   *Sotheby's*

the items already listed but nearly every component has its own characteristic features which will indicate the identity of the maker.

J. SMITH AND SONS, CLERKENWELL, LONDON

Clerkenwell has for almost two centuries been one of the leading centres of clockmaking in London and even today there are more clockmakers and ancillary businesses such as hand makers, engravers, dial restorers and material suppliers in that area than anywhere else in London, but their numbers have inevitably dwindled over the years as the ever increasing rents have driven them out into the suburbs or the provinces.

In the days when Smith's were flourishing clockmakers, c.1850-1900, the whole area must have been a hive of activity and to gain an insight into clockmaking at that time one cannot do better than read the account contained in *The Illustrated London News* of 20th September, 1851, the year of the Great Exhibition at which Smith's were showing their wares. (*See* Appendix 1, p.260.)

Figure 3/45a, b. A two train skeleton clock with floral frame by Smith's of Clerkenwell with five spoke wheelwork and hour strike on a bell. (Note the halberd type of hammer on the clock, typical of Smith's work, which is not very well drawn in their catalogue.) The top of the spire is missing from above the bell, probably having been reduced to enable a replacement dome to be fitted. In the clock shown a different chapter ring has been employed from that seen illustrated in the catalogue, which usually appears on the Brighton Pavilion clocks.
Height excluding dome 17½in. (44.5cm).

Sotheby's

It is very fortunate that one of Smith's catalogues of which the cover is shown in Figure 3/41, should have survived, as it gives us a positive guide to not only the clocks they were making at that time but also their prices (Figure 3/42). It is interesting to note that whereas most of the timepieces were only £2.10s.0d. to £3.10s.0d. complete with base and dome, striking clocks were £9.0s.0d. to £12.0s.0d. and chiming clocks more than double this amount.

Shown in Figures 3/43-3/46 are examples of Smith's clocks alongside the relevant drawings from the original catalogue and in Figure 3/47 additional designs are shown. Figures 3/45, 3/48, 3/49, 3/50 and 3/52 illustrate further clocks which may safely be attributed to them and in Figure 3/53 is their version of Brighton Pavilion. Figure 3/51 shows a fine quality three train

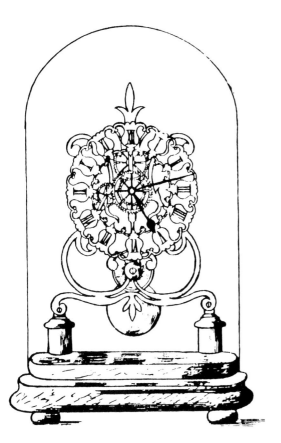

Figure 3/46a, b, c. Figure 3/46a is a further extract from Smith's catalogue and 3/46b is a clock which corresponds very closely to it. At first sight 3/46c looks quite different but in fact the only alterations are the fitting of another chapter ring and the addition of passing strike. Smith's production of a limited range of basic designs but with a variety of alternatives such as different styles of chapter ring, hands, feet, bases and the addition of passing strike is in some ways akin to modern motor manufacturing techniques.

Figure 3/46b

Figure 3/46c

Figure 3/47a, b, c, d. Four further designs from Smith's catalogue. Figures 3/47a, b and c are probably what Smith refers to in his catalogue as his Gothic designs and 3/47d, judging by the three spires and one or two other features, appears to be a very simple rendition of York Minster.

skeleton clock by Smith's with six spoke wheelwork which bears the inscription in longhand and capitals roughly 5in. x 3in. (12.7cm x 7.6cm):

'J. Smith & Sons
CHURCH, TURRET AND MUSICAL CLOCK MAKERS
St. Johns Square,
Clerkenwell.'

The chapter ring is very similar to those employed by them on their version of St. Paul's Cathedral (Figure 2/34) and the magnificent clock shown in Plate 35.

By 1900 Smith's production of skeleton clocks must have declined dramatically, although they did exhibit at least one quarter chiming skeleton clock at Chicago in 1910, and by the beginning of the First World War in 1914 production had virtually ceased.

[In the author's possession is a letter from Mr. Pearson who was taken on

Figure 3/47c

Figure 3/47d

by Smith's as an apprentice in 1912, in which he states that by that year they had ceased to manufacture chiming and striking skeleton clocks and were just making timepieces, still producing the frames by sandcasting using wooden patterns. He lists some of the clockmakers he knew who used to make the skeleton clocks in the previous century such as Bob Sawyer and Messrs. Collier, Rayner and Forrest, commenting that although they worked for a mere pittance they were absolutely dedicated to their jobs, finishing every part meticulously by hand.]

Plate 21. Figure 3/49. A further two train clock by Smith's with more pronounced Oriental features than Figure 3/48 (opposite) including two flying dragons.

Plate 22. Figure 3/50. A two train skeleton clock by Smith with hour strike on a bell and the mock gridiron pendulum which he frequently employed. Signed by the retailers 'G. Groom, Windmill Rd, Croydon'.

Figure 3/48. A two train skeleton clock by Smith with five spoke wheelwork, typical stepped base and a somewhat Oriental appearance to the frame (*see also* Plate 1). (Note the extreme delicacy of the chapter ring typical of much of Smith's better work.) A clock, very similar in all other respects, has been seen with six spoke wheelwork, something which occurs fairly frequently with Smith's finer clocks.
Height 19in. (46cm).

Figure 3/51a, b. A fine quality three train skeleton clock by Smith's, probably made in the 1870s, with a particularly well executed chapter ring similar to that used on the St. Paul's clock shown in Figure 2/34. (Note the large great wheels with six spoke crossings.) It is signed 'J. Smith & Sons, Church – Turret and Musical Clock Makers, St. Johns Square, Clerkenwell'. (For a similar clock retailed by Ulrich *see* Figure 6/5).

Figure 3/51b

Figure 3/52. A two train skeleton clock by Smith's with hour strike on a bell mounted on the backplate, a skeletonised snail, six spoke wheelwork and a chapter ring built up in two layers; the silvered diamond shaped plaques rest on a gilt background.

Figure 3/53. One of Smith's most elaborate skeleton clocks based on Brighton Pavilion (formerly in the collection of Major Heathcote) which has a finely fretted chapter ring typical of their work; a very similar one is illustrated in their catalogue (*see* Figure 3/45b). The eagle and lions seen on this clock are frequently missing from other examples.

Figure 3/54b. The reverse side of the clock illustrated in Plate 23 (opposite).

Plate 23. Figure 3/54a. A fine quality and rare three train skeleton clock by Smith's based on St. Paul's Cathedral. (Note the bells nestling happily inside the dome, the fine clickwork and all the detail on the underdial work, where everything is far more elaborately shaped and finished than it needs to be on strictly functional grounds.) It is similar to, but not quite so elaborate, as that seen in Figure 2/34. In this example seconds and chime selection have been omitted. Height excluding dome 25½ in. (64.8cm).

EVANS OF HANDSWORTH

In 1805 Boulton & Watt, of the Soho Foundry, Handsworth, Birmingham, decided to discontinue the manufacture of clocks and handed this side of their business over to John Houghton who had been their foreman. Houghton established himself in Soho Street and called his business 'The Soho Clock Factory', where trade flourished and in due course his son-in-law William Frederick Evans joined him. Houghton retired in 1843 leaving Evans to run the business and died some twenty years later.

Figure 3/55. Evans' trade cards and an advertisement of W.F. Evans and Sons which gives some idea of the wide range of clocks they marketed.

The Scott Memorial

In 1850 Evans produced his famous skeleton clock based on the Scott Memorial which he showed at the Great Exhibition and which is now in The City Museum and Art Gallery (Figure 2/18). This clock proved extremely popular and so he started producing the Scott Memorial clocks in large numbers, but whereas the original was a two train clock with balance wheel, having a relatively detailed frame and an elaborate marble base, those which he subsequently produced varied greatly. Some were single train (Figure 3/56), some two train (Figure 3/57a), some had a pendulum whilst others had a balance (Figure 3/57b) and the size and complexity of the frame varied

142

Figure 3/56. Scott Memorial skeleton timepiece with six spoke wheelwork and vertically mounted pointed tooth lever escapement.
Height 18in. (45.7cm).   *Sotheby's*

Figure 3/57a

Figure 3/57a, b. The largest of Evans' Scott Memorial clocks (other than that made for the Great Exhibition of 1851) bears a plaque on the base 'Evans Fecit, Soho St., Handsworth' (*see also* Plate 24). The chain fusee movement which has maintaining power, strikes and repeats the hours on a bell, and has a lever escapement with mono metallic balance mounted vertically at the top of the frontplate.
Height 23½in. (59.7cm).

Figure 3/57b

Plate 24. Evans' Scott Memorial clock (*see* Figure 3/57, p.143).

appreciably, even the way in which Scott and his dog were displayed was frequently altered (Figures 3/56 and 3/57). A limited number of relatively large two train clocks were also produced with pump action quarter chime on two bells on the first three quarters.

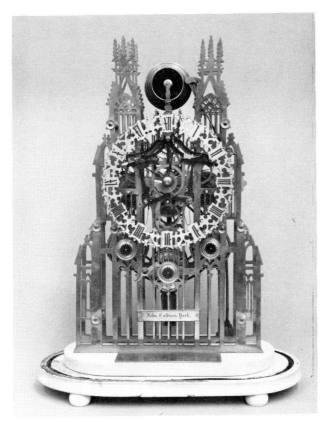 

Figure 3/58a, b. A three train York Minster skeleton clock chiming the quarters on eight bells, which is now in the Victorian parlour at the Castle Museum, York, bears the plaque of John Colburn of York who is recorded as working as a clockmaker in the mid-1860s, but he would only have retailed this clock. A presentation plaque reads 'Presented by the Corporation of York for the best short horn cow or heifer exhibited at The Yorkshire Fatstock Show, 1864. Won by John Radcliffe, Stearsby, York'. The clock was presented to the museum in 1960 by J.R. Radcliffe, one of the winner's descendants.

Castle Museum, York

Westminster Abbey and York Minster

As a result of his success with the Scott Memorial, Evans decided to produce clocks inspired by other buildings of which York Minster (Figures 3/58 and 3/59) and Westminster Abbey (Figures 3/60 and 3/61) are the best known. Having designed these clocks, he varied them remarkably little over the years, using virtually the same frame whether the clock had two or three trains, and kept the size constant, the overall heights varied because of the design of the base and were usually around 24in. (61cm) excluding dome. The Westminster Clocks are a little more complex than those depicting York Minster, a third frame generally being provided to carry the dial and a small fourth one representing the porch.

The quality of the clocks is always excellent, the frames being substantial and very well executed. The designs were varied a little by providing different chapter rings, either a simple silvered ring (Figure 3/61); a cast gilt chapter with raised numerals, usually silvered (Figure 3/60); a chapter ring which was fretted out, generally fairly simply, the commonest design being that seen in Figure 3/58, or occasionally raised white enamelled plaques with blue

Figure 3/59. A York Minster skeleton clock with full hour strike on a gong and passing half hour strike on a bell (not shown here). Relatively rare features are the use of raised white enamelled plaques for the numerals and the substantial brass base on which it rests, which may not be original.
Height 22in. (56cm).
Christie's

numerals were employed (Figure 3/59). No matter which pattern was used the dial was always substantial, being at least ⅛ in. (3mm) thick, which is almost twice those seen on Smith's products. Indeed nowhere in the design or execution of his clocks did Evans try to save on materials, time or money. The majority of the clocks made to this design were two train with full hour strike on a gong and passing half hour strike on a bell. In the case of the York Minster clock this was usually a conventional clock bell but with the two train Westminster clock an attractive church style bell was often used (Figure 3/60).

Figure 3/60. One of the most attractive of Evans' cathedral clocks is his two train Westminster Abbey. The use of a third frame to carry the dial and a small fourth frame representing the porch adds much to the perspective and the church style bell suits the clock well, which has passing half hour strike on the bell and full hour strike and repeat on a gong.
Height 24in. (63cm).

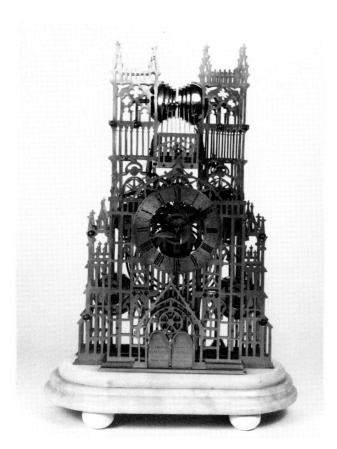

Figure 3/61. A quarter chiming Westminster clock with hour strike on a gong and mercury compensated pendulum, which bears the inscription 'Presented to the Rev. S. Edward Bushy M.A., L.L.D.T.C.D. Rector of St. Andrew's Belfast by the Churchwarden's Select Vestry and Parishioners March 1881'. Although the use of a simple chapter ring such as that on this clock is considered by some to be the sign of an early skeleton clock, this inscription would seem to contradict this, and indeed another clock with the same chapter ring has been seen dated 1888. The probable explanation is that a range of chapter rings was offered from which the retailer or customer could choose.

Christie's

Figure 3/62. A Gothic style skeleton clock with hour and half hour strike on a bell. A good quality English lever platform is mounted vertically at the top of the frontplate and maintaining power is provided. The clock is signed by Charles Shepherd of London (fl.1832-63) but would have been made by Evans of Handsworth, all the mechanical components being very similar to those used on his Scott Memorial clock. *Norman Langmaid Collection, U.S.A.*

With the quarter chiming clocks, which again had hour strike on a gong, the layout of the bells varied. On the Westminster Abbey clock the eight bells were generally mounted transversely (Figure 3/61) as two nests of four with the smallest bells being in the centre, whereas with the majority of the York Minster clocks the bells were mounted front to back, with the concave side of the smallest bell facing forward (Figure 3/58), although on occasions they are placed transversely (Figure 2/26), but they look more cramped and the layout is not as attractive as on the Westminster clocks.

Besides those based on known buildings Evans produced a series of clocks, both single and two train which might be termed Gothic clocks and these employed either a pendulum or a balance wheel (Figure 3/62).

The Detented Escapement

It is thought that Evans' detented escapement, which is described in more detail on p.185 (Figure 5/6), was introduced c.1860, first being fitted to some of the Scott Memorial clocks and later to an attractive scroll design with a floral influence (Figure 3/63). Because of the design of the escapement the train was inverted and thus the large seconds ring appeared in the bottom half of the dial. The escape wheel, as on a chronometer, is released only every other beat (coup perdu) and therefore full seconds are recorded on the dial even though the pendulum is beating half seconds. The majority of these clocks were timepieces which usually employed a chapter ring with shield shaped numerals, but Evans also produced a few two train clocks which were somewhat larger and had passing half hour strike on a bell, and hour strike on a gong (Figure 3/64) and at least one three train clock has been seen (Figure 3/65).

A rare clock, employing the same frame as those with pendulum and detent but having a full chronometer escapement is that shown in Figure 3/66; to date this is the only example seen.

The Arabesque Frame

Undoubtedly the most attractive clock frame produced by Evans was his arabesque which was a complete contrast to all his other designs, having great delicacy and balance, with the chapter ring and frame complementing each other perfectly. The vast majority of these clocks were timepieces, sometimes with the addition of passing strike (Figure 3/67). Some had only two frames but the best had a third frame which supported the chapter ring; at least two two train clocks have been seen but the addition of a second train in many ways mars the original concept and whether any quarter chiming clocks were produced is not known. A rare example with regulator dial layout may be seen in Figure 6/14.

Plate 25. Figure 3/63a. Evans' scroll frame skeleton clock (*see* Figure 3/63b opposite).

Plate 26. Evans' arabesque skeleton clock (*see* Figure 3/67, p.154).

Figure 3/63b. An Evans' scroll frame skeleton timepiece with detented escapement mounted low down on the backplate, which necessitates the inversion of the train, which is achieved by mounting the fusee at the top of the frame and connecting it to the spring barrel by a particularly long run of chain. Although it is fitted with a half seconds beating pendulum it records seconds on the large seconds ring because of the coup perdu (lost beat) escapement (*see* Plate 25 opposite).
Height 18in. (46cm).

Figure 3/64. A fine two train skeleton clock by Evans with passing half hour strike on a bell and hour strike and repeat on a gong; as is indicated by the position of the seconds ring it is fitted with his detented escapement, and also has maintaining power.
Height 23in. (58.5cm).

Pendulums

Evans generally employed one of four main types of pendulum:

1) A conventional design similar to that used on English bracket clocks at that time with a flat brass rod and a lenticular brass cased bob which in some clocks had the regulating nut placed below the bob, whereas in others, particularly those with detented escapements (Figure 3/63b) it was situated above the bob where it was easier to adjust.

2) A pendulum, presumably designed to be compensated, which had a turned wood rod and a cylindrical pewter bob (Figure 3/68), which was used on many of his better clocks.

These two pendulums were used on the vast majority of Evans' clocks, but he occasionally used two fully compensated pendulums.

3) A well made mercury compensated pendulum with a jar made either of glass or iron.

Figure 3/65a

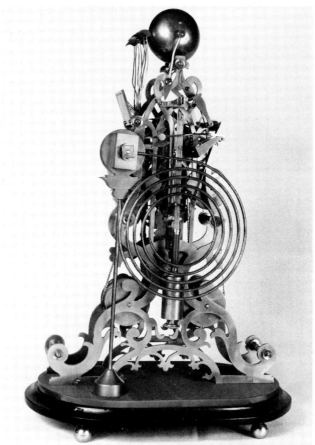

Figure 3/65b

Figure 3/65a, b, c. A similar clock to that shown in Figure 3/64 with detented escapement and the seconds ring at six o'clock, but which chimes the quarters on eight bells and has had the lower part of the frame extended to accommodate the barrels of the three mainsprings. As can be seen the fusees are mounted high up in the frame necessitating a long run of chain. In the close up of the escapement, which is illustrated in Figure 3/65c, the top part of the zinc and steel compensated pendulum may be seen. The clock is signed on a plaque by the retailer, C.C. Lowe of Manchester.

Norman Langmaid Collection, U.S.A.

Figure 3/65c

Figure 3/66a, b. A rare skeleton clock made by Evans, c.1870. Although similar in many respects to that shown in Figure 3/63 it has a large spring detent chronometer escapement mounted horizontally at the top of the two frames. Note the unusually large spring barrel which is an indication of the power absorbed by this type of escapement. Maintaining power is provided and the seconds ring is below twelve o'clock.

Figure 3/66b

Figure 3/67. Evans' arabesque, one of the most attractive skeleton clock designs ever produced (*see also* Plate 26), here seen as a timepiece with passing hour strike which was sometimes omitted, as also was the third frame which carries the chapter ring. (A virtually identical clock to the one illustrated bears the inscription 'This clock was presented to A.J. Moore, Esq. of Appleby Hall as his wedding present by the small tenantry of his estate, October 6th 1874'.)
Height 20in. (51cm).

4) A zinc/steel compensated pendulum which may be seen on the clock illustrated in Figure 3/65.

The heyday of Evans' skeleton clock production seems to have been from the early 1850s to c.1890, as most of the presentation plaques seen on the clocks bear dates varying from 1860 to 1885. In 1899 W.F. Evans died at the age of eighty-one and the business was then carried on by one of his sons, also named William Frederick Evans, who died on 22nd February 1904. The business was to continue for another thirty years until, on 27th September 1934 it was closed down and the contents disposed of by public auction (Figure 3/69).

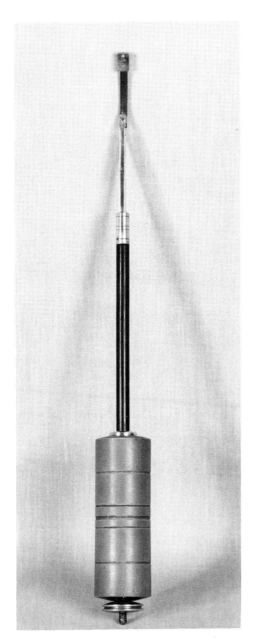

Figure 3/68. Evans' well executed compensated pendulum with wood rod and pewter bob which he employed on many of his better clocks. Just how effective the compensation was is not known.

Figure 3/69. The end of an era: the announcement by Bright Willis & Son of the sale of the contents of The Soho Clock Factory and the Auctioneers' Note relating to the sale.

Birmingham Reference Library

*By direction of Messrs. W. F. Evans & Sons
who are retiring from business.*

"The Soho Clock Factory"

154, SOHO ROAD, HANDSWORTH, BIRMINGHAM, 21.

Catalogue

of the

HIGH—CLASS

CLOCKMAKERS' PLANT,

MACHINERY and STOCK

To be Sold by Auction without reserve

on

Thursday and Friday, September 27th & 28th, 1934.

AT 11 A.M. EACH DAY

Auctioneers

BIRMINGHAM.   - - - -   SOLIHULL.

NOTA BENE:

The Auctioneers are confident that this Sale will prove of outstanding interest both to the Trade and the Public.

The Soho Clock Factory was established in 1805 by one John Houghton, the great-grandfather of the present proprietors and the business has had an uninterrupted career under the control of the family ever since.

It is very interesting to note that John Houghton originally worked in the clockmaking section of Boulton & Watt's famous Soho Foundry and when this section was discontinued he commenced business on his own account as a clockmaker.

Since it's establishment the firm has been renowned for the production of high quality clocks and timepieces, an important section of the business being the making of turret clocks and timepieces for public buildings, etc.

Clocks and Timepieces from the Soho Clock Factory are to be found in all parts of the British Isles and have been exported throughout the World.

Figure 4/1. A small and excellently proportioned great wheel skeleton clock which would have been made by Condliff but bears the plaque of Litherland, Davies & Co. Note the extreme delicacy of the wheelwork, those in the upper part of the train in particular being very finely crossed out with rims taken down to the absolute minimum thickness compatible with adequate strength. This is complemented by the narrow chapter ring and beautifully executed hands.

Michael Cox

4. Wheelwork

The skeleton clock displays the clockmaker's skill and ingenuity more completely than any other type of clock and for this reason is usually made and finished to a higher standard than the equivalent bracket clock. The frame of the clock provides the initial visual impact, but it is the quality and design of the wheelwork, the escapement used, the complexities which have been added and the detailed treatment and finish of the smaller components such as the cocks, bridges and levers, etc., which will intrigue enthusiasts and make them marvel on occasions at the wealth of detail utilised to make the components attractive. A classic example of this is Condliff's serpent (Figure 3/16c) sometimes used for regulating the balance of his escapements. Many other examples may be seen on the clock illustrated in Figure 6/1.

In this chapter attention is drawn to the fine wheelwork used on many clocks and the numerous different designs employed for what is basically a simple component. Probably the most common method used to improve the wheelwork was to cross the wheels out more carefully, tapering the spokes and keeping the rims as thin as possible (Figure 4/1). Instead of using four spoke wheels as on most English bracket clocks, five and six crossings were frequently employed. Evans generally used six and Smith's of Clerkenwell mostly five, sometimes four and occasionally six. Most attention was given to the hour wheel, a central feature of the clock, and the escape wheel, but it was not uncommon to use wheels with different numbers of crossings in the same train, for instance the great wheel may have six and the intermediate wheel four or five.

Great Wheel Skeleton Clocks

Some of the most attractive skeleton clocks made were those employing a larger than usual great wheel. The earliest examples were produced in France (Figure 4/2 and Plate 27) and with these clocks it was not just the size of the great wheel which was so spectacular but also the way in which it was crossed out (Figure 4/3). The frames employed with these clocks were usually the inverted 'Y' or the glass plate (Figure 4/3). In Figure 4/4 is an example which is unusual for a French clock in that it has a chain fusee; there is a skeletonised barrel, an extremely large great wheel which has beautifully tapered spokes and an intermediate wheel which is much larger than normal. Although some great wheel skeleton clocks were made in Austria (Figure 4/5) and their wheels were often beautifully crossed out their diameter was not usually nearly as great as on the French clocks.

Most of the English great wheel skeleton clocks were produced prior to 1850 and it is interesting to note that several of them had a going barrel and only a simple frame frequently based on an inverted 'Y' (Figure 4/6). The diameter of the great wheel was often the same as the chapter ring and never reached anything like the proportionally much larger size seen on the French clocks.

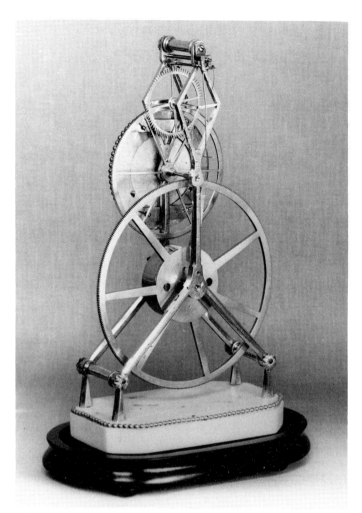

Figure 4/2b. A French early 19th century skeleton clock with an inverted Y frame (*see also* Plate 27). The clock has only three wheels, the seven spoke great wheel some 6¼in. (16cm) in diameter; a six spoke 4¼in. (10.5cm) intermediate wheel which has been designed to be a little larger than the dial so that it appears to run around it and a large 'scape wheel. The train count is:

Great wheel	372	: 10
Intermediate wheel	276	: 6
Teeth on 'scape wheel	80	
Overall height	13in. (33cm)	

Figure 4/3. An early 19th century French glass plate skeleton clock, the 10in. (25.4cm) great wheel with Y shaped spokes being exactly twice the diameter of the enamelled dial. Overall height 18in. (46cm).   *Sotheby's*

Plate 27. Figure 4/2a. French 19th century skeleton clock.

Plate 28. Figure 4/8a. An epicyclic skeleton clock (*see* p.164).

Condliff's beautiful series of great wheel skeleton clocks (Figure 4/1) were some of the best made in this country, the extreme delicacy of the wheelwork leaving little to be desired.

Three English clockmakers produced skeleton clocks with such individual wheelwork that it virtually became their hallmark:

1. Messrs. Strutt & Wigston employed epicyclic gearing.
2. Mr. McDowall made use of helical gearing.
3. James Edwards of Stourbridge used wheels with delicate rims and beautiful cut glass centres.

EPICYCLIC GEARING AND MESSRS. STRUTT AND WIGSTON

The word epicycle is derived from the Greek and literally means 'upon' and 'a circle' and epicyclic or 'sun and planet' gearing as it is sometimes called is basically the use of a sun or central wheel with planeting wheels which run around it and an outer annular ring with teeth on its inner aspect (Figure 4/7a). The epicycle was a device first used by ancient Greek astronomers as a representation of the apparently irregular motions of the planets and the epicyclic principle was recorded by Ptolemy in his treatise known as 'The Almagest'. The principle lends itself to gear train design and was in use as early as the Middle Ages. It has the advantage that, for engineering applications, far more power can be transmitted, relative to the size of the components than with conventional gearing (Figure 4/7b). Its main application in clockmaking has been in connection with the construction of the astronomical work of complex clocks, where the ability to gear up and gear down at the same time is of great value. Giovanni de Dondi[1] used it in his famous clock in the fourteenth century as also did Richard of Wallingford over a century earlier. An article by Karlsen and White[2] describes several other such clocks. Whereas many clockmakers had applied the principle of epicyclic gearing to the motion work of clocks, none until William Strutt's time had used it on the going train of a clock (Figure 4/8 and Plate 28).

William Strutt, [3, 4, 5, 6] who was born in Belper in Derbyshire in 1756, was a gifted engineer and inventor who seems to have turned his hand to a wide

1. Lloyd, M.A., 'Giovanni Dondi Dell' Orologius Astronomical Clock of 1364', *Antiquarian Horology,* Vol. III, No.7, June 1961.
2. Karlsen, H.B.J. and White, G., 'Unusual Differentials in Renaissance Clockwork', *Antiquarian Horology,* Vol. XIII, No.5, Sept. 1982.
3. Hacker, C.L., 'William Strutt of Derby', *Derby Archaeological Journal,* Vol. LXXX, 1960, pp.49-70.
4. Tilley, Joseph. Biographical notes compiled in the 1900s which are written on cards and stored in a file system by the Central Library, Derby.
5. *Derby Mercury,* 12.1.1831.
6. Wright, H. 'Biographical Notices', 1829.

Figure 4/4. All the wheelwork on this clock is beautifully executed with spokes which taper to a minimum, and very delicate rims; it has a pin wheel escapement and a skeletonised barrel with chain fusee. The enamelled chapter ring is signed by Jefferys & Gilbert, but unfortunately no trace can be found of this partnership.

In the first half of the 19th century a limited number of clocks were made in England in the French taste by some of the better makers such as McCabe, Arnold and Viner. Examples which spring to mind are the chariot clocks mostly by McCabe, and the boulle mantel clocks and the porcelain clocks by amongst others, Payne, Arnold & Frodsham. It is possible this clock is one of that group with many of the components imported, but it seems more likely that it was made entirely in France. *Keith Banham*

number of problems. That his ability was generally acknowledged is confirmed by the fact that he was elected a Fellow of the Royal Society in 1817. Amongst his sponsors were such famous names as Watt and Brunel; he was also a friend of Dr. Erasmus Darwin. The achievements he is probably best remembered for are the design of the first 'fireproof' mills and the construction of the Infirmary at Derby.

He was a close friend of William Wigston[7, 8], a machine maker who manufactured parts for steam engines, but unfortunately little is recorded about him. It is noted that he was working in Cavendish Street, Derby in 1831

7. Pigot's *Directory of Derby (and Derbyshire)*, 1831.
8. Pigot & Co., *Commercial Directory*, 1835.

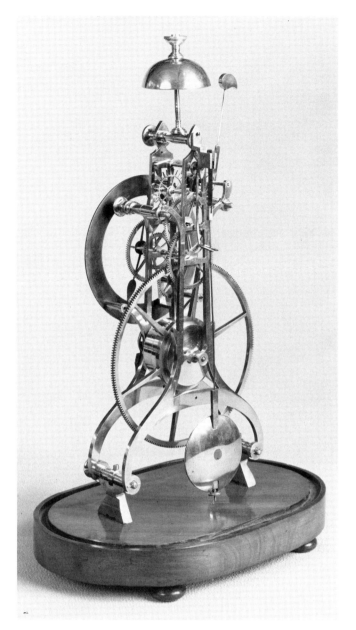

Figure 4/5. An anonymous early 19th century Viennese weight driven skeleton clock of one day duration which has only one wheel in the train besides the 'scape, an eight spoke great wheel, delicate dead beat pallets and a mercury compensated pendulum (the mercury being contained in the two glass tubes which form the pendulum rod). Winding is achieved by pulling a cord which passes down through the marble base. Height 20¾in. (53cm).
Osterreichisches Museum Fur Angewandte Kunst, Wien.

Figure 4/6b. The back view of the clock opposite, on page 163.

as a lace maker and in 1835 as a lace manufacturer and machine maker. This was a highly unusual partnership for the manufacture of clocks, although it must be remembered that appreciable numbers of clockmakers were employed in the weaving industry, making and repairing the more delicate parts of the machinery such as the yarn testers and measurers and various other devices.

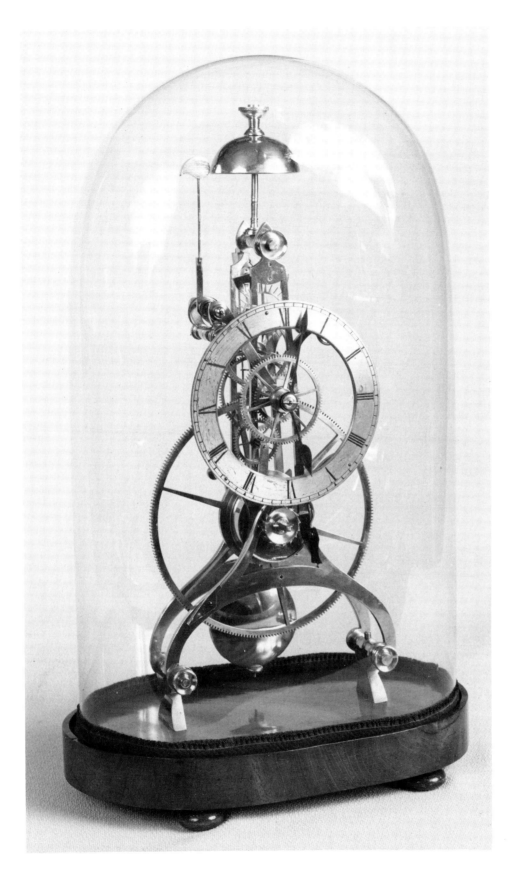

Figure 4/6a. An English great wheel skeleton clock with inverted Y frame probably made c.1830, with a going barrel and passing strike on the hour.

Figure 4/7a. An aircraft epicyclic test rig drive with a 6in. (15.2cm) annulus: power transmitted 97hp, input r.p.m.9752, output 1950. *J. Martin*

Figure 4/7b. Models showing the relative sizes of epicyclic and wheel and pinion gearing designed to the same parameters: input r.p.m.9000, output 3000. *J. Martin*

Figure 4/8b, c. An epicyclic skeleton clock resting on a black slate base signed 'W. Wigston, Derby. W. Strutt Esq. Invt.' (*see also* Plate 28 and Figure 4/8c). All the edges of the massive frame are carefully chamfered, the wheelwork is five spoke and indeed the whole clock is beautifully finished. One of the fascinations of this type of clock is that one can actually see the planetary wheel moving.
Height 14in. (35.5cm).

Figure 4/8c. Detail of the epicyclic skeleton clock seen opposite and in Plate 28.

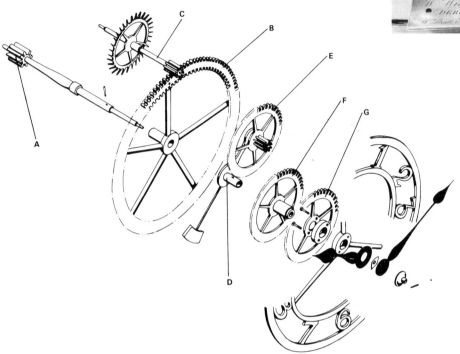

Figure 4/8d. An exploded view of the clock. The centre pinion (A) of eight leaves is directly driven from the fusee wheel and carries on it an annulus ring (B) freely mounted. The outside diameter of this ring is cut with 168 teeth meshing directly with the 'scape pinion of six whose arbor (C) carries a 'scape wheel of thirty-four. Pinned to the centre arbor and mounted directly in front of the annulus ring is a counterpoised carrier (D) which carries a single planet wheel (E) of sixty-eight. This meshes with the 144 inner teeth of the annulus. The planet wheel in turn carries a pinion of eight. Meshing with this pinion are two solar wheels (F) and (G). The wheel (G) of sixty-six is screwed through a spacer directly to the fixed centre spider of the dial, thus providing the stationary reaction member for the epicyclic train. The wheel (F) of seventy-two runs freely on the centre arbor on an extended pipe carrying the hour hand. The setting of the hands on such a clock must be carried out independently as each is mounted with its own friction setting.

The train is calculated as follows:

The centre arbor rotates once per hour as also does the carrier. The planet wheel rotates 8.25 per hour and the hour wheel (F) is driven forwards six teeth per hour and, therefore, rotates once in twelve hours. Applying epicyclic calculations, the planet wheel drives the annulus ring onwards (i.e. anticlockwise) 3.8958 per hour by its own rotation. However, in one hour the carrier has completed one revolution and this must be added to the work done by the planet wheel: therefore the annulus rotates 4.8958 per hour. This action, therefore, drives the 'scape arbor anticlockwise 137.0924 per hour (i.e. 2.2847 per minute or 155.36 beats per minute) necessitating a pendulum length of 5.8in. (14.6cm.).

Figure 4/9. An epicyclic skeleton clock signed on a plaque on the base 'W. Wigston. Derby. W. Strutt, Esq. Invt.' The dial (which is easier to read than on most skeleton clocks) has blued Arabic chapters and white hands. The plinth is attractively decorated with a band of gilt metal oak leaves and acorns. Height 10in. (25.5cm). Although it would have been expected that the train count of all Strutt & Wigston's clocks would have been the same this is by no means the case, the 'scape wheel for instance varying from thirty-one to thirty-four teeth. (This clock was bought by James Watt of Doldowlod, the son of the famous inventor, and remained with his family until 1978. A virtually identical clock, signed in the same way, bears the inscription 'A token of regard to my friend Mr. Daglish. for the improvement he has made in the working of my Colliery. E. J. 1831.' Mr. Daglish was the owner of a brass and iron foundry and engineering business which produced machines and winding gear for the cotton, wool and mine industries; E. J. may have been Edward Jackson, a local colliery owner.)   *Sotheby's*

Strutt became fascinated with the principle of epicyclic gearing and proceeded to design a clock based upon this principle which he persuaded his friend William Wigston to manufacture (Figure 4/8). An entry in the *Derby Mercury*[9] very shortly after his death gives us a clue as to the date when these clocks were produced, and also gives us some idea of the high regard in which he was held in the community at that time. It reads as follows:

> 'The invention of a machine somewhat similar in , external appearance to the sun and planet wheels, which were formerly used in steam engines, and its application to clocks and machines for indicating and registering the revolutions of rotary machinery was one of his latest efforts and the simplicity, accuracy and complete novelty of his powerful genius and comprehensive mind'.

9. *Derby Mercury,* 12.1.1831.

Figure 4/10a, b. An anonymous epicyclic clock very similar to those produced by Strutt and Wigston, but without the oval brass base and probably dating some thirty years earlier. Six spoke wheelwork is employed with recoil escapement and an indirect fusee. The bottom pair of pillars is appreciably heavier than that at the top. An interesting variation on Strutt's original design is that the inner and outer teeth on the annulus are set at right angles to each other instead of in the same plane but opposed 180°.
Height 9½ in. (24cm).

Unfortunately, because of the complexities involved in producing epicyclic gears and the consequent high cost of manufacture very few of the clocks were ever produced by Strutt and Wigston. However, the fascination of the principle of epicyclic gearing has never died and copies of Strutt's clocks have been produced intermittently, either commercially or by amateur horologists, up until the present day. An interesting variation of Strutt's original design is that shown in Figure 4/10 and Figure 4/11 is a clock signed 'J. Brookhouse Derby. Wm Strutt Esq Invt.' which has detail design differences to those signed by Wigston which may indicate that this clock was indeed made by Brookhouse. One other epicyclic clock has been seen which was also signed by Brookhouse.

One of the most recent epicyclic clocks made was that of Dent's[10] who produced a limited edition of one hundred (Figure 4/11) between November 1973 and February 1974. These were copied from one of Strutt's original clocks (which was at that time in the possession of Major Heathcote) and they were sold, mostly in the U.S.A., for some $3,500 each. A plate on each clock carried the familiar Dent triangle and the first owner's name.

10. *A Rare and Fascinating Georgian Timepiece.* A catalogue produced by E. Dent & Co. Ltd., in 1973 to publicise their limited edition of one hundred Strutt epicyclic clocks. (Printed by Fine Art International, Inc., 180 West Tenth Street, Wilmington, Delaware, 19801, in co-operation with E. Dent & Co. Ltd., 41 Pall Mall, London. S.W.1.)

Figure 4/11a. An epicyclic skeleton clock signed 'J. Brookhouse, Derby. Wm. Strutt Esq. Invt.' Although there are details which are different from those on the clocks signed by Wigston such as the slightly thinner plates which do not have chamfered edges, the glass dial, the use of a circular instead of a wedge shaped block to counterbalance the planetary wheel and the different treatment of the base (which by raising a relatively squat clock undoubtedly enhances its appearance) the overall design of the clocks including the construction of the pendulum is very similar. It is possible that Brookhouse took over the construction of the clocks after Wigston died or that this clock and another which is similarly signed was made for Brookhouse by Wigston to Strutt's design.

All the wheelwork is five spoke; the planetary wheel is carried by a counterbalanced arm and the double toothed outer wheel some 5in. in diameter is supported by a well finished five legged spider to which it is fixed by short feet.
Height 16in. (39.6cm).

Figure 4/11b. Detail of epicyclic skeleton clockface and gears.

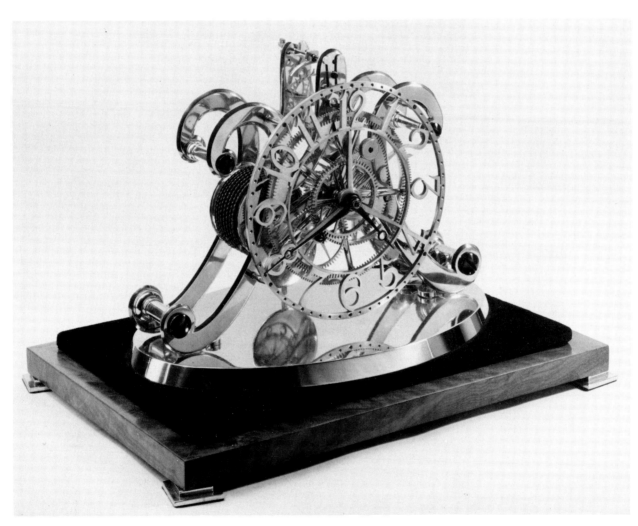

Figure 4/12. A reproduction by Dent of London of one of Strutt and Wigston's original epicyclic clocks (which was formerly in the possession of Major Heathcote). One hundred of these reproduction clocks were made between November 1973 and February 1974, the majority being sold in the United States for $3,500 each. *Sotheby's*

Figure 4/13. A skeleton timepiece now in the Time Museum, Rockford, U.S.A. signed on the silvered brass dial 'C. MacDowall's Patent Helix lever, No. 168, St. John's, Wakefield', c.1830-5. Although the train comprises only three wheels it has, because of the helical gearing, a duration of one month. Note the very substantial nature of the frames with the screws securing the pillars recessed into them. There is a large spring barrel with a chain fusee with a relatively flat profile for two thirds of its length.
Dial diameter 3³/₁₆ in. (8.1cm). Height of clock excluding base 9½ in. (24.1cm).
The Time Museum, Rockford, U.S.A.

Figure 4/14. A close up view of a similar clock to that shown in Figure 4/13, in which the helical gearing which is applied to all the wheelwork may be clearly seen. There is a wood rod pendulum approximately diamond shaped which follows the contours of the backplate and small steel plates are inserted where the crutch pin engages. Timekeeping may be adjusted by means of a nut above the pendulum and beat regulation is also provided. An unusual feature is the pivoting of both the pallets and the crutch between the plates; the crutch which surrounds the 'scape wheel arbor is in the form of a hollow sector made from brass, and can be seen immediately in front of the backplate. An extension at the bottom of the crutch carries the pin which passes through a slot cut in the backplate and engages the pendulum rod. The wheels are far thicker than on a conventional clock and possibly because of this only two and three crossings are used. The eighteen tooth 'scape wheel which has dead beat pallets spanning half its diameter, is of small size to reduce the power required. *Albert Odmark Collection, U.S.A.*

HELICAL GEARING AND MR. MACDOWALL

The word helical is derived from the Greek and may be translated as 'having the form of a spiral'. In helical gearing a spiral groove is cut in the arbor or pinion which meshes with teeth angled to match it. Sometimes called oblique tooth gearing, it has these advantages: a) Power is transmitted by pressure and rolling without any sliding friction. b) The contact bearing area is increased, enabling far heavier loads to be dealt with more smoothly, but this consideration is not normally of importance in clockwork. c) A much greater reduction in gearing may be achieved than with the conventional wheel and pinion. (If the length of the spiral, for instance, which produces one turn of the arbor is equal in length to one of the teeth with which it meshes, then every tooth on the wheel will rotate the arbor once. Thus if the wheel has forty-eight teeth, the arbor will rotate forty-eight times whereas if a conventional wheel of forty-eight teeth meshes with an eight leaf pinion the arbor would only rotate six times.)

The practical application of this in horology is that either one wheel and pinion may be omitted from the train, longer duration may be achieved, or possibly some combination of the two, but in practice it is doubtful whether it is of any appreciable value. Helical gears, because of their high ratios, absorb more power than a conventional train even with an extra wheel and pinion, and the complex machining required to cut them, utilising both a rotary and a progressive action, makes them far more expensive to produce. A further disadvantage is the lateral or end loads which helical gears impart to a train which is one of the main causes of power loss in a clock and is why end caps are frequently employed on the upper part of the train of regulators.

Whereas in horology the disadvantages of helical gearing far outweigh the advantages, in general engineering it has been used extensively, virtually since the start of the Industrial Revolution, in gearboxes and power transmissions of all kinds where a heavy tooth loading is to be expected.

CHARLES MACDOWALL

Charles MacDowall, the son of a watchmaker, was born in Pontefract in Yorkshire on 16th April, 1790 and later moved with his parents to Leeds where he carried on the family business on the death of his father. He subsequently opened his own clockmaking business in Saint John's, Wakefield, where he first devised his helical clock gearing.

His inventive nature must have been evident from the beginning as the contents of his window attracted a continuous crowd and were described as 'By no means least of the attractions of Merry Wakefield'. One particular item 'An endless gravitating and revolving gravitating timepiece with quiescent armillary escape, without springs, chains, barrels, fusees or keys' defies the imagination.

His 'Helix lever' attracted the attention of a Dr. Birkbeck (Physician, Philanthropist and Professor of Philosophy at the Anderson Institute, Glasgow, and President of the London Mechanics Institute) at whose insistence MacDowall moved to London in 1836. He first resided at Church Street, Kensington from where in 1839 he moved to St. James's Street, Pall Mall and in 1848 to 4 Hyde Street, Bloomsbury, and it is this address which is referred to in the Great Exhibition Catalogue of 1851.

He invented, or developed and improved many other instruments during his lifetime, adapting for instance the spiral drill for use in dentistry by adding a rose drill to the tip. In 1858 he moved to Jermyn Street, St. James's and it is here that he died at the age of eighty-three.

Whether MacDowall was the inventor of helical gearing on clocks is difficult to prove as the mechanism has appeared on several occasions, but he would certainly appear to be the first to have put it into regular production, as he featured it at the Great Exhibition in 1851, where he also displayed his 'single-pin escapement' the patent for which was acquired by Dent's.[11] In view of the relatively small number of these clocks which still exist it would seem likely that the project was not commercially viable, probably because of the high cost of manufacture.

That Dr. Birkbeck had no doubts regarding the quality of MacDowall's clocks can be ascertained from the following extract from a letter which he wrote to him in October 1836:

11. The escapement is described in some detail in the *Horological Journal* of September 1873.

Figure 4/15. A simple skeleton timepiece which although unsigned has a frame which is typical of the work of James Edwards of Stourbridge and would date c.1840-5.

Figure 4/16. An attractive two train clock with hour strike on a bell, a skeletonised snail and a good brass inlaid mahogany base, made by Edwards towards the middle of the 19th century (*see also* Plate 29).
Height 17½in. (44.5cm).

'It affords me great pleasure to state to you my very favourable opinion, both of the principle and action of your helix lever clocks. Two of them I have now tried for several years, and they have moved with so much precision, although unprovided with any compensation, as nearly to approach the accuracy of a good chronometer and regulator with which I have compared them. Indeed, the larger clock, notwithstanding the inconvenience of having for its maintaining power a spring wound up only once a month, has delighted me by its great precision, and it certainly far exceeds any clock which I have seen of the ordinary construction; indeed, this might be expected by anyone who will carefully attend to the mode in which motion is transmitted, the unvarying equality of pressure, and the continued preservation of a straight line, of the important line of centres. I have little doubt that this mode of gearing, if well executed, would be found the most advantageous for large machines; for small ones, such as clocks, the superiority cannot be questioned. The action of the wheel and pinion, with all the mechanical refinement that has, as yet, been expended upon the tooth of the one and the leaves of the other is still most variable and irregular.'

One slight enigma remaining is that although MacDowall exhibited his helix lever at the Great Exhibition in 1851 all his clocks are signed either Leeds or Wakefield from which he moved in 1836. It would therefore seem likely that

Figure 4/17. A somewhat more compact two train clock than that seen in Figure 4/16 with a halberd for the hammer, hour strike and repeat, and skeletonised barrel covers, signed by R.H. Sager of Blackburn, the distributor, who is recorded as working c.1824, but this clock would have been made by James Edwards c.1840-5. Height including dome 15¼ in. (39cm).

either production ceased in 1836 or that he retained his factory at Wakefield or possibly even opened another one in Leeds, although this seems most improbable.

JAMES EDWARDS OF STOURBRIDGE

In Vol. I of C.H. Baillie's *Watchmakers & Clockmakers of the World* a James Edwards is recorded as working in Stourbridge, Worcestershire, c.1795 but in Vol. II Loomes records a James Edwards of Stourbridge as working between 1828-60. Whether or not this is the same man or possibly father and son is difficult to assess as no records could be found of the birth, marriage or death of James Edwards, but he is mentioned in various directories and from these it is apparent that he was definitely working in Stourbridge between 1829-53, first in the High Street and later in Hagley Road, but no record of his place of work exists from 1860 onwards which leads one to believe that by then he had ceased business or possibly died.

Like many of the early skelcton clock manufacturers, James Edwards standardised on one basic frame design (Figures 4/15-4/18) and used it with only minor modifications on all his clocks. Although others were making skeleton clocks in limited numbers before him, Edwards was probably the first clockmaker to manufacture skeleton clocks on a relatively large scale, most of his clocks having been made between 1830-55, which predates Evans and Smith by some ten to fifteen years.

Figure 4/18. A skeleton clock by James Edwards (formerly in the collection of Major Heathcote); the inside of the door bears a watch label inscribed 'James Edwards of Stourbridge, Watch & Clockmaker, Worcs.' The wheelwork, which varies in diameter from $3^{1}/_{12}$ in.-6in. (7.7cm-15.2cm) has beautifully cut centres which are attached to their tapering arbors by screwed collets. The pendulum rise and fall mechanism with the regulation taken through to the front may just be seen at the top of the frame and the stopwork is attached to the bottom right. The front door of the mahogany box on which the clock rests slides to the left to reveal the mainspring. Below six o'clock can be seen the front one of the two plates which carry the fusee arbor, which may be unscrewed to allow removal of the fusee without dismantling the clock.
Height 21in. (53.5cm).

Figure 4/19b. A glass wheeled skeleton clock by James Edwards of Stourbridge (*see* Plate 30 opposite) in which the design, whilst very similar to that seen in Figure 4/18 has been somewhat simplified, for instance the fusee is not detachable and the rise and fall mechanism for the pendulum is less complex, which makes one wonder whether Figure 4/18 was the prototype and the one shown here was one of a series which he produced in very small numbers after the design had been finalised.

Other points to note are that the stopwork is no longer on display; the six pillars which reduce in size from the top to the bottom of the frame are all of the same design whereas on Figure 4/18 the bottom two are of a different pattern and the collets are of relatively conventional form rather than being dished. The opaque glass dials on these clocks had the numerals and minute marks cut into them and these would originally have been filled with gold leaf.

In this clock the rear view shown with the door removed shows on the right the large mainspring and to the left a striking train without fusee which has presumably been added at a later date.

Plate 29. Two train clock made by Edwards (*see* Figure 4/16, p.173).

Plate 30. Figure 4/19a. Glass wheeled skeleton clock by James Edwards (*see* opposite).

The majority of his clocks were either simple timepieces (Figure 4/15) or occasionally two train clocks (Figure 4/16) with hour strike on a bell mounted above the frame, which was of a simple, delicate and pleasing scroll design. The wheelwork, usually five or six spoke, was well executed and on the striking clocks the snail was often skeletonised.

James Edwards is best known for the beautiful skeleton clocks he produced called 'transparent clocks' which employed cut glass wheels with brass rims and cut glass pendulum bobs. He exhibited several of these at the 1851 Exhibition and although none appear to be signed by him (as was usual with his clocks) one, in Figure 4/18, bears his label pasted inside the front door and certainly the transparent clocks can all be safely attributed to him. An example which sounds particularly interesting is described in the Great Exhibition Catalogue as 'A new (quarter day) spring timepiece made of cut flint glass centres hooped with brass tooth rims, having engraved glass dial plate and pendulum bell, it goes three months and is kept in motion by a new clock movement propellor'. So far as it is known, no trace of this clock still exists.

In many ways James Edwards' clocks epitomised the Victorian era in being not only beautifully made but also showing great originality and ingenuity and being spectacular to look at. The principal feature of Edwards' clocks was, of course, the large cut glass centres to the wheelwork, the great wheel for instance being some 6in. (15.2cm) in diameter, but they had many other interesting features:

a) So as not to mar the overall appearance and possibly to add a little air of mystery, the mainspring was concealed in the wooden box on which the clock rested.

b) Because it would have been fairly difficult to drill through the cut glass bob (and this would certainly have marred its appearance) a pendulum rise and fall mechanism was provided.

c) On at least some of the clocks the fusee was held in position by independent plates screwed to the front and back frames (Figure 4/19) and could thus be removed without dismantling the clock.

d) The motionwork was concealed in a drum situated behind the opaque glass dial, presumably so that no conventional wheelwork could be seen.

e) Edwards positioned the wheels one behind the other so as to display them as attractively as possible and not, as on most clocks, by placing the third wheel just behind the frontplate.

Although the frames of his transparent clocks were very substantial, being some ⅜in. (10mm) thick, they were also very delicately pierced out to show off the wheelwork to the best possible advantage, the basic design of which was exactly the same as that used on his ordinary clocks.

5. Escapements

Whereas the design of the frame and the execution of the wheelwork, racks, levers, cocks, bridges, etc., illustrate the artistic skills of the clockmaker and the care and attention he puts into them, the construction of the clock's escapement is a display of his technical skill and ingenuity. With the majority of French skeleton clocks the pinwheel, in one of its various forms, is the escapement most commonly used, followed by the recoil and the conventional dead beat. Somewhat surprisingly it is rare to see an unusual escapement on a French skeleton whereas on the English clocks, although they are by no means common, a far wider variety is to be found.

Smith's of Clerkenwell were very conservative in their approach, using the recoil escapement almost entirely, whereas Evans of Handsworth was far more adventurous, employing a lever escapement mounted vertically on the frontplate of his Scott Memorial and other clocks (Figure 3/57). Evans designed his own form of pendulum controlled detented escapement (Figure 5/6), and on at least one occasion produced a full chronometer escapement mounted horizontally between the top of the two frames and on another clock employed Dennison's four legged gravity (Figure 5/4).

One of the most beautifully designed escapements was that produced by Condliff (Figure 3/16) in which a very large balance oscillates to and fro at the base of the frame.

Congreve's 'Extreme Detached Escapement' (Figure 3/7) is possibly the most ingenious, but unfortunately very few examples of it are still in existence. Another escapement produced by him was that which he employed on his rolling ball clock (Figure 5/15c). It is interesting that many of the most fascinating examples such as the chronometer escapement produced by Black of Alloa (Figure 5/7) or the table roller lever by Green of Wigan (Figure 5/10) were made by comparatively unknown makers or even appear on unsigned clocks.

In this chapter no attempt has been made to show all the different types of escapement in existence but to illustrate some of those examined and explain the way in which they work with the assistance of David Penney's excellent drawings to give readers some idea of the technical skill and ingenuity of the nineteenth century clockmakers.

Silent Escapements

The 'silent' escapement, which is comparatively rare, has always been assumed to have been designed for bedroom use but whether or not this is the case will never be known with any certainty, as this particular escapement is quite often seen on striking clocks (some of which have no strike/silent regulation) which does seem to refute this assumption. There are two main forms, both of which are very successful in that they can hardly be heard when in use, the first of which has sprung steel pallets and the second variety, shown here, makes use of gut line instead of the usual teeth on the 'scape wheel.

Plate 31. Figure 5/2a. A fine French skeleton clock of long duration made around the turn of the 19th century, which has an attractive fire gilt frame and engine turned inner and outer bezels to the enamelled dial which is signed 'Royelle, Paris'. There are centre sweep hands for seconds, minutes, hours and a thirty day calendar which has a very attractively fretted out star wheel; it has a relatively large pin wheel escapement, a drawing of which is shown in Figure 5/2c on p.182.   *Richard Wauson Collection, U.S.A.*

180

Figure 5/1a, b. An anonymous mid-19th century ivy leaf skeleton clock with passing strike on the hour, six spoke wheelwork, six graduated pillars, chain fusee and a brass rod pendulum with the regulating nut contained in a triangular space above the bob. A rare feature is the 'silent escapement', the 'scape wheel of which consists of two discs of brass between which gut has been stretched to take the place of the teeth.
Height 21in. (53.5cm).

Figure 5/2b. The rear view of the clock in Plate 31 (opposite) showing the pin wheel escapement.

Pin Wheel Escapements

The pin wheel escapement, in which the teeth of the 'scape wheel are in the form of pins projecting from it at right angles, was invented by Amant of Paris in 1749, and was mostly used in France on good quality clocks including longcase and table regulators but is seldom seen on English clocks other than turret clocks. Its advantage is that, although it is a form of dead beat escapement, it absorbs less power than the type used on most English clocks. The only problems which arise are the difficulty of keeping the pins lubricated and their fragility, as it is all too easy to bend them by careless handling of the clock.

Amant's original escapement is basically the same as that shown in Figure 5/2c and because the pins are only on one side of the 'scape wheel the pallets are of unequal length. In 1753 J.A. Lepaute modified the design by putting semi-circular pins alternately on either side of the 'scape wheel and thus made it possible to have pallets of equal length, but this would seem to be more of a theoretical than a practical advantage.

A later development of the pin wheel escapement is the coup perdu (lost beat) illustrated in Figure 5/3, in which the 'scape wheel is only released every other beat and thus permits seconds to be indicated on the dial even though a half seconds pendulum is employed.

Figure 5/2c. **Amant's pin wheel escapement.**

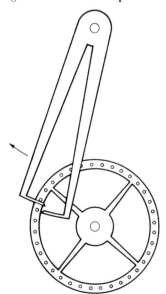 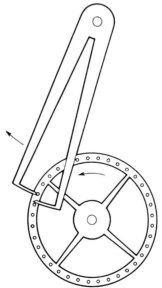 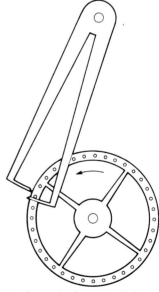

1. The pendulum is starting its swing to the left and at that stage a pin on the 'scape wheel is firmly locked on the left hand pallet.

2. As the pendulum continues its swing to the left the pin on the 'scape wheel is unlocked and impulses the left hand pallet and thus the pendulum.

3. At the end of the pendulum swing to the left the pin which impulsed the left hand pallet drops on to the locking face of the right hand pallet.

As the pendulum swings to the right the same sequence of events is repeated.

Figure 5/3a

Figure 5/3a, b. **Coup perdu (lost beat) pin wheel escapement.**
(A) and(B) are stops and (C) the counter weight. In Figure 5/3a the escapement is not in
a functional position.

Figure 5/3b

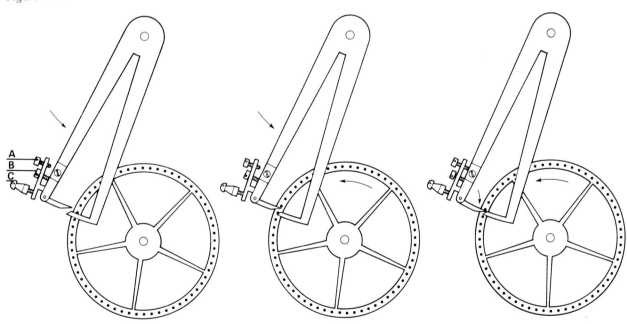

1. As the pendulum commences its swing to the right the pin is locked on the fixed right arm and the pivoted left pallet is raised by the counterweight.

2. As the pendulum continues its swing to the right the pin moves on to the impulse face of the fixed pallet just before the next pin falls on the pivoted left arm.

3. When this happens the pallet is depressed until the stop screw (A) comes into action, at which stage it is locked at the same level as the other pallet. As the pendulum returns the pin moves from the left to the right locking faces and the counterweight (C) then raises the left hand pallet.

Figure 5/4a

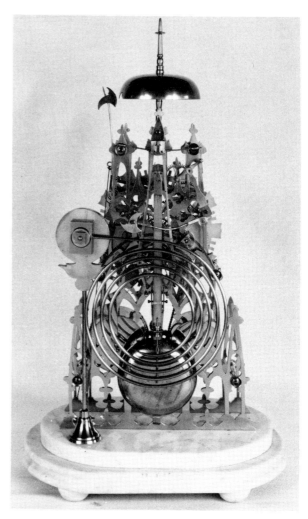

Figure 5/4b

Figure 5/4c

Figure 5/4a, b, c. **Gravity Escapements.**
An interesting and rare skeleton clock with four legged gravity escapement which may be safely attributed to Evans of Handsworth, (*see also* Plate 32). The two train chain fusee seven pillar movement has five and six spoke wheelwork. The clock is in many ways similar to his skeleton clocks with pendulum controlled detented escapements (Figure 5/6) the dials being virtually identical, with a large seconds ring at six o'clock; the fusees also are mounted high up with a long run of the chain from the barrel. As on most of Evans' clocks this has passing half hour strike on a bell and hour strike on a gong. A wood rod pendulum is employed with adjustable brass plates fitted to either side (Figure 5/4c) where the pins of the gravity arms engage.

A refinement not usually found on gravity escapements is the adjustable weights provided at the top of the gravity arms which may be seen in Figure 5/4b. A further improvement is that the bottoms of the arms may be adjusted merely by slackening off the locking screw, which greatly simplifies the setting up of the clock as on most longcase regulators employing a gravity escapement the arms have to be bent.
Height 21in. (53.3cm).

Figure 5/5a. This skeleton clock (formerly in the collection of Major Heathcote) signed by W. Tritschler & Co. Carlisle, the retailer, would originally have been fitted with Evans' detented escapement. In 1969 it was converted to Thwaites & Reed's design of six legged gravity escapement by Peter Bonnert of Maidstone, a purpose for which it was eminently suited because of the train layout with the high position of the fusee, the large seconds ring placed at the bottom of the dial, the provision of maintaining power and the use of a compensated wood rod pendulum with a relatively large pewter bob.

Evans' Pivoted Detent Escapement

This escapement is very similar in many ways to that used on some chronometers in that it employs a pivoted detent where the 'scape wheel is only released every other beat, thus enabling seconds to be indicated on the dial even though a half seconds pendulum is employed. It was probably first used by Evans on his Scott Memorial skeleton and at a somewhat later date on his scroll frame (Figure 3/16) and Gothic style clocks.

Figure 5/5b. In this close up illustration one of the lifting pins is about to raise the right hand gravity arm and the adjustable brass strips on which the gravity arms finally come to rest may be seen as well as the long run of the chain to the fusee.

Figure 5/5c. (A) is one of the lifting (set up) pins, (B) a locking piece, (C) one of the six legs of the escapement, (D) a gravity arm and (E) a fixed block.

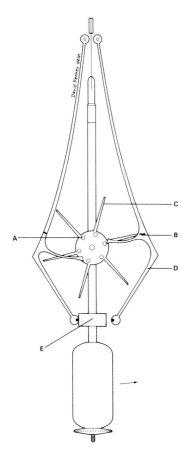

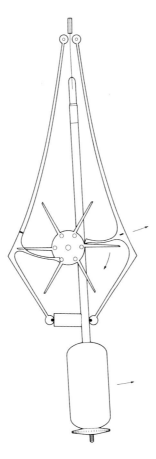

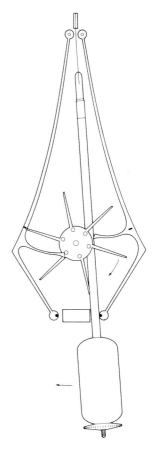

1. The pendulum is shown swinging free to the right through bottom dead centre with the 'scape wheel locked on the right hand locking stone (B) and the right hand arm (D) in its set position.

2. As the pendulum continues its swing to the right it picks up the right hand arm which releases the train to set up and lock on the left hand arm.

3. The pendulum now starts its return swing to the left and as it does so receives an impulse from the right hand gravity arm until this is arrested by the fixed block (E). Thus the distance between the set up position and the fixed block equals the gravity impulse.

Figure 5/6a, b. It seems likely that Evans considered this clock to be akin in many ways to a table regulator in that he employed a detented escapement (which theoretically at least should be as good as or better than a conventional dead beat), provided maintaining power and fitted the clock with a compensated pendulum in the form of a wood rod with pewter bob. Moreover there is a large subsidiary seconds dial on which, because of the escapement chosen, seconds as opposed to half seconds are indicated.

Due to the design of the escapement the train has to be inverted with the fusee mounted at the top of the frame. Although the layout of the escapement (Figure 5/6c, p.188) is a little different from that seen on the clock, functionally it is the same. *Mr. and Mrs. R. Seitz*

Figure 5/6b

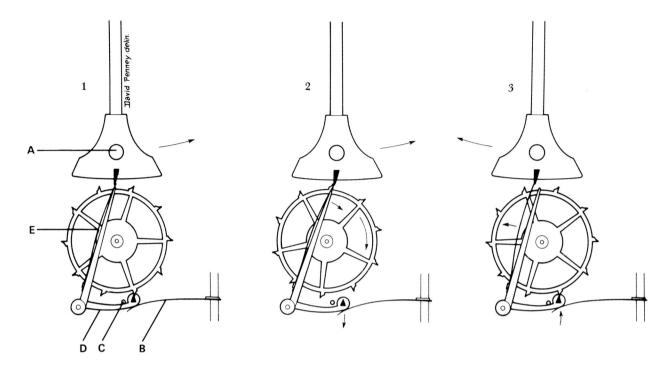

Figure 5/6c. (A) crutch pin (B) blade spring (C) banking pin (D) pivoted detent (E) passing spring. In (1) the pendulum and crutch are swinging freely to the right and are just about to engage the top of the pivoted detent and unlock it. When this happens (2) the 'scape wheel rotates and engages and impulses the tongue at the base of the crutch, following which the detent is returned to its original position by the blade spring and relocks the 'scape wheel. As the pendulum swings back to the left (3) it merely flexes the passing spring (E) leaving the 'scape wheel locked.

Chronometer Escapements

The chronometer escapement is in many ways the ultimate expression of the clockmaker's art in possibly being the most accurate escapement devised for spring driven clocks. Its principal use was in boxed ships' chronometers where it continued in employment for the best part of 200 years with, in the main, very little alteration; it was also used in pocket chronometers and on occasions in other high grade watches and clocks. The basic principle of its design is to detach the balance wheel as completely and for as long as possible from the influence of the movement which is providing the power to keep it beating. In this way the even beating of the balance will be disturbed as little as possible.

In view of the foregoing when related to the desire of the best skeleton clockmakers to display their skills to the utmost it is surprising that the chronometer escapement is seen so seldom on skeleton clocks. Evans is known to have made at least one (Figure 3/66) and possibly made a small series, and Andrew Black of Alloa (Figure 5/7) produced a limited number. One also occasionally sees isolated and frequently highly individualistic examples but the total number in existence must be very small.

188

Plate 32. Skeleton clock attributed to Evans of Handsworth (*see* Figure 5/4, p.184).

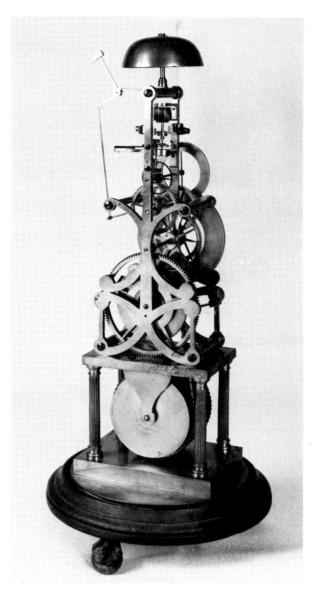

Figure 5/7a, b, c. Just how many of these highly individual clocks were made is not known, but possibly a very small number as only three have been seen in some twenty years. That Andrew Black was proud of his chronometer escapement is evinced by the fact that he signed his clocks 'And Black Alloa. Chronometer.' The clock is certainly fascinating to look at, with the complex series of rods for the passing hour strike, for instance, being more than a little bizarre. Although it is only a small eight day clock, standing some 11½ in. (29cm) high, it has a massive mainspring suspended independently below the brass plate on which the rest of the clock sits. The size of the mainspring gives some idea of the power absorbed by this type of escapement, and credence is given to the title 'chronometer' by the very large seconds ring immediately above the main dial. The layout of the escapement is visually excellent and makes it fascinating to watch. There is a large helical hairspring at the top, a split compensated bimetallic balance with regulating weights below this, and then the escapement which can be seen very clearly; the function of which is described in Figure 5/7d.

Norman Langmaid Collection, U.S.A.

Figure 5/7c.

1. The balance is moving clockwise and the unlocking stone (D) is about to push on the passing spring (A).

2. Unlocking occurs which pushes the detent locking stone (C) out of the way and allows the 'scape wheel to rotate and engage on the cut out in the roller (E) and give it impulse.

3. Immediately after unlocking the detent (B) returns to its original position and the next tooth on the 'scape wheel is arrested by the locking stone (C). The balance, which is now moving anticlockwise, returns, and as it does so moves the weak passing spring out of the way. Thus, as with all chronometer escapements, the 'scape wheel is released and the balance receives an impulse only every other beat, i.e. in just one direction.

Figure 5/7d. **Earnshaw's Spring Detent Escapement.** (A) passing spring (B) detent (C) detent locking stone (D) unlocking stone on unlocking roller (E) impulse cut-out in impulse roller (F) the thin part of the detent which acts as a spring.

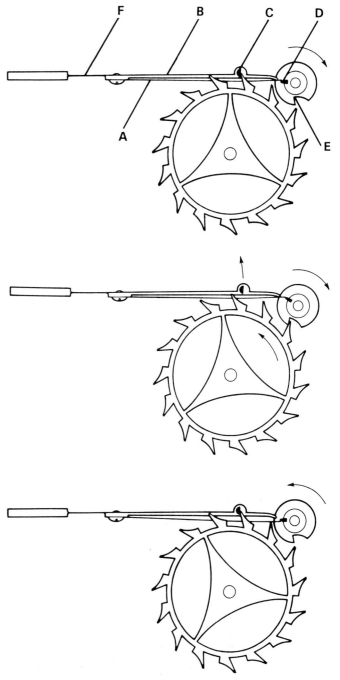

191

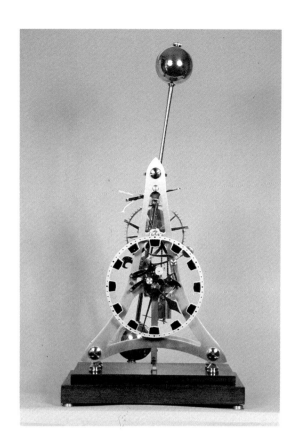

Plate 33. Skeleton clock signed 'E. Dent & Co. Ltd. London, England'. (*see* Figure 5/14, pp.204-5)

Plate 34. Congreve's rolling ball clock (*see* Figure 5/15, pp.207-8).

Figure 5/8a, b. **Chronometer Variant.**
A small English ivy leaf fusee skeleton timepiece
fitted with maintaining power and signed 'Arnold,
London' on a disc above twelve o'clock. It is fitted
with an unusual form of chronometer escapement
(Figure 5/8d) in which the passing spring used in
Earnshaw's Escapement (*see* Figure 5/7d) is
replaced by an additional pivoted lever; possibly
the basic purpose of this design was to try and
reduce the power absorbed by the standard
chronometer escapement, but there is still the
spring to deflect plus the friction of a pivot and
the additional inertia of the unlocking lever (F) so
it seems doubtful if any less power would be
required.
Height 11in. (28cm).

Norman Langmaid Collection, U.S.A.

Figure 5/8b

Figure 5/8c. Chronometer escapement of timepiece on previous page.

Figure 5/8d. (A) free axis of rotation of unlocking lever (B) fixed axis of rotation (C) counterpoise (D) return spring (E) locking detent (F) unlocking lever (G) unlocking stone (H) impulse roller with cut out.

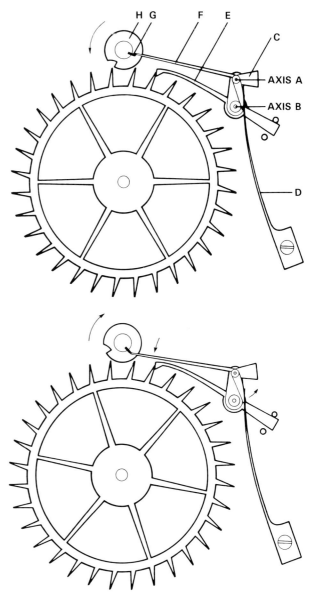

1. The 'scape wheel is locked. As the balance turns the unlocking stone (G) lifts the unlocking lever (F).

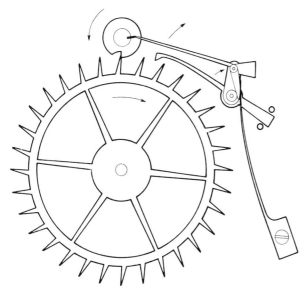

2. As a result of this axis (A) rotates around axis (B), which is fixed and lifts the locking detent (E). Impulse will then take place as the 'scape wheel rotates and engages the cut out in the impulse roller (H).

3. Passing action. On returning the stone on the impulse roller engages on the unlocking lever which can now rotate on its own axis and is thus moved out of the way.

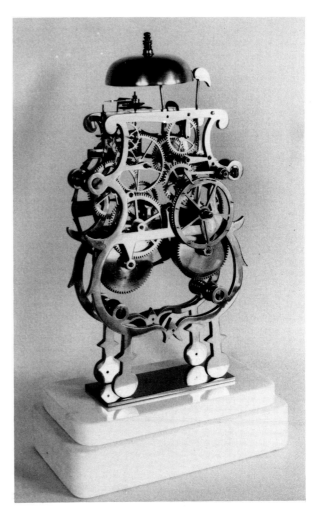

Figure 5/9a, b. This interesting and highly individual mid-19th century skeleton clock which is signed 'W. Jackson London' on a plaque at the bottom of the frame, has many unusual features; for instance it has no fusees, which is rare on an English 18th or 19th century clock. The pin wheel for the strike is mounted externally on the backplate, a large brass pinion is employed in the striking train and it is fitted with a de Baufre type escapement with two steel 'scape wheels and a plain steel balance.

Albert Odmark Collection, U.S.A.

De Baufre Escapement

The principle of this escapement is the mounting of two 'scape wheels on a common arbor. Seldom seen on English clocks it was only ever employed in limited numbers because of the additional expense involved in its production.

Figure 5/9c

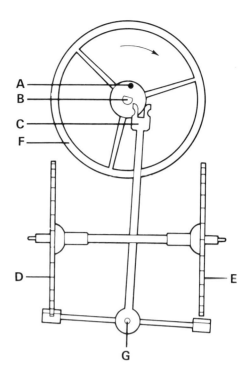

Figure 5/9d. (A) impulse pin mounted on impulse roller (B) balance arbor with a flat, for safety action (C) fork (D) and (E) 'scape wheels (F) balance wheel (G) pivot point of fork and pallets.

1. The left wheel is locked and the balance is swinging clockwise.

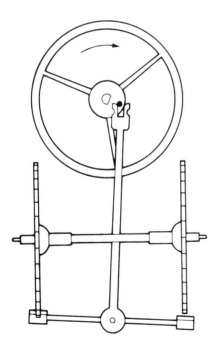

2. Impulse pin (A) engages in fork moving it to the left and taking the left hand pallet away from the 'scape wheel.

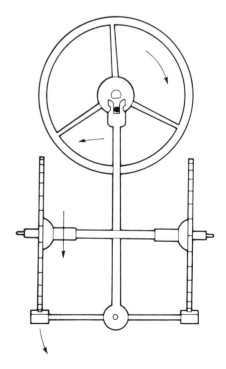

3. As this starts to unlock it receives impulse on its inclined plane; when the balance returns the process is repeated on the right hand pallet.

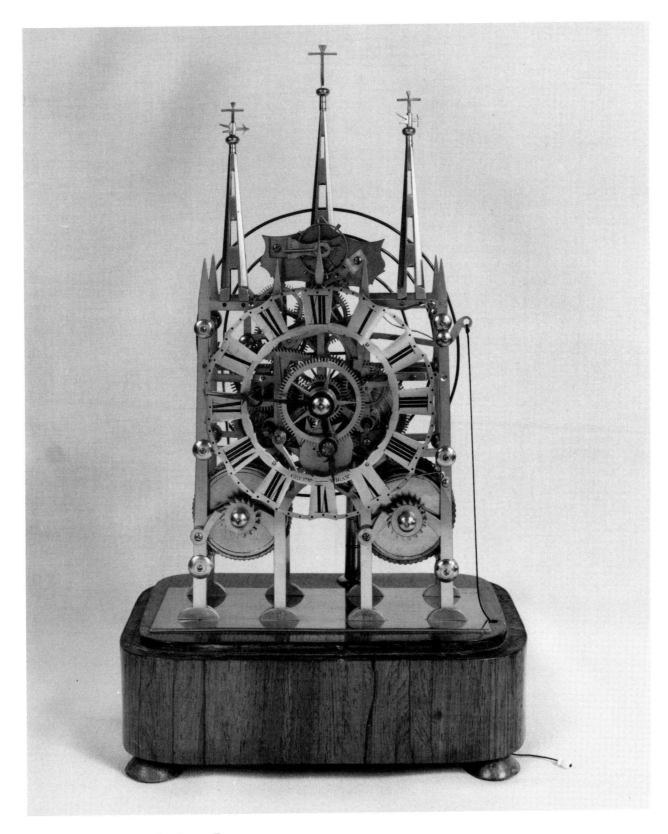

Figure 5/10a. **Table Roller Lever Escapement.**
A good two train skeleton clock based on Lichfield Cathedral, striking and repeating the hours on a gong. The six pillar movement which is signed 'Green of Wigan' on the inner aspect of the chapter ring has a lever escapement mounted vertically above the movement.

Albert Odmark Collection, U.S.A.

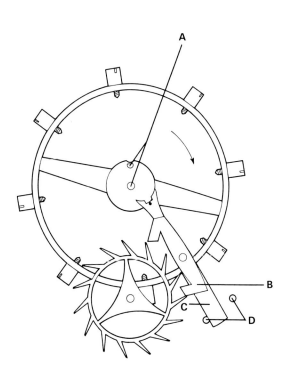

1. The balance is swinging free clockwise.

Figure 5/10b

Figure 5/10c. (A) impulse pin and roller, which has a notch in it for safety action whilst the pin is engaged by the lever (B) pallets (C) lever (D) banking pins.

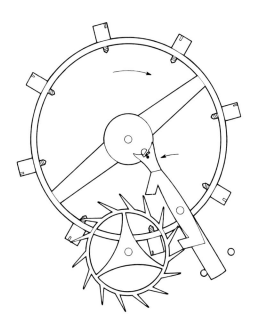

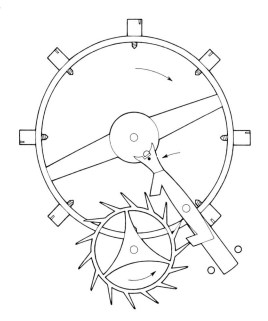

2. The impulse pin (A) meets the fork and thus moves the pallets and starts to unlock the 'scape wheel.

3. As this turns, impulse is given to the balance via the slope on the faces of the pallets, the lever and the impulse stone.

Figure 5/11a. **Lever Variant Straight Line Type with Two Impulse Pins.**
Unsigned mid-19th century skeleton clock with scroll frame, delicate six spoke wheelwork, maintaining power, half seconds balance and dead beat pallets to the lever escapement which is excellently displayed at the top of the frame.
Height 14in. (35.6cm).

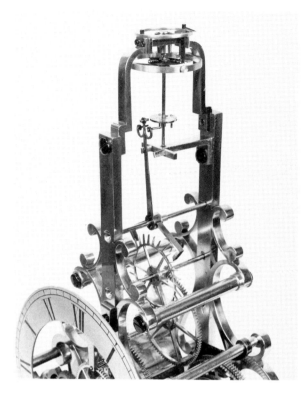

Figure 5/11b. Lever variant straight line type with two impulse pins.

Figure 5/11c. (A) impulse pin (B) safety pin and crescent.

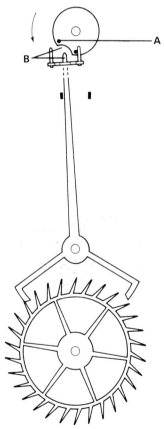

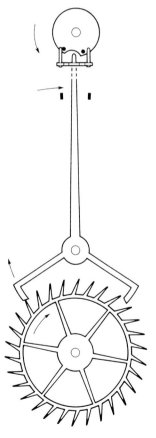

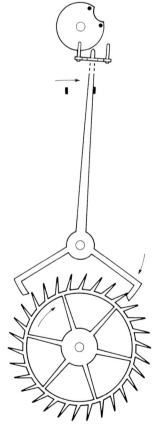

1. The balance is swinging anticlockwise and about to move the lever.

2. The balance is receiving impulse via the left hand pallet, lever and impulse pin (A).

3. The escapement is locked as the balance continues its swing anticlockwise.

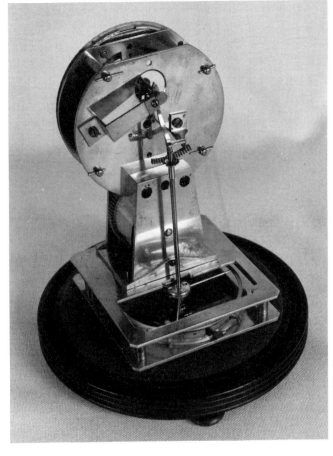

Figure 5/12a. **Rack Escapement (not lever), Pin Wheel Type.**
A very interesting little skeleton clock probably made in France towards the end of the last century, employing undrilled French clock plates, which has a very large plain three arm horizontal balance fitted into the base with its spring immediately below it. Regulation is achieved by moving a curved brass strip at the rear which is provided with a knob and has guides on either side. The escapement is illustrated in Figure 5/12b.

Figure 5/12b. (A) the pallets, one of which is in front and one behind the 'scape wheel (B) the six sided 'scape wheel which has pins fitted alternately to either side at the tips of its angles, i.e. three pins on either side (C) the rack and pinion (D) balance wheel (E) balance spring.

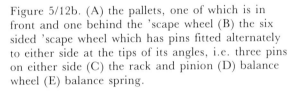

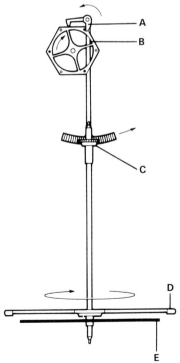

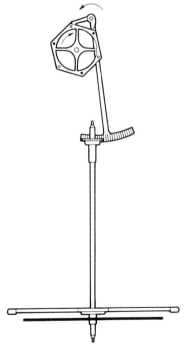

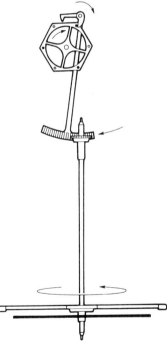

1. The balance is rotating clockwise and receiving impulse from the pin on the 'scape wheel engaging the front pallet.

2. After impulse the 'scape wheel is arrested by the rear pallet, the balance comes to rest and starts to return.

3. The back pallet now releases the 'scape wheel and the next front pin drops on to the front pallet.

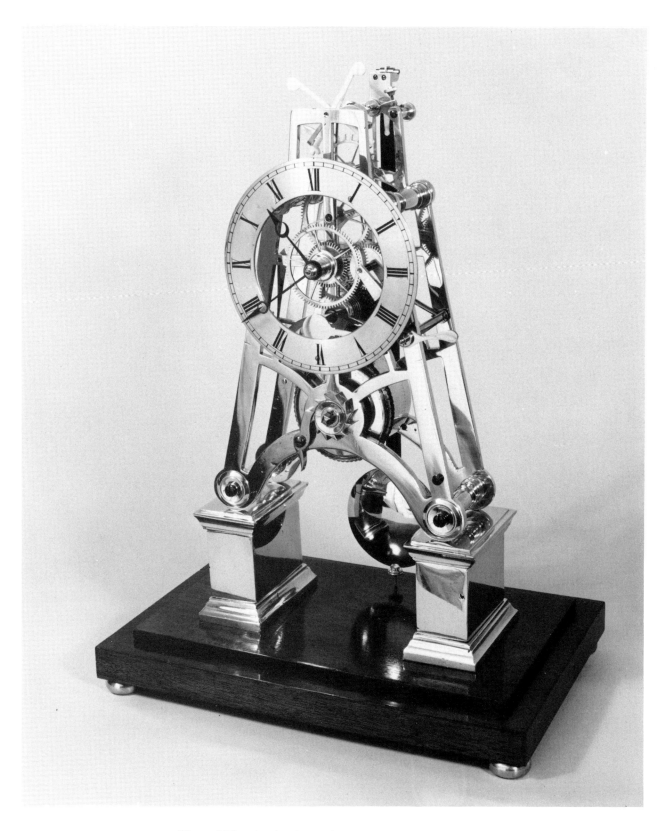

Figure 5/13a. A rafter frame skeleton clock (formerly in the collection of Major Heathcote) which in 1968 was fitted with a grasshopper escapement by Peter Bonnert; at the same time bolt and shutter maintaining power was added and a locking device acting on the 'scape wheel. A half seconds beating ebony rod pendulum was used and beat regulation incorporated in the pallet arbor, the actual pallets being made of ivory.

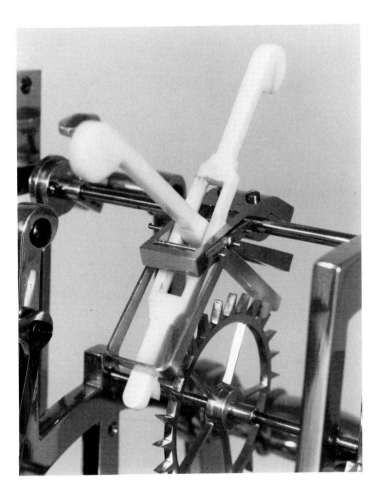

Figure 5/13b

The Grasshopper Escapement

It is not known for certain whether it was John Harrison or his younger brother James who invented the grasshopper escapement. The earliest clock which incorporates this device is believed to be a turret clock constructed by James but is was undoubtedly John who made it so well known.

This relatively complex escapement takes its name from the abrupt movement similar to that of the hind legs of a grasshopper and was originally incorporated in Harrison's longcase regulators made c.1726 which gave such amazing performances: John Harrison claimed that they kept time to within a second a month, a performance which was not surpassed for at least one hundred years. The escapement was also incorporated in his famous sea clocks which paved the way to the recording of accurate time at sea and thus enabled longitude to be determined accurately, an invaluable aid to navigation (which was to assist Britain in maintaining its mastery of the seas) and the production of accurate charts and maps.

The great advantages of the grasshopper escapement were that it gave a practically continuous impulse with a minimum of friction and never required oiling which meant not just that it did not require cleaning and re-oiling regularly but that friction remained constant over a long period of time and thus the accuracy of the timekeeping did not change. This was achieved by using brass working against lignum vitae which is self lubricating. A proof of the efficiency of the design is the fact that Harrison's first sea clock went on running in his home without ever stopping for some thirty years.

Figure 5/14a. A large and highly individual skeleton clock believed to have been made in limited numbers in the early 1970s, signed on the backplate 'E. Dent & Co. Ltd., London England. No Jewels, No.028' (*see also* Plate 33). 'Whitlock' also appears on the plate, possibly the employee of Dent's who was responsible for its construction. (This particular clock was formerly in the collection of Major Heathcote.)

As can be seen from the rear view (Figure 5/14b) an electric remontoire is provided which is triggered and rewinds the weight every time it reaches the bottom and tilts a platform which is supported by a large stud mounted on the backplate. A long drive down from the 'scape wheel advances the minute and hour hands which are both independently actuated and controlled by ratchets. Immediately below the plaque on the backplate is a lever which may be tilted by a knurled screw to immobilise the massive compound seconds beating pendulum. The grasshopper escapement, which is copied from an original model by Martin Burgess, is illustrated in Figure 5/14d, p.206.   *Sotheby's*

204

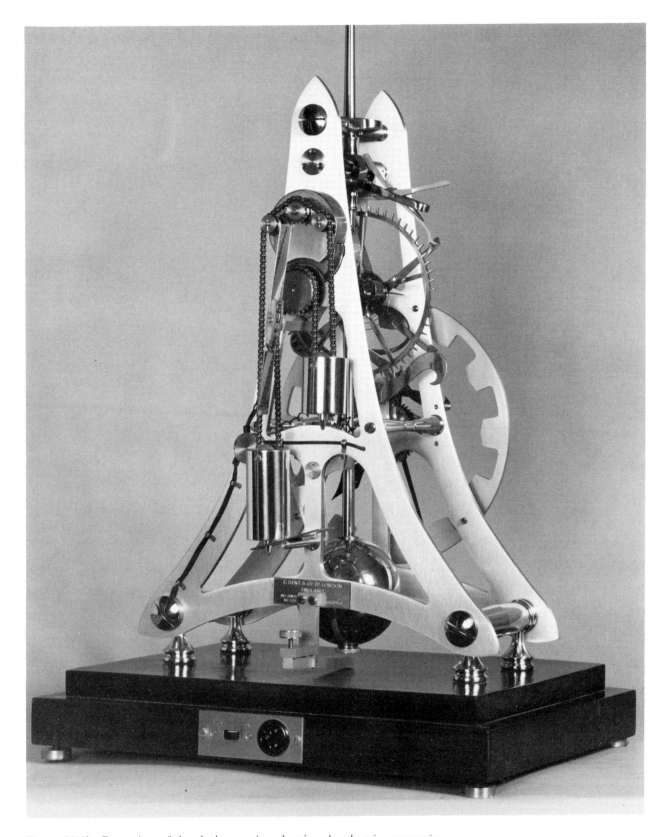

Figure 5/14b. Rear view of the clock opposite, showing the electric remontoire.

Figure 5/14c.

Figure 5/14d. (A) compound pendulum (B) pivot point for pallet arms (C) pins which act as controller stops (D) pallet controller, which positions the pallets precisely and acts as a damper on pallet movement.

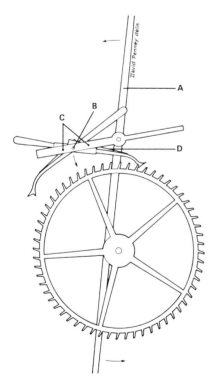
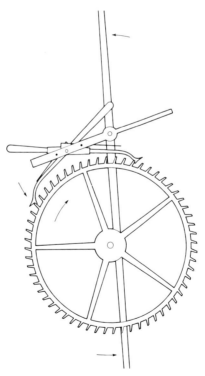
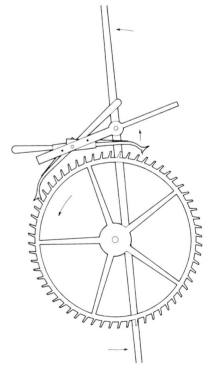

1. The compound pendulum is swinging anticlockwise, and the 'scape wheel which is rotating clockwise is locked on the right hand pallet giving it a 'push' impulse.

2. The pendulum is now almost at the end of its swing and the left hand pallet engages a tooth of the 'scape wheel.

3. The pendulum completes its swing which recoils the 'scape wheel enough to release the right hand pallet. As the pendulum swings in the reverse direction exactly the same process is repeated.

Figure 5/15a, b. **Congreve's Rolling Ball Clock.**
This clock has already been mentioned
earlier (*see* pp.78-82) as have the other
escapements which Congreve designed
including his 'Extreme Detached
Escapement'. The escapement used on his
rolling ball clock is described in Figure
5/15c to complete the picture. This clock is
a particularly attractive example (probably
made in the mid-19th century) with a brass
strung base covered in red tortoiseshell and
a silvered brass frame (*see also* Plate 34).
The table is skeletonised and an interesting
refinement is the provision of leaf spring
bumpers (to either side of the table) which
engage just before it comes to rest and help
it to tilt back in the other direction. The
chain fusee movement has four pillars, five
spoke wheelwork and three dials which are
from left to right, hours, minutes and
seconds. The clock has a plaque inscribed
'Invented by Sir William Congreve Bart.
Patented in 1808'.
Height 15in. (38.1cm).
Albert Odmark Collection, U.S.A.

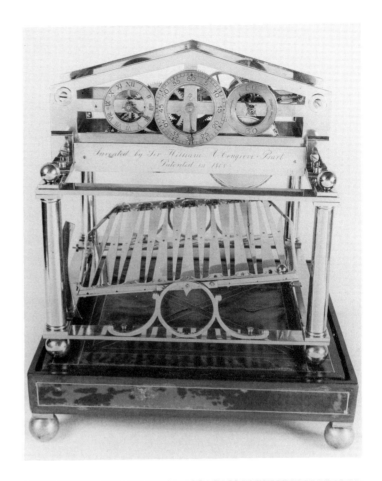

Figure 5/15b

207

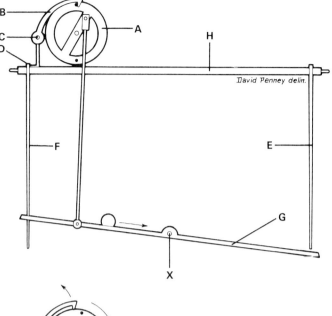

Figure 5/15c. (A) 'scape wheel which runs on the same arbor as the seconds hand is released every thirty seconds (on some clocks this may be every fifteen seconds) (B) locking pawl (C) pivot point of pawl (D) a tongue (not seen here) is attached to the back of the arbor (H) so that the bottom of the pawl may be depressed (E) and (F) release arms (G) table (H) arbor on which the release arms are mounted (X) axis of table.

1. The ball is rolling down the inclined plane and the train is locked.

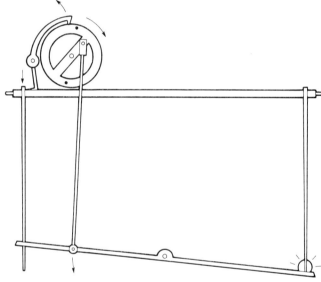

2. The ball tilts the release arm (E) which rotates arbor (H) and via the tongue attached to the back of it (D) depresses the base of the locking pawl (B) which then pivots around its axis (C) releases the train. The seconds wheel (A) now makes half a turn and in doing so rocks the table around its axis (X) and reverses its tilt.

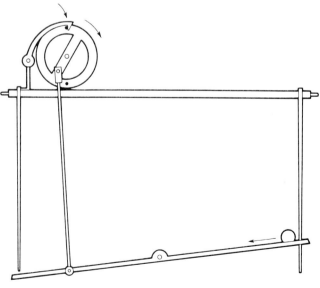

3. The seconds or 'scape wheel is now locked by the second pin and the ball starts its return journey towards the other release arm.

208

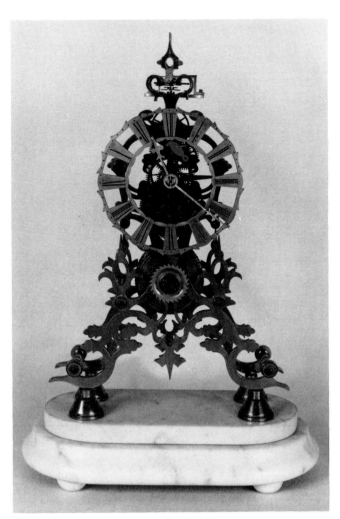

Figure 5/16b

Figure 5/16a, b. **Duplex Escapement**

A rare anonymous mid-19th century English skeleton clock with six spoke wheelwork, six pillars and a duplex escapement mounted horizontally between the two frames. Although it is impossible to attribute this clock with certainty it seems extremely likely that it was made by Evans of Handsworth as the frame is very similar to that shown in Figure 3/63 and the style of chapter ring used has also been seen on clocks made by him. A further factor is that Evans is known to have produced skeleton clocks with many different types of escapement, possibly as part of a limited series. The duplex escapement was conceived and evolved in the second half of the 18th and the first part of the 19th centuries by several makers such as Dutertre, Pièrre Le Roy and Thomas Tyrer. A demanding escapement both in its manufacture and its maintainence, for these reasons the duplex really found favour. The basic principle of the duplex is the employment of two sets of teeth, the outer ones for locking and the inner ones for providing impulse, but the way in which they are laid out varies appreciably. The escapement is like that of a chronometer in that it receives impulse in one direction only, i.e. at every other vibration, and when it is made to the highest standards produces results which are only a little inferior to the chronometer.

Plate 35. This clock, which must have been one of the finest English skeleton clocks produced, would have been made by Smith's of Clerkenwell, as many of the components, including the chapter ring, are readily identifiable as their work. In basic design and execution it bears marked similarities with their St. Paul's and Brighton Pavilion clocks and may just possibly have been modelled on a building (*see* Figure 6/1, pp.211-14).

6. Complex Clocks

In this chapter are included not only skeleton clocks but also a few examples of clocks such as regulators which have been skeletonised to display the movement as completely as possible. For convenience they have been divided into the following groups:

1. Quarter chiming clocks.
2. Musical clocks.
3. Table regulators and astronomical clocks.
4. Skeletonised longcase regulators.
5. Clocks with calendarwork and other unusual features.

1. Chiming clocks

The vase majority of English clocks which chime the quarters have three trains, the exception being that interesting group which are two train and have pump action quarter chime, i.e. they chime the first three quarters but prior to the hour the mechanism is pumped over so that just a single hammer strikes the hour. Examples of these are the two clocks made by Moore (*see* Figures 3/29 and 3/30).

Most clocks which chime the quarters do so on eight bells, but just two are occasionally used; four are employed fairly frequently, usually as Westminster chimes, and on rare occasions nine, ten, twelve or even more are incorporated in the chime. Most of those which were in common use are listed in de Carle[1].

The clocks illustrated in this chapter together with those elsewhere in the book, such as Figures 2/23, 2/26c, 2/34, 3/20, 3/54 and 3/65, will give some idea of the range of chiming clocks produced.

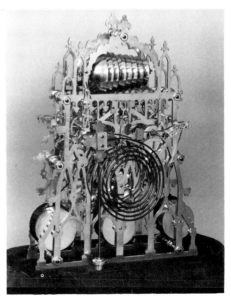

Figure 6/1b. The reverse side of the clock opposite.

---

1. de Carle, D., *Watch & Clock Encyclopedia*, N.A.G. Press Ltd., London, 2nd ed., 1959.

Figure 6/1a (*see* Plate 35). The solid silver plaque fitted to the velvet covered base which is surrounded by attractively engraved silver fretwork bears the inscription 'Presented to Joseph Norton Esquire on retiring from business by his Numerous Work People as a Testimonial of Their Regard and Esteem. May 1864'. It also carries the name 'Cooper, New St, Huddersfield', the distributor.

The clock, which is basically a straightforward quarter chiming clock but finished to an extremely high standard, looks far more complex than it really is because almost every component is fashioned in a far more elaborate way than is necessary for strictly functional purposes. This also holds true of course, but to a far lesser extent, of virtually all English 17th and 18th century clockmaking and also many of the clocks produced in Southern Germany over a century earlier.

Figure 6/1c. The bells are beautifully displayed in a cutout and the end of each hammer is carefully finished in a rosette. The long pin barrel (the vertical drive to which may be seen to the right) adds to the visual attraction, particularly when the clock is chiming.

Figure 6/1d. This view displays much of the quarter work including the rack and its tail which are carefully fretted out, the quarter snail, and the vertical drive to the pin barrel which employs a six spoke contrate wheel supported by a substantial, attractively pierced out bracket.

Figure 6/1e, f. In Figure 6/1e may be seen the gathering pallet scarcely recognisable as such and the hour rack below it and in Figure 6/1f the tail of the rack resting on the skeletonised snail. Immediately behind this is the star wheel and jumper and to the top right may be seen the motion work.

Figure 6/1f

Figure 6/1g. The clickwork: even at this magnification, the quality and detail of finish cannot be faulted.

Figure 6/2a, b. A large unsigned and highly individual skeleton clock probably made in the 1840s, which chimes the quarters on four bells laid out in a most unusual way, three being mounted from front to back with the fourth bell placed horizontally above them. The fifth or very top bell is for striking the hours.

Figure 6/3. A scroll frame skeleton clock with five spoke wheelwork chiming the quarters on eight bells and striking the hours on a further bell mounted on the backplate. Height 20in. (51cm)

Christie's

Figure 6/4. A very substantial three train clock chiming the quarters on eight bells and striking the hours on a gong. The barrels are skeletonised and all the wheelwork is six spoke. An unusual feature which looks somewhat out of keeping is the addition of finials to the scroll frame. The chapter ring, which is simply fretted out, blurs into the background and makes good the adage that one cannot read the time on a skeleton clock.
Height 23½in. (59.7cm).   *Sotheby's*

Figure 6/5. A quarter chiming skeleton clock by Smith's of Clerkenwell, probably made c.1880, which is fairly unusual in having a seconds ring, signed by Ulrich, the London retailer. The elaborate numerals are fretted out to one of Smith's standard designs but have been laid upon a conventional chapter ring. For a very similar clock see Figure 3/51.
Height 23in. (58.4cm).   *Christie's*

Figure 6/6b. A good unsigned mid-19th century three train chain fusee skeleton clock chiming the quarters on eight bells and striking the hours on a gong, which has a relatively delicate open scroll frame which rests on two brass plinths (*see* Plate 36 opposite). The six pillar movement has five spoke wheelwork throughout the train and a conventional pendulum. The left hand pillar immediately below the chapter ring has a loose bushing surrounding it which acts as a roller for the fusee chain thus reducing friction and preventing it rubbing the pillar when it is coming off the small end of the fusee. The only alternative would have been to move the pillar which would have destroyed the symmetry of the layout. On the gong block is inscribed 'Conversion by Nome, Notting Hill, London', but little would seem to have been altered on the clock since its manufacture.
Height 24in. (61cm).

Plate 36. Figure 6/6a. Three train fusee skeleton clock (*see* opposite page)

Plate 37. Figure 6/7. A fine quality skeleton clock with a fretted and engraved chapter ring with raised numerals, gilded wheelwork and frames. The plinths on which it rests are engraved and there is brass fretwork in front of the pendulum bob. The movement which chimes the quarters on eight bells and strikes the hours on a ninth mounted behind the main nest has dead beat escapement; an unusual feature is the elimination of the need for slots in the heads of the screws holding the frame pillars by holes drilled in them through which a tommy bar may be placed for tightening.
A relatively rare refinement is the provision for winding all three trains through the elaborate and well carved base. It is interesting to compare and contrast this clock with that seen in Figure 6/9 and to speculate whether the clocks were both executed by a clockmaker to his own basic design over a twenty to thirty year period or whether, for instance, different clockmakers used components bought in from a common source.

Figure 6/8. A fine and relatively large three train skeleton clock with fully engraved frame which chimes and repeats the quarters on eight bells (attractively displayed in a cutout at the top of the frame) and strikes the hours on a gong. Great attention to detail has been paid to the clock, with even the barrel covers decorated. Signed in full at the base of the frame 'Roskell, Church Street, Liverpool', the bold way in which the signature is executed, and the fact that it is so obviously part of the overall design of the engraving, leaves one in little doubt that this clock was actually made by one of the Roskell family and that they were very proud of their work. The Roskells, famed for their fine watches and chronometers, were working in the first half of the 19th century. Gilded chapter rings such as the one on this clock were used by some of the finest makers around the mid-19th century and invariably had painted numerals. An attractive refinement is the fitting of a spirit level to the front of the brass plate on which the clock rests.
Height 22in. (56cm). *Phillips, Edinburgh*

Figure 6/9. Another Liverpool clock, also of high quality and with some similar features to the one made by Roskell, such as the finely engraved frame and the gilded chapter ring which is signed 'Penlington & Hutton, Liverpool'. The three train movement which has six massive baluster pillars screwed at both ends, chimes the quarters on eight bells and has a gong for the hours. The escapement is dead beat and the pendulum has a lenticular bob overlaid on both sides with chased acanthus scrolls. The four rectangular plinths on which the clock rests are profusely engraved with leaves and flowers. The frame design is very similar to that used on the musical clock signed by McFerran of Manchester (Figure 1/21) which although far more flamboyant in its concept, also employs dead beat escapement and has an overlaid pendulum. An interesting and rare feature is that it still has its black painted travelling case fitted with a velvet covered securing bar and is complete with original cruciform winding key and dome.
Height 23in. (58.5cm).   *Sotheby's*

Figure 6/10. A beautiful quality quarter chiming skeleton clock signed 'James Condliff, Liverpool 1862. International Exhibition' on plaques affixed to the base. This clock is typical of Condliff's work with a fine balance with helical hairspring mounted in a cutout at the top of the attractive scroll frame which rests on a rectangular gilded base. Items to note are the detail finish to the hammer heads and the fact that it has strike/silent regulation and a choice of chimes. The walnut base is excellently executed and complements the frame perfectly.

Merseyside County Museums

Figure 6/11. A most ingenious skeleton clock of eight days duration signed 'W. Wilson, Maryport' (who is recorded as working from 1869-79) which has four spring barrels and four fusees, the outer two being for the going and striking trains with the fusees mounted high up in the frame and the inner pair with the fusees situated at the bottom below the spring barrels, which work in tandem to supply power to the Swiss musical movement via a drive shaft and a series of bevel gears. The movement plays every two hours. The clock, which has a pin pallet lever escapement with blued steel spiral hairspring, is fitted with maintaining power and in addition to the main dial has subsidiary dials for the days of the week, days of the month and months of the year.
Height 22in. (55.9cm). *The Time Museum, Rockford, U.S.A.*

2. Musical Clocks

Very few musical skeleton clocks seem to have been made, the reason for this possibly being in part the high cost of manufacture but also probably because the large number of components required tends to mar the overall concept of the skeleton clock, making it appear far too solid.

Figure 6/12a, b. A highly individual musical clock with time indicated on a delicate chapter ring with Arabic numerals situated immediately below the cupola. Six spoke wheelwork is employed and the dead beat escapement, which may be seen in the rear view between two of the bottom pillars of the cupola, has a bimetallic balance with hair spring and silvered regulation sector. The music is played once every hour or at will employing sixteen bells and two sets of sixteen hammers, one set being muted. Most unusually there are two pin barrels working together, one large and one small. The tune selector, which is signed 'Ross Fecit', gives a choice of fifteen different tunes.
Width of base 18in. (46cm).   *Peter K. Weiss, and Christie's*

There are three basic types of musical skeleton clocks.

a) Those in which the musical train is incorporated within the clock itself. These are basically similar to but more elaborate than the standard quarter chiming clock.

Figure 6/12b

b) Those in which a separate musical movement is fitted in or on top of the base and is triggered off by the main movement at set intervals, usually every one or three hours.

c) Four train clocks which are basically quarter chiming and musical clocks with separate trains for each function.

In addition there are variations on this theme such as two train musical clocks in which the striking train also supplies power for the music and three train clocks in which by means of pump action a chime is played on the first three quarters and music on the hour.

One musical clock has already been illustrated in Figure 1/21 and others will now be described.

Plate 38. Figure 6/13a. A complex fully skeletonised four train musical and quarter chiming bracket clock which might equally well be termed a four train skeleton clock, contained within a mahogany bell topped case inlaid with floral marquetry. Brass fretwork has been used to close the space between the case and what is, in effect, the frame of the clock, which adds to the appearance of complexity. As with several complex clocks because of the lack of space the pendulum has been omitted and a lever escapement employed.

Plate 39. Figure 6/13d. The various subsidiary dials are for:

Top left　　　Music and chime silent.
Top centre　　Days of the month.
Top right　　Cambridge/Oxford chime.
Bottom left　　Music selection.
Bottom centre　Year calendar.
Bottom right　Days of the week.

Figure 6/13b. The clock chimes the quarters on either eight bells or four gongs and plays one of seven tunes employing sixteen bells and twenty-one hammers, i.e. five bells have two hammers and the others one only. A possibly unique feature is the provision of two extra gongs to play 'Amen' after the hymn, which should be set to play on Sunday when the clock is on automatic change. There is also a provision for manual change, the tunes available being 'God Save the Queen', 'The Blue Bells of Scotland', 'The Minstrel Boy', 'March of the Men of Harlech', 'Auld Lang Syne', 'Home Sweet Home' and the hymn 'Great God What do I see and Hear'.

Figure 6/13c

The levers seen in Figures 6/13c and 6/13d (see Plate 39) are for:
Next to III, repeating hours and quarters.
Next to IX, repeating music.
Next to VIII, automatic or manual tune change.

Figure 6/14a. A skeletonised table regulator by Evans with his arabesque frame, in which can be seen a 'regulator' dial layout but with the positions of the seconds and hour rings reversed, due to his pivoted detent escapement, a drawing of which may be seen in Figure 5/6c. (The same layout is usually employed when Dennison's gravity escapement is used.)

The clock is fitted with maintaining power and a zinc/steel fully compensated pendulum. Seconds, as opposed to half seconds, are indicated on the large seconds ring because the train is only released every other beat as with chronometer escapements.

Dr. S.P. Lehv Collection

3. Table Regulators and Astronomical Clocks

Whereas in England the longcase regulator led the field in precision timekeeping, in France table regulators were produced at least in equal and possibly greater numbers than longcase regulators, throughout the second half of the eighteenth and the first part of the nineteenth centuries. However, a few table regulators were made in England such as the hump backed clocks by Jump and Barwise, the lovely series made by Dent's in the mid-nineteenth

Figure 6/14b. Reverse side of clock on previous page.

century (Figure 6/15) and various others which were produced on a one off basis.

Evans, in his overall approach and constant search to maintain and improve the standard of his products, was the only large scale skeleton clock manufacturer to give serious consideration to improving the accuracy of his clocks. He produced his wood rod pendulum with pewter bob which whilst not a fully compensated pendulum, was an approach in this direction and he also constructed clocks with mercury and zinc/steel compensated pendulums. His clocks with pivoted detent escapement which were also fitted with maintaining power (Figure 5/6) should really be classified as skeletonised table regulators and he made at least one clock with a similar frame which was fitted with a chronometer escapement (*see* Figure 3/66). In Figure 6/14 is seen a table regulator by him which has a fully compensated pendulum.

Figure 6/15a, b. In the mid-19th century Dent's produced a beautiful series of highly individual skeletonised table regulators, all similar in their construction but varying in detail; for instance two had Airy's escapement whereas the rest had a conventional dead beat and two were fitted with a remontoire; the amount of jewelling employed varied and there were minor differences in the design of the frames which gave each regulator its own character. Just how many were made is not known but it is believed to be around six or seven.

Dent No.860, illustrated here, is a fine, skeletonised table regulator with silvered brass dial, jewelled dead beat escapement, a mercury compensated pendulum supported by a relatively massive brass bracket and provided with beat regulation (*see also* Plate 40). The movement, which is fitted with maintaining power has a spotted backplate and fully jewelled train.
Height 18½ in. (47cm).

Figure 6/16a, b. A fine table regulator by Adam Thomson of London (who is recorded as working between 1839-57) which has a wood rod pendulum with brass lenticular bob, a graduated rating nut, a beat scale and beat regulation. The movement has dead beat escapement and maintaining power and rests on a substantial brass plinth which in turn rests on a mahogany base fitted with levelling screws and a spirit level.

The dial layout is both interesting and attractive with centre sweep minute and hour hands, subsidiaries at the bottom for days of the week and month, and below twelve o'clock a most unusual dial in the centre of which are displayed the moon's phases with a lunar calendar immediately above. To enable true seconds to be shown with a half seconds pendulum the outer ring has been calibrated twice, 0-30 and 30-60.

Asprey

Figure 6/17. Charles Edward Viner was undoubtedly one of the finest English 19th century clockmakers. He was apprenticed to Thomas Savage of Red Lion Square, Clerkenwell, London, on 22nd September 1802, became free of the Clockmakers' Company on 3rd May 1813, and was a liveryman from 1819-40. He formed a partnership with Hoskins in 1832 and the business Charles Edward Viner & Co. is recorded as being in existence from 1828-69, but it seems likely that Viner died in the 1840s.

The variety of work he produced, its concept and the superb way in which it was executed was almost unsurpassed by any other clockmaker. Thus it is surprising that so little is known or has been written about him. He produced fine watches, some excellent carriage clocks (a limited number of which were of great complexity) some exquisite bracket clocks, usually of relatively small size and often with delicately engraved silvered or gilt dials, and a few regulators.

The skeleton clock illustrated here which is typical of his work is indoubtedly one of the best ever produced in this country; it is of year duration and has two very large skeletonised spring barrels the chains from which rise to the two fusees which have large great wheels. All the wheelwork is of very fine quality and dead beat escapement is employed with a pendulum. The dials, as on many of Viner's clocks, are gilt brass, the upper one showing seconds, the main dial has concentric steel hands for minutes and hours and an additional gold plated one for the equation of time. The lower dial is a year calendar giving days of the month, months of the year and also has a concentric lunar date calendar. Days of the week are shown in an aperture immediately below twelve o'clock. The clock rests on a marble plinth with ormolu decoration and bears a plaque inscribed 'This Twelve Month Clock designed and constructed by C.E. Viner 235 Regent Street, London 1830.' (Viner was working at this address from 1829-42.)   *G. Daniels, Isle of Man*

Plate 40. Skeletonised table regulator by Dent (*see* Figure 6/15, p.231).

Plate 41. Figure 6/18. A good quality English table regulator signed 'Alexr. Watkins, 67 Strand London' (who is listed as working 1844-81) which has a very decorative dial with a true regulator layout. The substantial chain fusee movement, seen here with the chain detached, has eight pillars and frames some 3¹/₁₆ in. (6mm) thick. A conventional dead beat escapement is fitted which is controlled by a large compensated balance mounted at the top of the plates.
Height 15in. (38cm).
   Norman Langmaid Collection, U.S.A.

Figure 6/19a, b, c. A compact and fine quality two train skeleton clock with particularly delicate six spoke wheelwork, signed on the dial 'McMaster & Son, Dublin, No.3675' (who worked and traded at 97 Grafton Street c.1847-79) has a well executed spring detent chronometer escapement with blued steel helical hairspring and is fitted with maintaining power. All the wheels and levers are screwed on to their collets. *Private Collection*

Figure 6/19b

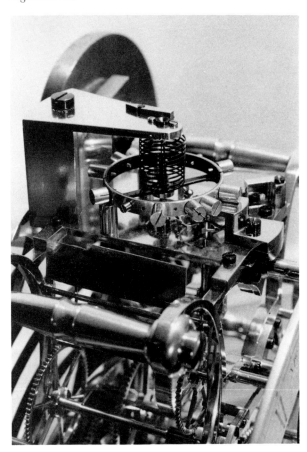

Figure 6/19c

Figure 6/20a, b. A two train skeleton clock made to regulator standards with pump action quarter chime on two bells. The delicate wheelwork is six spoke, a wood rod pendulum is used with a large brass lenticular bob; beat regulation is provided at the crutch pin and it is signed on the silvered beat scale 'Snosswell, Farringdon Street (London)'. Two Snosswells are recorded: William (working 1828-57) who was known for his musical clocks and C. Snosswell who was in business a little later. The pin wheel escapement, a form of dead beat, may be seen in the close up. The dial which is of English regulator layout appears as three large overlapping rings but is actually taken out of one piece of metal.   *Christie's*

Figure 6/20b

236

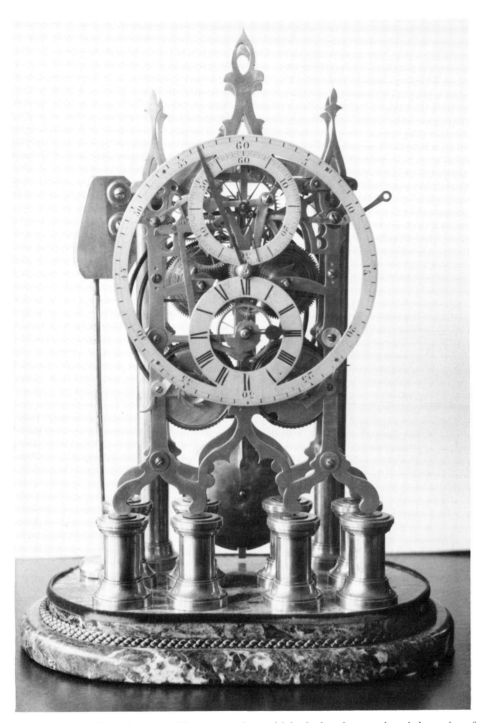

Figure 6/21a. It is not known with any certainty which clockmaker produced the series of skeletonised table regulators such as those illustrated here. Although several examples have been seen over the years, only one, that of which the rear view is shown in Figure 6/21c has been signed. It bears the name A. de B. Savory which could have been Adey B. Savory (recorded as working 1815-25) or A.B. Savory & Sons, presumably his successors, who were active in London from 1839-63. All these clocks appear to be two train with hour strike and repeat on either a bell or a gong and all have an English regulator dial layout. An unusual feature is that the pendulum, generally with wood rod, is supported by a substantial cross bar (either curved or straight) which rests on two heavy vertical free standing pillars. The movements of all these clocks are almost identical with only minor differences to such items as the collets and the type of feet they rest on, which are always eight in number.

J.B. Hawkins Antiques, Australia

Figure 6/21b. Side view of the two train clock with hour strike, shown on the previous page.

238

Figure 6/21c. Rear view of a similar clock to Figures 6/21a, b, marked with the name A. de B. Savory, c.1815-25. (Note the cross bar which rests on two vertical pillars and supports the pendulum.)

Figure 6/22a, b. This superb quality skeleton table regulator is signed by Walsh of Reading who was working in the mid-19th century, and has a regulator dial layout with separate rings for seconds, minutes and hours. The movement is supported by four pillars and a further pair somewhat higher than the rest carry an elaborate bridge from which the mercury compensated pendulum is suspended, much in the fashion of the regulators illustrated in Figure 6/21. The grasshopper escapement, which is beautifully executed, has two wheels, one for locking and the other for impulse.

Franklin Institute, U.S.A.

Figure 6/22b

Figure 6/23a, b. A most unusual mid-19th century skeleton clock, signed by Charles Frodsham and numbered 885, which was probably used by Frodsham's for exhibition and demonstration purposes. It has two 'scape wheels each with its own seconds dial, that on the left being dead beat and the one on the right recoil — either may be engaged by shunting the third wheel across to mesh with the relevant pinion — all that remains to be done is to change the position of the pendulum. There are four levelling screws and a spirit level at the base of the frame.

Private Collection

Figure 6/23b

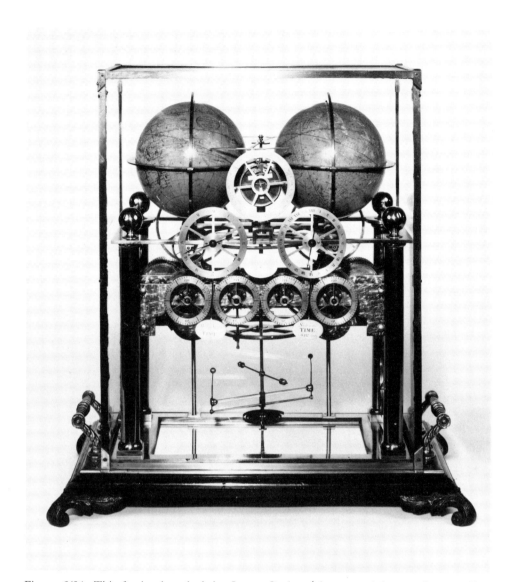

Figure 6/24. This fascinating clock by James Gorham[1] has two globes, each some 6in. (15.2cm) in diameter. The terrestrial globe on the left is signed 'G. & T. Cary'[2] and dated 1835, whereas the celestial globe, similarly signed, is dated 1822. Below the terrestrial globe are second, minute and twelve hour dials which show mean solar time whereas those on the right show siderial time and have double twelve hours; between the two globes is a year calendar. The movement has a high count train with six spoke wheelwork, Harrison's maintaining power and a detached lever escapement with dead beat 'scape wheel and an elaborate mercurial balance with steel regulation crossbar spectacularly displayed beneath the main body of the movement. A thermometer and magnetic compass are also fitted.

(This clock was made for the mathematician John Herapath (1790-1868) of Kensington, and remained with his family until a few years ago.)   *Christie's*

Astronomical Skeleton Clocks

It was originally thought that only one of these fascinating astronomical skeleton timepieces existed but comparatively recently a second was recorded, and a third has been discovered in Norway.[3] That seen in Figure 6/24 is signed 'James Gorham, Kensington, Watch & Clock Maker to the Queen' whereas the other in Plate 42 (opposite) is signed by James Shearer who was working in London from 1825 to 1840.

Plate 42. The principal differences between this clock which is signed by Shearer and that in Figure 6/24 are that is has no year calendar between the two globes, and the mean time dial on this clock is a twenty-four hour one. The terrestrial globe on the left gives the position of the moon in its various phases and being synchronised with mean solar time can give exact time in any part of the world whereas the celestial globe gives the position of the sun and stars. (This clock is believed to be the one which Shearer is recorded as having sold to the Duke of Sussex, an uncle of Queen Victoria, but it was Gorham who was clockmaker to the Queen.)   *Private Collection*

1. Ward, F.A.B., 'A Mean and Siderial Time Clock', *The Horological Journal,* Vol. LXXXVII, No.1058, Nov. 1946, pp.466-7.
2. Gunther, R.T., *Early Science in Oxford,* Vol. III, p.262 concerning C.J. Carey.
3. Rössaak, Tor E., 'James Shearer, Devonshire Street, Queen Square, London', *Antiquarian Horology,* June 1987. (Letter to Editor.)

Figure 6/25a. A fully skeletonised longcase regulator with fine six spoke wheelwork, pulley offset and a double three legged gravity escapement mounted high up in the frame to permit seconds to be displayed below twelve o'clock, instead of at six o'clock as on most regulators with gravity escapement.

4. Skeletonised Longcase Regulators

It was not unusual on English longcase regulators to skeletonise the dial and also sometimes the movement to a greater or lesser extent so as to show off the superb craftsmanship so often put into these clocks.

   Possibly the best example is that seen in Figure 6/25 in which the movement is just like a skeleton clock; another fine quality piece is shown in Figure 6/26. The dial has been skeletonised, the plates shaped and the movement mounted on heavy brass brackets, as opposed to a seatboard, to display everything as completely as possible. Figure 6/27 shows a relatively late regulator by Moore of Leeds with many interesting technical features.

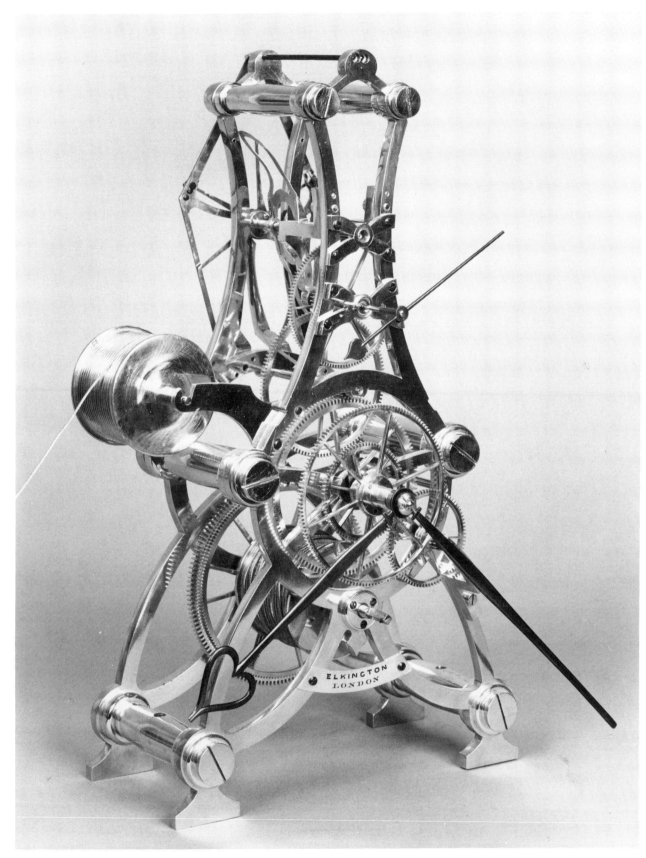

Figure 6/25b. The clock mechanism of Figure 6/25a removed from its case.

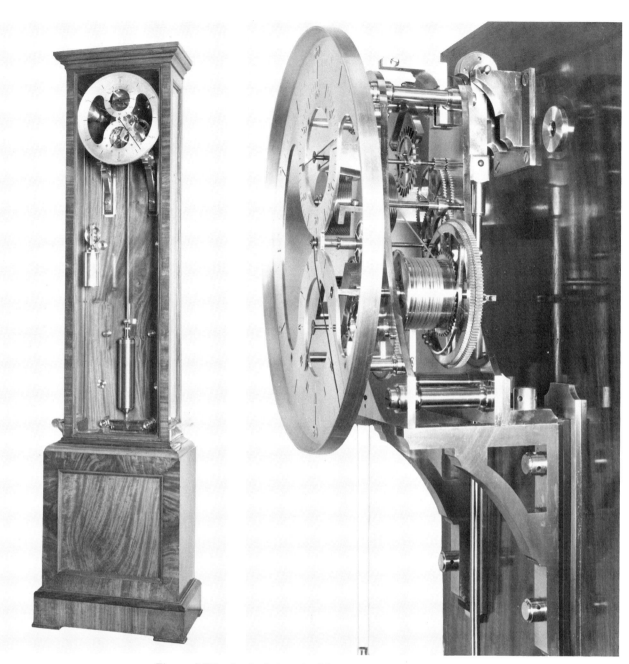

Figure 6/26a, b. A skeletonised longcase regulator made to the highest standards. The whole of the top of the case excluding the backboard may be removed using the carrying handles on either side to give complete access to the movement. Points to note are the mercury compensated pendulum with steel jar which is protected from excessive movement by a guard at the base; the provision for electrical contacts with insulating blocks behind the movement and pendulum supporting brackets, so that slave clocks may be used; and that the bolts for the brackets are tightened with a tommy bar to avoid the use of slots.

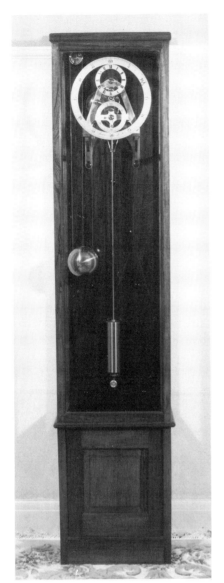

Figure 6/27a, b. A longcase regulator by Moore of Leeds of massive construction. (The plates are ½in. (12mm) thick, 8in. (20.3cm) high and 9in. (30cm) wide.) As with other regulators by this maker, lantern pinions are used and epicyclic winding and maintaining power is incorporated in the great wheel. The train contains fourteen jewels, the pallet 'scape wheel arbors have end stones and the other arbors run in three screwed bushes with end screws. The pendulum and weight are replacements.   *Private Collection*

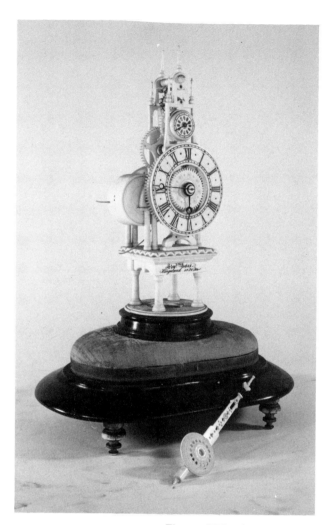
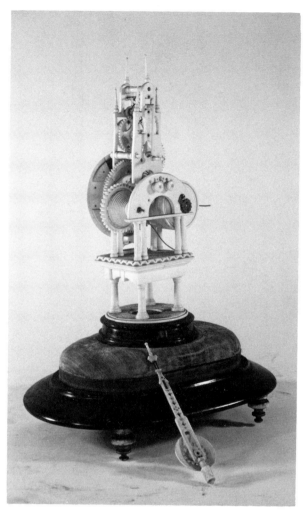

Figure 6/28a, b. The attractive little fusee timepiece shown here, which is only 10in. (25.4cm) high overall, has a seconds hand above the main dial which goes round every twelve seconds. Virtually every component except the hands, arbors and clickwork are made of ivory; it is signed above and between the two front columns 'Edward Bates, Kingsland' and dated 1858.

Dr. S.P. Lehv Collection, U.S.A.

5. Unusual Skeleton Clocks

In this section are included various skeleton clocks which exhibit considerable ingenuity in either their design or construction. Indeed in no other type of clock does one find such a fascinating variety.

Ivory Clocks

Occasionally skeleton clocks are seen which are in part made of unconventional materials such as glass, wood or papier mâché; ivory and bone were sometimes used largely for their decorative value. The majority of clocks made of ivory were of French origin but the examples shown here would appear to be English.

Plate 43. Figure 6/29. A small ivory (or possibly bone) skeleton timepiece dismantled prior to restoration, in which even the pinions and pillars are of ivory and only components such as the arbors and click spring on the fusee are made of steel.   *Albert Odmark Collection, U.S.A.*

Plate 44. Two train skeleton clock with hour strike on a bell and calendar work (*see* Figure 6/32, p.254).

Figure 6/30a. An English skeleton timepiece of extremely robust construction probably made c.1850, which has a massive mainspring and six heavy pillars. There is a circular cut out in the front frame for the fusee stop and the chain on the spring barrel only just clears the baseplate. A large lever escapement is mounted on top of the frames. Although the fusee only takes twelve turns of the chain, this gives a duration of 120 days on one winding.

Height 12½ in. (32cm)

Albert Odmark Collection, U.S.A.

Figure 6/30b. Rear view of timepiece opposite.

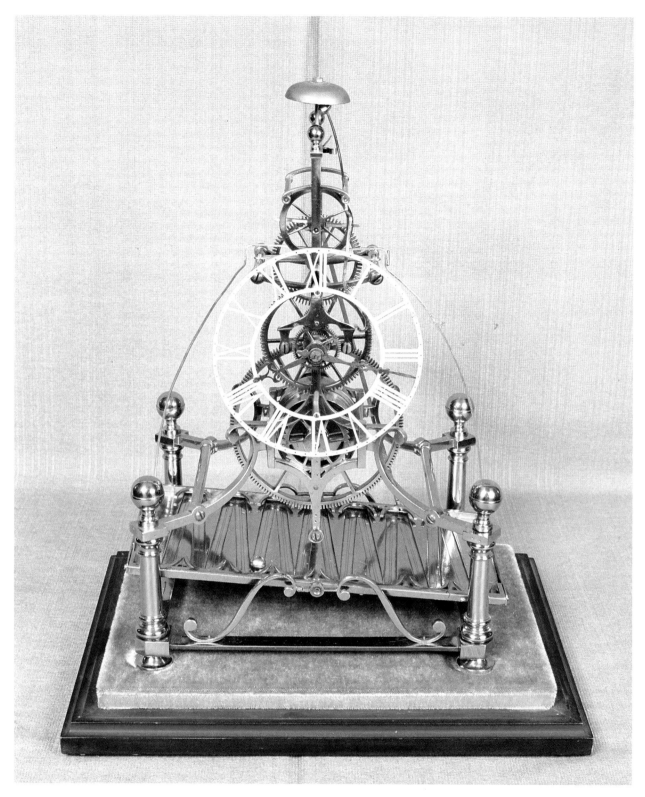

Plate 45. Congreve rolling ball clock, c.1840 (*see* Figure 6/37, p.258).

Figure 6/31. This good quality skeleton clock which is signed on the base of the frame 'Tritschler & Co, 402 Oxford Street, London' has a gilt chapter ring engraved with leaves and flowers and with a star shaped border. The two train movement which strikes and repeats on a gong may be wound through the base, thus avoiding the necessity to remove the dome. The vertical shaft connecting the winding squares to the fusees may be seen on either side of the pendulum, which is most unusual in that it employs a glass rod which has a very low coefficient of expansion. (This clock may well be the one referred to in the Great Exhibition Catalogue when describing Tritschler's exhibits.)
Height 17½ in. (44cm).   *Sotheby's*

Figure 6/32. A two train skeleton clock with hour strike on a bell and three subsidiary rings for days of the week, days of the month and strike/silent (*see also* Plate 44).

Figure 6/33. Thomas Cole produced a great variety of highly individual clocks (which are excellently described in *Thomas Cole & Victorian Clockmaking* by J.B. Hawkins) but the only series which concerns us here are his tripod clocks in which the movement rests at the centre of a tripod, which was formed in a wide variety of ways. Almost invariably the dial is beautifully engraved and a wood or brass rod pendulum is used with a heavy spherical bob. In the example shown here, as on all the tripod clocks, a going barrel is used which gives a duration of one month. Let into the base is a thermometer and aneroid barometer. Cole's pendulum locking system is provided and also a plumb line to ascertain when the clock is level, which is achieved by adjusting the feet with the spanner incorporated in the other end of the winding key.   *Christie's*

Figure 6/34. A most unusual skeleton clock signed 'Joyce, London' with separate overlapping rings for seconds, minutes and hours. The large subsidiary dial at the top of the clock, which shows the moon's age on its outer aspect, has a universal tidal dial within this. It employs a coup perdu pin wheel escapement (*see* Figure 5/3) which enables seconds to be indicated with the half seconds pendulum.   *Sotheby's*

Figure 6/35. A highly individual great wheel skeleton timepiece with a going barrel (i.e. no fusee) which has fine six spoke wheelwork, pin wheel escapement and a mock three rod gridiron pendulum. It is boldly signed on the front frame 'Robert Lenaghan, Antigua.' and most unusually has a solid silver chapter ring which bears a Glasgow hallmark for 1828.

Figure 6/36a, b. One cannot help wondering how and why this highly original and well-made clock (which in many ways resembles Siamese twins) was conceived. In effect it consists of two almost completely independent trains with identical frames, which are screwed together. One possibility is that just the time side was made first and the striking side added at a later date, but this does not seem very likely as the detail construction of both sides is identical and the time side would not stand very well on its own. The clock is fitted with maintaining power and has a fairly large horizontal balance mounted at the very top of the frame.

David Olson Collection, U.S.A.

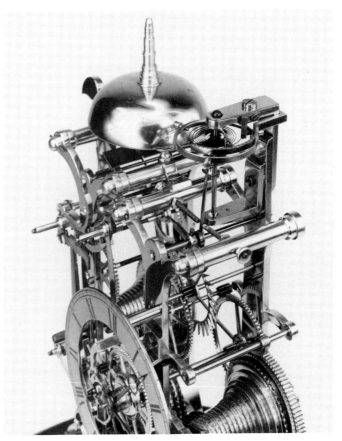

Figure 6/36b

Figure 6/37. This fascinating skeleton clock, c.1840, is possibly the only one made which employs Congreve's rolling ball escapement and could be unique (*see also* Plate 45). It has a going barrel with a fairly large six spoke great wheel from which the train runs up vertically as opposed to the conventional Congreve clock in which it is horizontal. The relatively light construction and the use of a conventional chapter ring in place of the architectural top with applied chapter rings employed on most Congreve clocks gives an appearance of delicacy which adds appreciably to its appeal. The duration of the clock is only thirty hours but this has probably been a deliberate choice on the part of its designer, as to achieve a duration of eight days would require a far heavier mainspring and probably a more substantial design, as this form of escapement absorbs far more power than, for instance, a conventional anchor. The bell is not original.

Height without cover 16¾in. (42.5cm). Table 9¾in. x 5in. (24.8cm x 12.7cm).

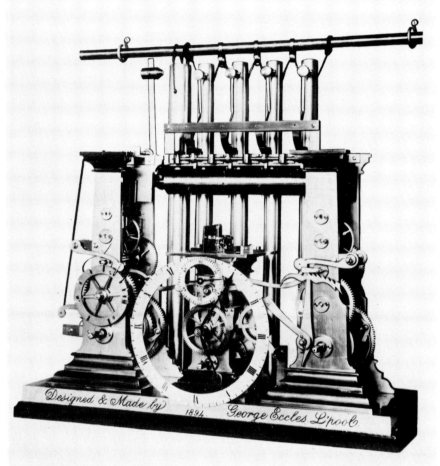

Figure 6/38. In 1891 an educational model of a clock was constructed by George Eccles to the order of the Rev. Henry Higgins, the Chairman of the Museums Committee, who wrote a thirty-three page book which accompanied it when it was sent round to the local schools. Following the success of this project the clock, shown here, was designed and made by Eccles in 1894 for the Liverpool Museum. All the components are positioned so that they may be seen as clearly as possible and their functions fully understood; moreover, as many different types of mechanism as possible are incorporated in the design. Thus a rack is seen controlling the weight driven quarter chiming on the right hand pillar, whereas a count wheel (weight driven) is used for the hours, on the left. In contrast the going train, which is powered by a mainspring with fusee and chain, is fitted with maintaining power and has a seconds beating chronometer escapement with compensated balance. (This clock, which was unfortunately destroyed during the Second World War, was displayed on the Museum's main staircase.)   *Prescot Museum*

Appendix 1

Visit to a Clerkenwell Clock Factory

Clerkenwell has long been noted for the manufacture of every description of clocks. There are, however, not more than about half a dozen clock manufactories on a large scale, the work being, for the most part, done by those who are known as small masters, employing one or two journeymen or apprentices, and who attend entirely to particular branches of the trade; for instance — there are the dial enameller, the hand maker, the pinion maker, the wheel cutter, the fuzee cutter, the spring maker, the movement maker, the pendulum and barrel maker, the carver, the case maker, the clock-glass maker, the French polisher, and the finisher: so that, when a clock of a particular construction is ordered of one of the small masters, he has to depend on more than a dozen workmen, living in various parts of the district, for the several distinct portions of work required to complete the clock. Delay after delay is the consequence. ''the wheel-cutter is so much engaged'', or ''the case-maker has deceived me'', and such like, are among the reasons for disappointing, again and again, the anxious inventor of some horological improvement. It is quite obvious, therefore, that a factory which embraces all the various branches of the business must possess considerable advantages, especially when all the operators are under the immediate superintendence and practised eye of the principals.

Our attention was lately directed to such an establishment in St. John's Square, Clerkenwell, belonging to Messrs. J. Smith and Sons, which occupies the site of the once famous clock manufactory of Colonel Magniac. One of the principals kindly attended to us during an entire day, which we spent in examining closely the various operations necessary in producing a clock, and also several beautiful machines employed in facilitating some of the more difficult and tedious processes.

We, in the first place, noticed the stock of mahogany which is introduced into the yard, around which the various workshops are placed, direct from the West India Docks. The mahogany logs, which are from 18 inches to 3 feet square, and from 8 to 20 feet in length, are in the first instance cut up into boards, varying from three-quarters of an inch to 2 inches in thickness, which, for the purpose of seasoning, are racked in the open yard, in a horizontal position, for about two years; after which period they are transferred to a shed, and placed in a vertical position, being separated from each other by a rack at top. Here they remain for three years, after which they are ready for use. For clockcases intended for hot climates, the additional precaution is taken of stacking the boards at about seven feet above the glass-bending kiln. There are three kinds of mahogany used — Spanish, Cuba, and Honduras; oak is also used, besides maple, rosewood, satin, and other fancy woods. At the saw-pit we observed some logs of oak being cut up, of a rich brown colour, which is only attained by great age; the logs in question were at least 200 years old.

The principal divisions in the manufacture of a clock are, the brass-founding, the glass-bending, the case-making and the clock making.

Figure 1. The turret clock shop.

Brass-founding. — Every piece of brasswork used in a clock made at Messrs. Smith and Son's establishment is cast in the foundry, at the east end of the yard, as seen in the Engraving. The furnace, which is under the level of the floor, is constructed chiefly of Stourbridge bricks; the ash-pit is in front, and covered over with a grating. Gas coke is sometimes used, but coke of a harder description, similar to that made for locomotive engines, is preferred. The casting-pots used are made chiefly of clay and powdered coke, and are formed with a small spout, but without any handle. When the metal is put into the melting-pot, the founder places it into the furnace by means of tongs of a peculiar shape. The pots are of conoidal form, some of which will hold 50lb. of metal, which consists of about two of copper and one of spelter, or zinc, for most purposes in clock-making; but the quality is altered at pleasure, for particular purposes, by changing the proportions of the copper and spelter respectively. For turret clock-work, gun metal is used instead of brass.

The casting trough is made of wood with sloping sides, and is placed opposite to the furnace. The sand used for taking the cast is from Hampstead Heath, and is mixed with loam from the same locality, in the proportion of about one half of the latter to one of the former. This is the only description of sand used by all London brass founders. All the various pieces of brass required in the construction of a clock can be cast at the same time. The impression of one side of the article to be cast is first taken in the sand from a suitable pattern, the sand having been firmly pressed into one half of an iron frame or mould; the same process is observed with regard to the other half. When the two half frames are put together by means of casting boards, one

Figure 2. The brass foundry.

at top and the other at bottom, and secured together by means of wood-screws, ridges are formed in the sand from each sinking or impression into the main channel which terminates with an opening on the side of the frame, through which the liquid metal is poured, and which fills up all the cavities. While the metal is being poured into the mould, it is placed with one side towards what is called a spilling trough, which receives the waste metal escaping from the pot. In a few minutes the boards are taken off, the sand removed, and the rough articles of brass are separated from each other, and removed to the various shops.

Brass-finishing shop. — In this department the clock rings, or bezels, are turned by the lathe, the hinges being let into the rings and soldered, and the whole subjected again to the operation of turning, and finally finished. Here, also, the dials are silvered. The cases for the clock weights and pendulums, which are of sheet-brass, are also made in this shop, at one end of which is a forge, which is principally used for forging the hammer stems, pulley frames, pinions, repeating work, &c., of turret clocks, which are brought to great perfection at this establishment. Here, also, the brazing and soldering are effected. The sheet brass is cut out by means of large shears, with as much ease as a piece of card-board with ordinary scissors. At the other end of the shop is a manumotive wheel cutting machine, specially used for cutting out from the solid brass the wheels for turret clocks. It consists of a large fly-wheel, which is turned by hand, communication from which is effected by a round band passing to a 4-inch pulley fixed on the spindle of the cutter, by which the teeth are formed: the frame containing the cutter is furnished with both a horizontal and vertical movement, by which the exact portion of the wheel to the cut is regulated. Underneath the frame is a projecting arm, the use of which is to keep the wheel in its place during the operation. The number and size of the teeth of a wheel of any given diameter are regulated by a circular brass plate of about 18 inches diameter, through which are perforated different series of holes, ranged in concentric circles.

Besides the wheel-cutting engine, there is another machine of a different construction, used for cutting the pinions for church clocks. It is furnished with a cutter, which rotates at considerable velocity on a stationary axis; the pinion is moved horizontally underneath the cutter, which is so constructed that it not only cuts the slit in the pinion, but also shapes the leaves at the same time.

The dials are made either of sheet tin, iron, or brass, the faces of which are coated with what is technically termed *white-flake,* a superior kind of white-lead, which is ground down with the finest description of copal varnish, and then put into a stove, similar to that used by japanners, until it becomes sufficiently hard to receive a polish, which is effected chiefly with pumice-stone, by which means a most perfect surface is produced, ready to receive the figures, which are painted with lamp-black, varnish, and turpentine.

The church clock dials are coated four times with black paint, and sized and gilt in the ordinary way; the gold, however, for this purpose, is of extra thickness. The divisions of the dials are set out by means of an index plate. Opposite to the wheel-cutting engine, as above described, is a simple and ingenious contrivance, for grinding the edges of clock and watch glasses. The operator stands in front of the work, with his right hand turning round a handle, placed vertically above the bench, and with his left hand holding a sort of hood, or, as it is called, cup, supplied with emery powder, by which the grinding is partially effected: the glass to be ground is temporarily fixed on a boxwood mallet, by means of cement, at the top of a spindle, which passes through the bench, and to which rapid motion is communicated by a round band from a horizontal wheel below the bench, turned by the right hand of the operator.

After the grinding is completed, the edge of the glass is smoothed with pumice stone, and finally polished with oxide of tin, usually called putty-powder.

The glass-bending shop is situated on the south side of the yard, and is fitted up with furnaces and an annealing oven.

The crown glass, used for enclosing the dials of clocks and watches, before being moulded or bent into the required form, is first cut into circular shape by means of a circle-cutter, which consists of a circular board, covered with wash-leather, which is made to revolve on a pivot by one hand of the operator, while with the other hand he presses down a diamond on to the glass; the diamond is fixed at the end of an adjustable arm, which traverses a slot, the exact diameter of the circular plate to be cut being regulated by an index fixed

Figure 3. The regulator and general clock shop.

at the side of the slot. The circular flat plates, which are removed to moulds
turned out of solid fire-stone, the sinking of the moulds being of flat elliptical
section, are put into one or other of the furnaces, according to the size of the
glass to be bent: while in the furnace, the mould is kept in continual circular
motion by the long iron rod of the operator, until the glass sinks into the
required form. The size to which glass is bent at this manufactory is equal to
30 inches in diameter. The grinding and polishing the edge of the glass is the
next operation, which has already been described as being carried on in
another part of the premises.

The close-case making department (of which we furnish an Illustration) is
situated on the floor above the "brass finishing shop". Here is manufactured
every kind of case, from the ordinary office dial clock to the elegant ornamental
case of the first-class regulator. The variety of designs followed to suit
particular tastes is rather astonishing.

In order to produce the most beautiful work, as well as that of the most
sound description, the external covering is produced by laying on veneers, an
operation requiring considerable care, by means of *cauls,* which are simply
pieces of wood of the shape of the articles to be veneered, made hot and
screwed down close to the foundation on one side, and the veneered lining on
the other: thus, the soundest work is produced, and the cracks and flaws so
commonly seen in inferior cabinet-work are thus avoided.

Each bench in this shop is furnished with a *German screw,* by which the work
is more firmly held together, and closer joints effected, than by the ordinary
screw attached to the English bench.

In the course of construction we observed a very handsome case for a first-
rate regulator, which is now to be seen at the Great Exhibition.

The buhl-work of brass and mother-of-pearl, &c., which is let into some of
the clock-cases, is produced by a machine called a "neddy", which derives its

Figure 4. The clock case shop.

name from the workman standing across the body of the machine. The pattern intended to be used is first cut out in brass, which serves as a type from which to print any number of copies on thin paper: these paper patterns are pasted on the brass, pearl, wood, or other suitable material intended to be used. By means of a treadle worked by the left foot of the operator, the work is readily shifted; while with his right hand he cuts out the work by means of a very fine saw, made of a watch spring, and having exceedingly fine teeth on one edge.

Adjoining the case-maker's shop is a department entirely set apart for the ''system plan'', each man attending continually to one particular branch of the business; thus, to one is assigned the barrel making, to another the pinion work, or what is known among clock-makers as filling in the movement, and so on.

There is one machine in this department which especially attracted our attention, and that is called a ''fuzee engine'', by which the spiral groove is cut in the solid brass intended for the fuzee. The brass is put upon a steel arbor, placed between two centres; the operator with his right hand presses a triangular sliding bar, furnished at the end with a steel cutter against the brass, while with his left hand he turns a handle in connexion with a sliding frame, on which is a brass bar placed at any given angle so as to regulate the size of the spiral groove; this bar is adjusted by means of a segment at either end. By this machine the grooves of fuzees of from three-quarters of an inch to the largest size required are readily cut.

On the south side of the yards are two clock-makers' shops — the one on the upper floor being entirely devoted to the finest and most delicate kind of work required for bracket clocks, regulators, &c.; and the lower one on the ground-floor solely for the works of turret and church clocks. (Views of both these shops are engraved in our present Number.) In the upper shop we observed every kind of tools required in making and finishing the various parts of a regulator, which we had the opportunity of examining in order. First, the frames, which are constructed of thick brass: these are hammered, and then pinned up and filed square; the pillars by which the two frames are connected, are next turned, and fitted with large screws; after this the arbors of the pinions are subjected to the turning process, by means of a turn-bench, worked by a drill-bow in the left hand of the workman. The back-cock and the crutch, the thumb-screws, and other brass works are then roughed out; and finally, the several parts are finished, chiefly by means of a hand-lathe turned by the workman's left hand, while the cutting tool is held in the right hand. For ordinary descriptions of work a common foot-lathe is used. After the several wheels have been finished by means of the ''throw'', or hand-lathe, they are fixed on to their respective arbors of steel, and the depthening tool is now brought into action, by which the exact positions of the centres of motion are determined, in order to make the necessary perforations in the frames for the pivots of the pinions to work in. This tool consists of two similar horizontal pieces of brass, hinged together and turned up at each end, to receive a socket-piece, also of brass, and placed horizontally; there are four of such socket pieces, on the inside of each of which is a *centre-piece* to receive the pivots of the wheels and pinions, and on the outside a steel pointer, by which the centres of motion are marked on the brass frames with the utmost accuracy. Thus the wheel and socket is placed on the arbor between the centre-pieces in one section of the depthening machine, and the pinion into which it is intended to work on the other: the relative position of wheel and pinion is regulated with great accuracy by means of an adjusting screw, by which the two portions of the machine are either brought nearer together or removed further from each other as required. The maintaining power, consisting of the barrel, the main-wheel, the going ratchet, and the two clacks, the brass dial plate, with the hands of steel, and the compensation mercurial pendulum of glass, with its steel rod and index, make up the several parts of the regulator. In the lower shop, in which turret work alone is constructed, the lathes are of a stronger description, and the tools generally more nearly resemble those in use in the best turning shops of the kingdom.

After visiting the various manufacturing departments of the establishment, we were finally conducted to the show-rooms, which contain an extensive assortment of eight-day skeleton clocks, representing various ecclesiastical edifices, some striking the hours on a cathedral-toned gong, and others chiming the quarters on eight bells. Then there are regulators, hall clocks, musical clocks, and bracket clocks, in cases of old oak, mahogany, and rose-wood, both carved and plain, many of which are of elaborate design, and all produced at this establishment. Nor are these clocks solely for the English market, but also for China, Turkey, and other parts of the world, as we discovered by the curious characters on the dials answering to our numerals.

This article appeared in *The Illustrated London News,* 20th September, 1851, and was reprinted in *Antiquarian Horology,* No.3, Vol.12, Autumn 1980.

Index

A

'Almagest, The', 160
Amant, 182; **5/2**
America, United States of, 13, 118, 169; **3/31, 4/12**
American clocks, 34
Antigua, 256; **6/35**
Arnold, 161, 193; **4/4, 5/8**
art deco influence, 48
art nouveau influence, 47
Asprey/Nielson Exhibition 1975, 94; **3/12**
astronomical clocks, 49, 164, 168, 169, 211, 229, 242, 243; **2/4, 4/8, 4/11, 6/14, 6/24, Plates 9, 28, 42**
Augsburg, 81
Austria, 11, 12, 13, 127, 157
Austrian clocks, 12, 13
Austro-Hungarian Empire, 13

B

balance
    bimetallic, 190, 224, 225; **5/7, 6/12**
    compensated, 234; **6/18, Plate 41**
    horizontal, 257; **6/36**
    mercurial, 242; **6/24**
    mono metallic, 143; **3/57b**
    seconds beating, 107
    three arm horizontal, 201; **5/12**
    wheels, 27, 53; **2/6**
balance springs
    helical, 98, 103, 107, 108, 109, 110, 222; **3/16c, 3/18e, 3/23, 6/10, Plate 18**
balance wheel regulation, 36, 39, 61; **1/18, 2/3, 2/18**
barometers, 255; **6/33**
Barraud, Paul Philip, 22, 114; **3/28**
Barrie, Andrew, 80; **3/3**
bases
    brass, 110, 129; **3/23, 3/43**
    wooden, 101; **3/18, Plate 17**
Bates, Edward, 248; **6/28**
beat regulation, 49, 51, 113, 171, 202, 231, 232, 236; **2/3, 3/26, 4/14, 5/13, 6/15, 6/16, 6/20, Plate 40**
Belgium, 13, 16
Bertoud, 12
Bird, Francis, 75; **2/33**
Birkbeck, Dr., 172
Birmingham, 142
Black, Andrew, 179, 188, 190; **5/7**
Blaylock of Carlisle, 49, 52; **2/5**
Bleachers 10 hour Bill 1860, The, 106; **3/20**
Bonnert, Peter, 73, 185, 202; **2/31, 5/5, 5/13a**
Boulton & Watt, 142
bracket clocks, 226-28, 233; **6/13, 6/17, Plates 38, 39**
Breguet, 12, 13, 104
Brighton, 72, 73, 74, 75; **2/30, 2/31, 2/34**

Brookhouse, J., 167; **4/11**
Brooksbank, William, 26; **1/7a**
Brunel, 161
Brussels, 10; **2**
Bryson (Edinburgh), 79, 80; **3/3**
Buckingham Palace, 83, 84; **3/5, 3/7**
Bury St. Edmunds, 90, 91, 97; **3/15, Plate 14**
Burgess, Martin, 204, 206; **5/14**

C

calendarwork, 12, 18, 19, 95, 180, 211, 226-8, 249; **1/2, 5/2, 6/13, Plates 31, 38, 39, 44**
Cambridge University, 77
Carlisle House, Soho Square, 17
Carlton House, 83, 84; **3/5, 3/6**
Carrara marble, 61; **2/17**
carriage clocks, 53, 233; **6/7**
Carter, 49
Castle Museum, York, 145; **3/58**
chamber clocks, 11; **1**
chariot clocks, 161; **4/4**
Chicago, 134
chiming clocks, *211-23,* 29, 38, 39, 41, 65, 68, 69, 75, 100, 103, 106, 108, 109, 115-18, 125, 134, 145-8, 149, 152, 211-13, 215-22, 225, 228, 236, 259; **1/17, 1/21, 2/23, 2/26c, 2/34, 3/17, 3/19, 3/22, 3/29, 3/30, 3/39b, 3/58, 3/60, 3/61, 3/65, 6/1-6/10, 6/13b, 6/20, 6/38, Plates 7, 16, 35**
'Chinese taste', 72; **2/30**
chronometers, 22, 99, 107, 114, 185, 188, 193, 220; **5/8, 6/8**
Civil War, 70
Clerkenwell 131, 260-7
clickwork, 214, 248; **6/1g, 6/28**
Clockmakers' Company, 233; **6/17**
Colburn, John, 145; **3/58**
Cole, Thomas, 255; **6/33**
compass, 55, 130, 242; **2/4, 6/24, Plate 9**
complex clocks, 34, 211-59
components, standardised, 128
Condliff, James, 13, 22, 26-9, 50, 56, 59, 98, 99, 101-3, 106-9, 112, 113, 116, 156, 157, 160, 222; **2/10, 3/16-3/23, 4/1, 6/10, Plates 15-18**
Condliff, John, 99, 113; **3/26**
Condliff, Joseph, 99, 113
Condliff, Thomas, 99, 103, 112, 113; **3/25**
Congreve, Ambrose, 80; **3/3**
Congreve, Sir William, 67, 78-85, 87, 88, 192, 207, 252, 258; **3/1-3/4, 3/6, 3/9, 3/15, 6/37, Plates 12, 34, 45**
Cooper (Huddersfield), 210, 212; **6/1, Plate 35**
Copenhagen, Siege of, 79
Corneily, Mrs., 17
count wheels (weight-driven), 259; **6/38**
Cox, James, 16
Cumming, 82

D

Darwin, Dr. Erasmus, 161
dated clocks, 36, 47, 111, 112; **1/14, 3/25**
de Dondi, Giovanni, 160
Dent & Co. Ltd., 27, 82, 114, 124, 125, 167, 169, 192, 204, 205, 229, 231, 234; **3/38-3/40, 4/11, 4/12, 5/14, 6/15, Plates 33, 40**
dials, *34-47*
    chapter rings, 27, 34, 42, 43, 44, 45, 66, 74, 130, 139, 145; **1/22, 1/23, 1/25, 1/27, 1/28, 2/32, 3/52, 3/61, 6/35, Plate 8**
    enamel, 46, 47, 78, 100, 145, 146, 158, 180; **3/1, 3/17, 3/59, 4/3, 5/2, Plate 31**
    glass, 101, 106, 176, 177; **3/18a, 3/19, 4/19, Plate 30**
    lunar, 55, 232, 233; **2/4, 6/16, 6/17, Plate 9**
    painted, 41, 50, 53; **1/21, 2/2, 2/6**
    regulator, 47, 149, 229, 234, 236, 237, 240; **6/14, 6/18, 6/20-6/22, Plate 40**
    siderial time, 242; **6/24**
    solar, 242, 243; **6/24, Plate 42**
    tidal, 255; **6/34**
    twenty-four hour, 39, 243; **1/18, Plate 42**
Dublin, 235; **6/19**
Durrant (London), 37; **1/16**
Dutertre, 209; **5/16**
Dwerrihouse, 49, 51
Dwerrihouse, Ogston & Bell, 50; **2/2**

E

Earnshaw, 191, 193; **5/7, 5/8**
Eccles, George, 259; **6/38**
Edinburgh, 61; **2/17**
educational clocks, 259; **6/38**
Edward the Confessor, 65
Edwards, James, 26, 126, 160, 173, 174, 178; **1/7, 1/12, 4/15-4/19, Plates 29, 30**
eight day duration clocks, 15, 18, 19, 24, 40, 120, 121, 123, 190, 223; **1/2, 1/6, 1/21, 3/32-3/34, 5/7, 6/11**
eighteen day duration clocks, 97; **3/15, Plate 14**
epicyclic clocks, 159, 160, 164, 165; **4/7, 4/8-4/12, Plate 28**
escapement
    Airy's, 231; **6/15**
    anchor, 18, 19, 22, 109, 125, 128; **1/2, 3/39**
    balance wheel, 27, 29, 63, 128; **1/14, 2/20**
    chronometer, 128, 149, 179, 193, 194; **3/66, 5/7, 5/8, 6/38**
    Condliff's, 98, 103, 104, 108, 110, 157, 179; **3/16, 3/18e, 3/18f, 3/23d**

Congreve's, 83, 84, 85, 88, 98, 179; *3/5,*
    3/7-3/9, 3/16c, 5/15
coup perdu (lost beat), 63, 149, 151,
    182, 183; **2/20**, 3/63, **5/3**
cross beat, 11; **2**
dead beat, 17, 41, 52, 60, 73, 95, 97,
    111, 113, 114, 125, 179, 219, 221,
    224, 225, 231, 232, 233, 234, 241;
    **1/21, 2/5, 2/16, 2/31, 3/14, 3/15,
    3/24, 3/26, 6/7, 6/9, 6/12,
    6/15-6/18, 6/23, Plates 14, 37, 40,
    41**
de Baufre's, 195, 196; **5/9**
Dennison's, 179
detented, 149, 151, 152, 184, 187;
    3/63-3/65, 5/6
detented coup perdu, 128; **3/63**
duplex, 209; **5/16**
Earnshaw's, 191, 193; **5/7, 5/8**
Evans', 149, 151, 187, 229; **3/63, 3/64,
    5/6, 6/14, 5/5a**
extreme detached, 78, 82, 83, 85, 88,
    179, 207; **3/5, 3/7, 3/8e, 5/15,**
Graham dead beat, 49, 75, 91, 122; **2/5,
    2/34, 3/35, Plate 20**
grasshopper, 202-6, 240; **5/13, 5/14,
    6/22**
gravity, 179, 184, 185, 186, 229, 244,
    245; **5/4, 5/5, 6/14, 6/25, Plate 32**
Lepaute's, 182
lever, 42, 98, 103, 115, 143, 144, 148,
    179, 226-8, 242, 250, 251; **1/22,
    3/16c, 3/18e, 3/29, 3/57, 3/62, 6/13,
    6/24, 6/30, Plates 24, 38, 39**
lever variant, 199, 200; **5/11**
pendulum controlled, 63; **2/20**
pin pallet lever, 223; **6/11**
pin wheel, 49, 51, 161, 179, 180, 181,
    182, 201, 236, 255, 256; **2/3, 4/4,
    5/2, 5/3, 5/12, 6/20, 6/34, 6/35**
pivoted detented, 185, 188; **5/5a, 5/6c**
rack, 201; **5/12a**
recoil, 23, 24, 27, 111, 123, 167, 179,
    241; **1/4, 1/6, 3/24, 4/10, 6/23**
remontoire, 12
rolling ball, 207, 208, 258; **5/15, 6/37**
'silent', 179, 181; **5/1**
'single pin' (McDowell), 172
spring detent, 83, 153, 191, 193, 235;
    3/5, 3/66, 5/7, 5/8, 6/19
table roller lever, 179, 197, 198; **5/10**
vertical, 62; **2/19**
vertical verge, 10, 11; **1**
with gut line, 179, 181; **5/1**
Evans & Sons, W.F., *126-130,* 13, 31,
    34, 41, 43, 45, 47, 50, 54, 56-8, 60,
    62-4, 68, 69, 107, 112, 126-8, 130,
    142-5, 148-51, 153-5, 157, 179, 184,
    185, 187-9, 209, 229, 230; **1/20, 1/24,
    1/29, 2/7, 2/11, 2/15, 2/19-2/21,
    2/26, 3/21, 3/55-3/57, 3/62-3/64,
    3/66-3/69, 5/4-5/6, 5/16, 6/14,
    Plates 6, 24-26, 32**

F

Far East, 16
First World War, 47, 134
Fitzherbert, Mrs., 73
Forbidden City (China), 16
Foster, Henry, (Liverpool), 109; **3/23,
    Plate 18**

frames
    arabesque, 11, 34, 40, 46, 57, 59,
        130, 149, 150, 154, 229; **1/27,
        1/31, 2/11, 3/67, 6/14, Plate 26**
    architectural, 34, 39, 49, 61, 62, 66,
        74, 75, 128, 142-9, 210; **1/18,
        1/20, 2/21, 2/31-2/34, 3/56-3/61,
        6/1, Plates 24, 35**
    egg shaped, 114; **3/27**
    floral, 34, 40, 49, 57, 58, 59, 60, 73,
        130, 149, 181, 193; **1/19,
        2/12-2/16, 2/31, 3/63, 5/1, 5/8,
        Plates 10, 11**
    fretted out, 60; **2/16**
    from wooden moulds, 47
    glass plate, 11, 157, 158; **4/3**
    Gothic, 10, 34, 39, 42, 44, 49, 50,
        53, 54, 61, 128, 134, 148, 149,
        185; **1, 1/14, 1/18, 1/22, 1/28,
        2/6, 2/7, 3/47, 3/62**
    inverted Y, 11, 13, 20, 22, 23, 24,
        26, 27, 34, 49, 50, 157, 158, 162,
        163; **1/3-1/6, 2/1, 2/2, 4/2, 4/6**
    lyre shaped, 39, 124; **1/18, 3/38-3/40**
    rafter, 11, 27, 34, 37, 49, 51, 52, 55,
        202, 203; **1/16, 2/4, 2/5, 5/13,
        Plate 9**
    scroll, 13, 25, 27, 32, 34, 36, 39, 49,
        50, 56, 59, 92, 94, 101, 104, 108,
        109, 111, 112, 122, 128, 130, 149,
        150, 151, 185, 216, 217, 218, 222;
        **1/7, 1/11, 1/15, 1/18, 2/9, 2/10,
        3/11, 3/12, 3/18, 3/23, 3/24,
        3/35, 3/63, 6/3, 6/4, 6/6, 6/10,
        Plates 5, 18, 20, 25, 36**
    transitional, 27, 39; **1/8, 1/17**
    with cupola and spire, 49, 50; **2/1**
    with fourth frame, 147; **3/60**
    with third frame, 64, 147, 149; **2/21,
        3/60**
France, 11-13, 16, 20, 127, 157, 180,
    229, 248; **5/2, Plate 31**
French clocks, 12, 13, 22, 34, 157, 159,
    179, 180, 201; **4/2-4/4, 5/2, 5/12a,
    Plates 27, 31**
French Academy of Art and Science, 16
French (Royal Exchange), 81; **3/4**
Frodsham & Keen (Liverpool), 73, 74;
    2/31
Frodsham, Charles, 83, 84, 161, 241;
    3/5, 3/6, 4/4, 6/23
fusee, with great wheels, 233; **6/17**

G

Gadsby Leicester), 54; **2/8**
Galileo, 79
gears
    bevel, 223; **6/11**
    epicyclic, 126, 159, 160, 164-7; **4/7,
        4/8, Plate 28**
    helical, 126, 160, 170-2; **4/13, 4/14**
George III, 74
George IV, 73, 79, **2/30**
German clocks, 34
Germany, 11, 13, 34, 127
Gibbons, Grinling, 75; **2/33**
glass clocks, 248
glass wheeled clocks, 176, 177; **4/19,
    Plate 30**
Gothic clocks, 10, 11; **1**
Gothic churches, 65
Graham, 49, 66, 75, 91, 122; **2/5, 2/34,
    3/35, Plate 20**

Grand National, 100, 108; **3/17**
Gratte, Henry, 22
Gravel & Tolkein, 78, 81; **3/1**
Great Exhibition Catalogue (1851), 91,
    95, 116, 172, 178, 253; **3/14. 6/31**
Great Exhibition of 1851,
    12, 13, 30, 60-3, 75, 76, 90, 95, 116,
    118, 131, 142, 143, 173; **2/16,
    2/18, 2/19, 2/34, 3/31**
Great Exhibition (Paris), 12, 123; **3/36**
Great Fire of London, 1666, 74
great wheel clocks, 12, 24, 26, 30, 56,
    58, 109, 111, 114, 138, 156-63, 247,
    256, 258; **1/4-1/6, 1/9, 2/10, 2/14,
    3/24, 3/28, 3/51, 4/1, 4/2, 4/4-4/6,
    6/27, 6/35, 6/37, Plates 11, 27**
Green (Wigan), 179, 197, 198; **5/10**
Greenwich Mean Time, 18, 19; **1/2**
Groom, G. (Croydon), 136; **3/50, Plate
    22**

H

hairsprings, 190, 223, 224, 225, 235;
    5/7, 6/11, 6/12, 6/19
Halifax Moon, 18; **1/2**
hammers, 130, 132, 174; **3/45, 3/67,
    4/17**
hammer springs, 130; **3/67**
Hammond, G. & T. (Manchester), 29;
    1/8a
Handley & Moore, 115
hands, 34, 41, 45, 47; **1/21, 1/30**
Hardy, 82
Harlow, Joseph, 122
Harlow, Samuel, 122
Harrison, James, 203
Harrison, John, 203, 242; **6/24**
Hatfield & Hall (Manchester), 56;
    2/9
Haycock (Derbyshire), 117, 122, 123;
    3/35-3/37, Plate 20
Haycock, Charles, 123; **3/37**
Haycock, Henry, 123; **3/37**
Haycock, John, 122
Haycock, Thomas, 122
Haycock, jun., Thomas, 122, 123
Haycock, William, 122, 123
Heathcote, Major, 73, 75, 94, 95, 140,
    167, 169, 175, 185, 202, 204; **2/31,
    2/34, 3/12, 3/13, 3/53, 4/12, 4/18,
    5/5, 5/13a, 5/14**
helical clocks, 17, 126, 170-2; **4/13, 4/14**
Herapath, John, 242; **6/24**
Hermitage Museum, Leningrad, 118;
    3/31
Holland, 13
Holland, Henry, 72, 74; **2/30**
Hornby (Liverpool), 99
Hoskins, 233; **6/17**
Houghton, John, 142
Howells, Wm., 22
hump backed clocks, 229

I

identification of clocks, 127
Illustrated London News, The, 131
imported clocks, 127, 161; **4/4**
Industrial Revolution, 99, 106, 172; **3/20**
International Exhibition of 1862, 106;
    3/20
Italy, 11, 13
ivory clocks, 248, 249; **6/28, 6/29, Plate
    43**

J

Jackson, W. (London), 195; **5/9**
Jamieson, George, 18, 19, 22; **1/2**
Janvier, 12
Jeffereys & Gilbert, 161; **4/4**
Jordan (Manchester), 30; **1/9**
Joyce (London), 255; **6/34**
Jump and Barwise, 229

K

Kemp, George Meikle, 62
Kenwood, 15, 17; **1/1c**
Knibb, Joseph, 103
Kunsthistorisches Museum, Vienna, 81

L

lantern clocks, 11; **1**
lantern pinions, 247; **6/27**
Lenaghan, Robert, 256; **6/35**
Lepaute, J.A., 12, 182
Lepine, 12
Le Roy, Pièrre, 16, 82, 209; **5/16**
Lichfield Cathedral, 62, 70-2, 76, 131,
    197; **2/27-2/29, 3/44, 5/10**
lignum vitae, 203
Lister and Son (Newcastle), 41, 68;
    1/20, 2/26, Plate 6
Litherland, Ann, 112
Litherland, Davies & Co. (Liverpool),
    27, 107, 111, 112, 156; **3/21, 3/24,
    4/1**
Litherland, Peter, 112
Litherland, Whiteside & Co., 112
Liverpool, 99, 103, 107, 108, 220-2, 259;
    6/8-6/10, 6/38
longcase regulators, 60, 84, 203, 211,
    244-6; **3/6, 6/25-6/27**
long duration clocks, 91, 95, 180; **5/2,
    Plate 31**

M

McCabe, 161; **4/4**
McDowall, Charles (Wakefield), 17, 27,
    126, 160, 170-3; **4/13, 4/14**
McFerran, Wm. (Manchester), 41, 221;
    2/21, 6/9
Magniac, Colonel, 260
McMaster & Son (Dublin), 235; **6/19**
maintaining power, 18, 19, 49, 51, 52,
    75, 83, 98, 100, 113, 114, 115, 143,
    144, 151, 153, 185, 187, 193, 202,
    223, 229, 230, 231, 232, 235, 242,
    247, 257, 259; **1/2, 2/3, 2/5, 2/34,
    3/5, 3/16, 3/17, 3/26, 3/27, 3/29,
    3/57, 3/64, 3/66, 5/5, 5/6, 5/8, 5/13,
    6/11, 6/14-6/16, 6/19, 6/24, 6/27,
    6/36, 6/38, Plates 15, 16, 24, 40**
mantel clocks, 27, 29, 34, 53, 161; **4/4**
Margraf, Christolph, 79, 81
Mayer, Joseph (Liverpool), 101; **3/18,
    Plate 17**
Mercia, kingdom of, 70
Merlin, John Joseph, 13-17, 21; **1/1,
    Plates 2, 3**
Merseyside County Museum, 106; **3/20**
Middle East, 16
miniature clocks, 124, 125; **3/39**
month duration clocks, 17, 116, 117,
    122, 123; **3/35, Plate 20**
Moore & Sons, John, 27, 115-18; **3/30,
    3/31, Plate 19**
Moore (Leeds), 244, 247; **6/27**
Moore, George, 116

Morgan (Manchester), 60; **2/14, Plate
    11**
movements
    eight pillar, 106, 109, 112; **3/20,
        3/23, Plate 18**
    four train, 225-8; **6/13, Plates 38, 39**
    going train, 259; **6/38**
    inverted train, 149, 151, 187; **3/63,
        5/6**
    musical, 34, 41, 118, 211, 223-8;
        1/21, 6/11-6/13, Plates 38, 39
    remontoire, 12, 204, 205, 231;
        5/14b, 6/15
    skeletonised, 98; **3/16; Plate 15**
    three train, 13, 101, 106, 132, 138,
        140, 141, 145, 149, 170, 217-21,
        225; **3/20, 3/51, 3/54, 3/58, 3/65,
        4/13, 6/4, 6/6, 6/8, 6/9, Plate 36**
Mudge, 22

N

Napoleonic Wars, 79
Nash, John, 74
navigation, 203
night timepiece, 91
Norway, 242
Norwich and Bury Post, 90
Norwich Union, 115, 117; **3/29, 3/31**
numbered clocks, 241; **6/23**

O

one day duration clocks, 162; **4/5**
120 day duration clocks, 250, 251; **6/30**
Oxford University, 76, 77; **2/35**

P

Pace, John, 90, 92, 93, 95, 97;
    3/13-3/15, Plate 14
Pace, Thomas, 90
papier mâché clocks, 248
Parker, Benjamin, 67, 91, 92, 94; **3/11,
    3/12, Plate 13**
Parker and Pace, 13, 27, 89, 90, 95;
    3/10
Paris, 81
Patterson, G. (Walworth), 49, 55; **2/4,
    Plate 9**
Payne, 161; **4/4**
pendulum clamp, 89, 125; **3/10, 3/39**
pendulum clocks, 107, 109; **3/21, 3/22**
pendulum locking system, 255; **6/33**
pendulums
    axe shaped bob, 95; **3/14**
    brass rod, 125, 151, 181, 255; **3/39,
        5/1, 6/33**
    compensated, 130, 148, 151, 152,
        155, 162, 187, 229, 230, 231, 240,
        246; **3/61, 3/65, 3/68, 4/5, 5/6,
        6/14, 6/15, 6/22, 6/26, Plate 40**
    conventional, 73, 151, 218, 219;
        2/31, 6/6, Plate 36
    cut glass bob, 178; **4/18**
    glass rod, 253; **6/31**
    half seconds beating, 60, 149, 151,
        185, 202, 232, 255; **2/16, 3/63,
        5/13, 6/16, 6/34**
    mercury compensated, 148, 151, 162,
        230, 231, 240, 246; **3/61, 4/5,
        6/15, 6/22, 6/26**
    mock gridiron, 129, 130, 136, 256;
        3/43, 3/50, 6/35
    regulation, 36, 87; **1/15, 3/8d, Plate
        5**

    rise and fall mechanism, 176, 177;
        4/19, Plate 30
    seconds beating, 84, 204; **3/6, 5/14**
    steel rod, 94, 122; **3/12, 3/35, Plate
        20**
    supported by a cross bar, 237-9; **6/21**
    true gridiron, 12
    wood rod, 49, 51, 52, 171, 184,
        237-9; **2/3, 2/5, 4/14, 5/4, 6/21,
        Plate 32**
        with cylindrical bob, 113, 122,
            3/26, 3/35, Plate 20
        with lenticular bob, 21, 130, 221,
            232; **6/16, 6/20**
        with pewter bob, 50, 57, 60, 68,
            130, 155, 185, 187, 230; **2/7,
            2/11, 2/15, 2/26, 3/68, 5/5,
            5/6**
        with spherical bob, 18, 19, 255;
            1/2, 6/33
Penlington & Hutton (Liverpool), 221;
    6/9
Pierce, Edward, 75; **2/33**
pillar clocks, 93, 98, 103, 109, 120, 121;
    3/16, 3/23, 3/32-3/34, Plates 15, 18
plinths, 30, 31, 37, 51, 55, 221; **1/10,
    1/13, 1/16, 2/3, 2/4, 6/9, Plate 9**
    brass, 50, 89, 218, 219, 232; **2/2,
        3/10, 6/6, 6/16, Plate 36**
    marble, 233; **6/17**
plumb line, 15, 17, 21, 255; **1/1c, 6/33**
porcelain clocks, 161; **4/4**
portico clocks, 10, 11; **2**
presentation clocks, 27, 34, 145, 147-9,
    210-12; **1/8a, 3/58, 3/61, 6/1, Plate 35**
Prince Regent, 72, 74, 78, 79; **2/30, 3/1**
Ptolemy, 160
pyramidical clocks, 91, 95; **3/14**

Q

quarter work, 213; **6/1d**

R

Radeloff, Nikolaus, 81
regulators, 11, 87, 99, 233, 244, 245;
    6/17, 6/25
Reid, 82
reproduction clocks, 169, **4/12**
Rhodes, M. (Bradford), 74; **2/32**
Richard (of Wallingford), 160
Rippin, James (Spalding), 114; **3/27**
roller skate, 17
rolling ball clocks, 192, 207, 208, 252,
    258; **5/15, 6/37, Plates 34, 45**
Rome, 81
Roskell (Liverpool), 220, 221; **6/8, 6/9**
Ross, 224, 225
Rotunda, Greenwich, 81
Royal
    Collection, 80; **3/2, 3/5, 3/6**
    family, 72; **2/30**
    laboratory, Greenwich, 79
    Pavilion, Brighton, 62, 72, 73, 74,
        128, 132, 140; **2/30-2/32, 3/45,
        3/53**
    Regiment of Artillery, Woolwich, 78;
        3/1
    Society, 79, 161
Royelle (Paris), 180; **5/2, Plate 31**
rubber, synthetic, 119
Rudolf II, Emperor, 81
Rutter, S. (retailer), 129; **3/43**
Russell, Benjamin (Norwich), 35; **1/13**

S

Sager, R.H. (Blackburn), 174; **4/17**
St. Chad, 70
St. Paulinus, 65
St. Paul's Cathedral, 62, 74, 75, 76, 128, 134, 138, 140, 141; **2/33, 2/34, 3/54, Plate 23**
Sarton, 16
Savage, John (Salop), 24, 26; **1/6**
Savage, Thomas, 233; **6/17**
Savory & Sons, A.B., 237, 239; **6/21c**
Schleswig, 81
Scott (Leeds), 26; **1/7b**
Scott Memorial, 61-3, 66, 127, 128, 142-5, 179, 185; **2/17, 2/18, 2/20, 3/56, 3/57, Plate 24**
Second World War, 259; **6/38**
Shearer, James, 242, 243; **Plate 42**
Shepherd, Charles, 148; **3/62**
Sheraton, Thomas, 12
16th century clocks, 11; **1**
six pillar clocks, 250, 251; **6/30**
Smith & Sons, J. (Clerkenwell), *126-41*, 13, 31, 39, 43, 47, 50, 56-9, 66, 69, 70, 71, 73, 74, 76, 107, 112, 126-33, 135-41, 146, 157, 179, 210, 211, 217, 260-7; **1/18, 1/25, 2/12, 2/24, 2/28, 2/31, 2/32, 2/35b, 3/21, 3/41, 3/43, 3/44, 3/47-3/54, 6/1, 6/5, Plates 1, 21-3, 35**
Smith, William (Musselburgh), 119-21; **3/32-3/34**
snails
    quarter, 110; **3/23c**
    skeletonised, 73, 74, 100, 107, 108, 139, 173, 214; **2/31, 3/16, 3/17, 3/21, 3/52, 4/16, 6/1f, Plate 16**
Snosswell, C., 236; **6/20**
Snosswell, William, 236; **6/20**
Society of Arts, Edinburgh, 119
Society of Friends, 90
Soho Clock Factory, The, 142, 155; **3/69**
Spain, 13
spherical clocks, 15, 18, 19, 22; **1/2, Plate 4**

spirit level, 52, 81, 220, 241; **2/5, 3/4, 6/8, 6/23**
spring driven clocks, 80, 81, 84; **3/2, 3/3, 3/5**
springs, 119-21; **3/32, 3/34**
Steell, John, 61; **2/17**
strike/silent regulation, 35, 222; **1/13, 6/10**
Strutt and Wigston, 13, 27, 92, 126, 160, 161, 164-9; **4/8, 4/9, 4/11, 4/12, Plate 28**
Suffolk Clocks and Clockmakers, 91
Sussex, Duke of, 243; **Plate 42**
Swarz, Franciscus, 11; **2**
Switzerland, 13
Syon House, 62, 77; **2/36**

T

table regulators, 49, 53, 113, 187, 211, 229-32, 234, 237, 240; **2/3, 3/26, 5/6, 6/14-6/16, 6/18, 6/21, 6/22, Plate 40, 41**
thermometers, 242, 255; **6/24, 6/33**
thirty hour duration clocks, 258; **6/37**
thirty second table, 81; **3/4**
Thompson, Adam (London), 232; **6/16**
three frame clocks, 57; **2/11**
three month duration clocks, 95, 178
three year duration clocks, 91, 95
Thwaites & Reed, 185; **5/5**
Thwaites, Jn. (Clerkenwell), 115
Time Museum, Rockford, U.S.A., 83, 84, 170; **3/5, 3/7, 4/13**
Tompion, Thomas, 66
Tom Tower, Christ Church, Oxford, 62, 76, 77; **2/35**
'transparent clocks', 178; **4/18**
travelling cases, 80, 221; **3/2, 6/19**
tripod clocks, 255; **6/33**
Tritschler & Co., E. (Carlisle), 185, 253; **5/5, 6/31**
Tsar of Russia, 118; **3/31**
turret clocks, 99, 203
20th century clocks, 47, 169, 204, 205; **1/32, 4/12, 5/14**

twenty four hour clocks, 108; **3/19**
two sided clocks (with identical frames), 257; **6/36**
Tyrer, Thomas, 209; **5/16**

U

Ulrich (London), 138, 217; **3/51, 6/5**
unusual clocks, 31, 248-59; **1/10**

V

Victoria, Queen, 242, 243; **Plate 42**
Vienna, 12, 162; **4/5**
Viner, Charles Edward, 49, 51, 161, 233; **2/3, 4/4, 6/17**

W

wall clocks, 34
Walsh (Reading), 240; **6/22**
watchmaking, 99, 107, 112, 233; **6/17**
Watkins, Alexander, 234; **6/18, Plate 41**
Watt, James, 161, 166; **4/9**
weight driven clocks, 81, 84, 162; **3/1, 3/6, 4/5**
Westminster Abbey, 62, 64-6, 69, 128, 130, 145-9; **2/21-2/24, 3/60, 3/61**
wheelwork, *157-178*
    arched crossings, 113; **3/26**
    cut glass centres, 126, 160, 178
Whitehurst & Son (Derby), 22, 23; **1/5**
Wigston, William, 161
Wilson, W. (Maryport), 223; **6/11**
winding (epicyclic), 247; **6/27**
Winstanley Hall, 103
wooden clock cases, 47, 48, **1/32**
wooden clocks, 248
Wren, Sir Christopher, 74, 75; **2/33**

Y

York Minster, 28, 41, 47, 57, 62, 65, 66, 68, 128, 130, 134, 135, 145, 146, 149; **1/20, 2/25, 2/26, 3/47, 3/58, 3/59**
year duration clocks, 94, 95, 233; **3/12, 3/13, 6/17**

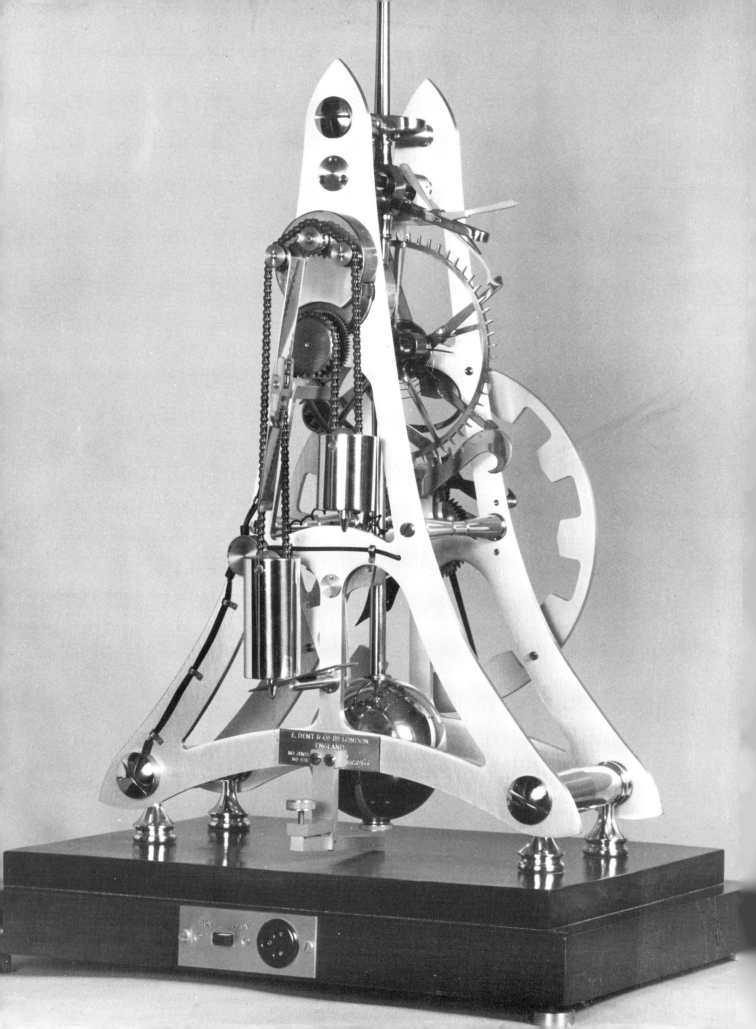